Romantic Writing
and the Empire of Signs

Romantic Writing and the Empire of Signs

Periodical Culture and Post-Napoleonic Authorship

Karen Fang

University of Virginia Press
Charlottesville and London

University of Virginia Press

Printed in the United States of America on acid-free paper

First published 2010

9 8 7 6 5 4 3 2 1

Library of Congress Cataloging-in-Publication Data

Fang, Karen Y.

Romantic writing and the empire of signs : periodical culture and post-Napoleonic authorship / Karen Fang.

p. cm.

Includes bibliographical references and index.

ISBN 978-0-8139-2874-6 (acid-free paper) — ISBN 978-0-8139-2890-6 (e-book)

1. English literature—19th century—History and criticism. 2. British periodicals—History—19th century. 3. Romanticism—Great Britain. 4. Imperialism in literature. 5. Orientalism in literature. 6. Periodicals—Publishing—Great Britain—History—19th century. 7. Authors and publishers—Great Britain—History—19th century. 8. Literature publishing—Great Britain—History—19th century. I. Title.

PR468.P37F36 2010

820.9′3581—dc22

2009021114

To Andrew, with love

Contents

Acknowledgments

This book could never have been completed without the support of my Houston community: Hosam Aboul-Ela, Margot Backus, Ann Christensen, Natalie Houston, Maria Gonzalez, Kasi Jackson, Ann Kennedy, Elizabeth Klett, David Mazella, Kat McClellan, Stacey Peebles, Jeanne Scheper, and Lynn Voskuil. I also found additional readers in Jason Goldsmith and Jerome Christensen. Hosam, Margot, and Lynn merit additional mention, as do Anne Frey and David Higgins, for gamely reading the entire manuscript, as did the two anonymous readers for Virginia. They all deserve tremendous credit for the final shape and achievements of this book. I could not have asked for a better editor than Cathie Brettschneidner, who was a patient and professional shepherd throughout this long process.

The Rosetta Stone was selected for the jacket art both because the stone is the subject of chapter 2 and because its three different scripts are an apt emblem for the various oriental motifs adapted by different authors during the Romantic era. I thank the Trustees of the British Museum for granting me permission to use the image.

The University of Houston and the Houstoun Grant for Literary Criticism at the University of Houston both provided financial support at the beginning and the end of this project. Very early research was conducted with the support of the Huntington Library, California; Winterthur Library, Delaware; and Thayer Library, UCLA. Portions of chapter 1 appeared in "Empire, Coleridge, and Charles Lamb's Consumer Imagination" and are reprinted with permission from *SEL Studies in English Literature 1500–1900* 43, no. 4 (Autumn 2003): 815–43. Portions of chapter 2 first appeared in "A Printing Devil, a Scottish Mummy, and an Edinburgh Book of the Dead: James Hogg's Napoleonic Complex," *Studies in Romanticism* 43, no. 2 (Summer 2004): 161–85, and are included here with the permission of the Trustees of Boston University. I am privileged to have started the first germ of this book under Antoinette Burton, Jerome Christensen, and Ronald Paulson. While any errors or shortcomings are of course my own, it is my sincere hope that this book shows some measure of what I have learned from them.

Romantic Writing and the Empire of Signs

Introduction

Empire, Periodicals, and Late Romantic Writing

This book is about the power accorded literary periodicals by late Romantic authors, who inhabited an era of tremendous growth in the periodical press. The "years between Waterloo and the passage of the first Reform Bill greatly enlarged the audience for periodicals," Richard Altick has already noted; this marked expanse in periodical publications was due to the era's "social and political turmoil" and was spurred by recent economic and technological developments, such as the invention of the steam press, the perfection of steel-plate engraving, and the reopening of Continental trade (which renewed access to paper rag), that enabled a sudden rise in publication and reading after the wars.[1] But if periodicals were a veritable index of contemporary sociodevelopment, this link between capitalism and literary form also is at odds with traditional characterizations of Romantic culture and suggests a late Romantic investment in periodicals as a vehicle of literary ambition that is counterintuitive. I would do "Any thing but Mortgage my Brain to Blackwood," Keats once declared, referencing a popular Tory monthly in a characteristically high Romantic rejection of the commerce and commodification represented by the periodical press.[2] His resistance to periodicals bespeaks the conflict between art and commerce that pervades so much Romantic writing, and it illustrates the challenge supposedly posed to Romantic idealism by the material dynamics of contemporary capitalism, the very process driving historical change in these years of post-Napoleonic economic and territorial growth.

The territorial expansion and economic development associated with imperial acceleration were a crucial component of the era's historical experience and thus play an important role in periodicals, albeit not in the ways that might typically be expected. Consistent with this "new imperial age," as it has been described by historians such as C. A. Bayley, the pages of the many periodicals launched and published between 1815 and 1832 teemed with references to contemporary territorial expansion, whether in the visual and verbal representation provided by journalistic reportage and accompanying illustrations, or in the advertisements that filled the back pages with announcements of new products and commodities available from abroad or with lists of necessary purchases for a journey into these exotic regions.[3] My interest, however, is in more subtle, less obvious instances of imperial involvement in literary magazines, but which would have been of particular use to the aspiring authors who also contributed to those pages. These are the many geographical motifs of exotic or foreign locations that occur in texts developed amid collaboration with periodicals, and whose topical, detailed, and often highly informed representations correspond with the growing knowledge of the imperial archive. In the broader context of periodicals as cross-sections of contemporary culture and history, these moments of geographical exoticism are analogous to the more specific visual and textual representation of empire within newspapers and magazines and are simply oblique reminders of an expanding imperial world. But for individual authors and their Romantic ambitions for literary posterity, these geographical references also were vehicles in calculated ploys for literary prestige, which reversed the prior, high Romantic resistance to the base commodification of periodicals and instead capitalized upon the contemporary interdependence of periodicals with empire to enact a sophisticated representational economy. In this system, empire was appropriated as a conceptualizing paradigm for the corporate enterprise of periodicals in which so many authors were involved, and the most sophisticated authors mastered the system by exploiting the imperial analogy within periodicals to effect their own authorial self-promotion.

"Ozymandias" perfectly illustrates this confluence of imperial imagery in literary contributions to post-Napoleonic periodicals. Shelley's famous sonnet, which was written as part of a sonnet competition between himself and Horace Smith, first appeared in the *Examiner* in 1818. It was occasioned by the colossal Egyptian fragments that had been acquired by Britain in its 1801 defeat of French forces at Aboukir and that in 1817 went on display in the newly reopened and expanded British Museum. Although the massive bust then known as "Memnon's Head" that is often associated with the sonnet would not arrive in England until the next year, all the Egyptian antiquities then displayed or still in the process of arriving in England were prominent legacies of the British campaigns against Napoleon, and therefore emblematized the nation's post-Napoleonic supremacy. For *Examiner* readers, then, Shelley's sonnet, with its famous description of "Two vast and trunkless legs of stone" glimpsed in a distant and "antique land," was a graphic indicator of the expanding British world, whose inclusion in the London weekly demonstrated how periodicals could chart a national sphere of influence through its depiction of numerous unconnected events within the globe.[4] Like the news and other reports from different world regions that also appeared in the *Examiner* pages, such as the American president's message on the reduction of the British naval force in American lakes, the "latest advices of the state of affairs in New Guyana . . . received by way of Trinidad," or the cover story on the thousands of impoverished sailors left in the English capital since war's end, this literary contribution on strange and enormous exotic antiquities of Egyptian provenance would have no relevance to *Examiner* readers except for the auspices of British imperial expansion.[5] They illustrate, through the "arbitrariness of their inclusion and juxtaposition," what Benedict Anderson shows to be periodicals' instrumental role in carving a national community. This occurs in the way that the haphazard, purely contingent meaning generated from their inclusion and adjacency to other reports "shows that the linkage between them is imagined," and exists only because of an imagined community that knows those distant locations belong to its own experience.[6]

But although "Ozymandias," in its general corroboration of contemporary imperial culture, fits easily into the miscellaneous contents of periodicals—what might be called their characteristic "din and clamor"—my interest lies in how the sonnet uses those imperial tropes to promote Shelley himself. The crux of the poem is the ironic contrast between the hubris of the motto carved on the colossal statue and the current state of the fragmented ruins, such that the statue's carved injunction to "those passions read" (line 6) refers not to the inscription nor to the famously egotistical pharaoh, Ramses II, who commissioned the statue, but to the poem itself, whose formal wroughtness as a sonnet asserts perfection and perdurability far beyond that of the visual icon the poem describes. It is for this claim to Romantic posterity that Shelley's poem is famed, but less commonly recognized is how that claim's reference to a historically topical icon of empire is enhanced through intertextual associations, or how the magazine's publication of the sonnet accorded Shelley topicality and reach far exceeding that of the statue or ruler named in the poem. Shelley's image of a traveler viewing antique fragments clearly references the *Ruins of Empires*, an influential 1791 treatise by French philosopher Constantin-François Volney, which depicts a wanderer in contemporary North Africa who believes that to "interrogate ancient monuments" will reveal *"by what secret causes do empires rise and fall"* (emphasis in the original).[7] Indeed, the *Ruins* had been much admired by Napoleon, who was inspired by the text to appoint the teams of scientists and intellectuals who accompanied his army into Egypt, and who thus enacted a real-life, contemporary version of Ramses' use of monuments to assert imperial power when his *corps des savants* unearthed the Egyptian antiquities that Shelley would later evoke. Shelley, of course, was a great admirer of the *Ruins,* as the text would later be the source of his famous characterization of poets as the "unacknowledged legislators of the world," but it is the *Examiner* that truly animated his Volney-based power. With its mass distribution and the topical meaning generated from its collective contents, the *Examiner* activates the multiple allusions to ancient Egyptian empire, recent French imperialism, and current, conquering British empire implicit in Shelley's sonnet, and therefore accords Shelley a literary or poetic power that far exceeds Ramses' statue in outreach and scope.

How does Shelley's Egyptian motif compare with other moments of geographical exoticism in writing by late Romantic periodical collaborators, many of whom were far more closely identified with periodicals than was Shelley? Do these authors' references to Egypt or to other sites of contemporary imperial ambition cohere with their politics or the politics of the periodical in which their work appeared? Do such moments of literary orientalism, with their close identification with imperial power, offer any insight into periodicals, a literary form and commercial publication often metonymic of contemporary capitalist enterprise? Are these connections between empire and periodicals true even of works not actually published in periodicals, but developed in conjunction with periodical collaboration? By raising such questions, I hope to merge the material concerns of imperial history and print culture studies with the traditionally idealist approaches of Romantic aesthetics, thereby highlighting some key issues in the intersection of empire, periodicals, and late Romantic writing. That there is a recurrent tendency toward geographical exoticism in late Romantic and early-nineteenth-century writing is not surprising given the era's imperial developments; nor is the fact, given the parallel expansion in the periodical press, that many of these works were developed by authors closely associated with periodicals, even if those works ultimately were not published in the periodicals themselves. This book proposes a constitutive relation between the content of such works and the context of their composition and publication. By tracking how contemporary authors use their geographical motifs as a method of activating imperial tropes already latent within the periodicals, I explore the extraordinary power that late Romantics accorded the periodical format. This power, so ubiquitous and omnipotent that periodicals are often compared with imperial capitalism itself, characterizes the mutual influence of empire and periodicals in the later Romantic era, and differs dramatically from the benighted status of periodicals among the high Romantics.[8] Indeed, in their deliberate, complexly orchestrated, and strategic investment in imperial culture and the periodical form, late Romantic writing invites an unprecedented application of postcolonial analysis to nineteenth-century literature. That is, in this study of geographical tropes in the late Romantic writing developed amid the periodicals, what looks like imperial commentary is often, more specifically, an insight into their authors' position in the contemporary capitalist enterprise most directly affecting their personal and professional lives—periodical publication.

In his seminal study of early-nineteenth-century periodicals, Jon Klancher describes a dense discursive landscape formed from the "colliding objects, events, and styles" of the countless new periodicals that launched in that period.[9] Embodied in the miscellaneous form of the periodical itself, this hybridity and multiplicity were further amplified by the product variation that each periodical cultivated to differentiate itself from their many commercial and ideological competitors. For Klancher, this complex and dynamic sphere of published discourse—a "force field for the power of thought"[10]—is more volatile and less coherent than the quasi-utopian public sphere that Jürgen Habermas once identified among eighteenth-century periodicals.[11] Rather, where Habermas imagined civil society taking shape amid the pages of newspapers and broadsheets, Klancher believes those earlier periodicals to have only extended an older, traditionally amateur relationship between authors and readers, and instead sees the professionalization and accelerated production of the early-nineteenth-century periodical marketplace as constituting a fundamentally different cultural economy. In this new ethos, individual voice is lost in the "essentially authorless text" of a collective "institution blending writer, editor, and publisher," and literary style assumes unprecedented importance as the only means by which authors and readers can reconstruct their relationship to each other and among themselves.[12] (Indeed, here Klancher is consistent with Habermas, who famously cited the nineteenth century's increasing commercialization of periodicals as a lamentable break or "transformation" in the public sphere.) In such a characterization of the diffuse, embedded, and numinous cacophony of contemporary periodicals, the periodical press is a literary microcosm of culture at large. And because post-Napoleonic culture was one of economic expansion, political dissent, upward mobility, and a "fascination with commodities," the contents of the periodical press were as varied and strewn with potent tokens or images as contemporary culture itself. "In the early nineteenth century, writers and readers became highly self-conscious about interpreting, constituting, and struggling over signs," Klancher thus observes. "A class will henceforth be defined by how it interprets signs," and the "text would become the counter in a serious game of symbolic reciprocity."[13]

Klancher's term for this discursive complex of resonant words and images is the "empire of signs," a phrase he derives from contemporary Romantic metaphors of the mind, but which I will show is also conveniently suggestive of the interdependent relationship of periodicals to post-Napoleonic imperial culture.[14] According to Klancher, all discursive sign systems were organized around a master sign, "a sign potent enough to represent all other signs."[15] Astute authors and readers established themselves by a deft positioning within that complex and interdependent system of reference, in which a "merely partial access to the empire of signs condemns the aspirant" to an incomplete, unfulfilled version of the personal and professional opportunities for self-advancement within that system.[16] As should be apparent by the opportunities for conquest and class mobility implied within the allusion to "empire," one of the most prominent of such master signs within the periodicals was the political and economic institution of territorial conquest referenced in the term and then an increasingly prominent aspect of British life. Although Klancher uses "empire" only metaphorically, it is characteristic of his groundbreaking analysis that it also anticipates a more focused approach, where magazines are also the site of corporate practices and other aspects of contemporary print capitalism that render the term far more concrete than abstract. Indeed, as a process whose institutional organization and cultural effects provide both the formal consequences of agency and commodity culture that Klancher describes, empire is the master sign that organizes so many late Romantic, post-Napoleonic periodicals.

It is with this focus on the specific and historically significant meaning of "empire" that this book takes up from where Klancher left off. With reports and illustrations of new territories and distant frontiers on every page, and latent evidence of a mounting imperial culture throughout all other contents, such as advertisements and literary references, contemporary periodicals harbored a deeply ambitious, highly topical content that some authors cannily exploited by further augmenting the imperial qualities always latent within periodicals through sophisticated motifs of geographical exoticism. In some cases their representations of empire were precise and explicit, such as in allusions to Napoleonic conquest or the mercantile trade with certain colonies and interests; and in some cases their references were more abstract, in the general sense of the geographical exoticism and vague interest in territorial location that was an inevitable by-product of global expansion.

One of the most obvious ways in which the late Romantics engaged this imperial motif was through visual, often starkly material emblems, as already illustrated in the opening example of "Ozymandias." In that poem, Shelley uses the explicitly topical reference to a prominent icon of contemporary imperial triumph to invoke imperial ambition as a metaphor for his literary aspirations, and through the poem's temporal coinciding with the exhibition at the British Museum, he implicitly aligns the *Examiner* with the architectural monument of imperial accumulation and display whose reopening that year was meant to crown the newly ascendant imperial nation.[17] Such a conceit is a remarkably pragmatic approach to the creation of literary or cultural capital, and it has a real historical analogue in the contemporary imperial servants and functionaries whom Maya Jasanoff has shown to have used collecting as a means of dramatizing their own class mobility.[18] But in calling attention to the *literary* motifs of imperial collecting within periodical publications, I also mean to reconceive the role of material culture in much recent imperial and postcolonial studies. The visual and physical objects associated with empire are compelling and accessible reminders of the larger political and economic processes in which they were embroiled, and hence they have received considerable scholarly attention because of their overt distillation of the processes by which those items came to be (but which are not themselves so easily portrayed).[19] Literary uses of imperial icons, by contrast, reverse this ontology, and instead suggest that authors and editors were early progenitors of the triumphal rhetoric and display implicit in periodicals. With this insight into the originary responsibility of periodicals in the formulation of late Romantic motifs of empire—yet another instance of the intimate relationship between empire and periodicals—post-Napoleonic Romanticism suggests literary production as a constitutive element of imperial culture, and not the other way around.

At play in the imperial motifs within early-nineteenth-century periodicals is an oft-noted custom of using their titles to liken the literary format to the many physical centers of accumulation and exhibition then erected to display those physical items. Scholarly histories of periodical magazines have long noted this rhetorical tradition. Most recently, Judith Pascoe has observed how Romantic enthusiasms for collecting were textually rendered in the periodical format, whose titles "equated magazines to museums or cabinets of collectible objects."[20] In this physical and even architectural emphasis upon the term, Pascoe's interpretation of magazines as a literary analogue to contemporary cultures of collecting implicitly heralds the form's new role in fostering original literature, and it reiterates a point made as early as 1930 by Walter Graham—that nineteenth-century magazines differ from their eighteenth-century predecessors in this modern sanctification of authorship and the individual imagination.[21] The difference between these two eras in periodicals is encapsulated in the dominant terms for the form. Eighteenth-century periodicals often bear titles emphasizing a reflective and purely visual scopic engagement with the world, such as the *Spectator* or the weekly Edinburgh *Mirror.* These periodicals were often ad hoc productions jumbled together from amateur contributions and meteorological and mercantile data, suggesting an older notion of the periodical format as a reflective window or "mirror" upon society. By contrast, most of the new journals that blossomed during the post-Napoleonic years were the venue of professional writers and frequently went by institutional terms such as "magazine," "museum," and "repository."[22] In periodicals such as the *London Magazine*, the *London Museum*, or the *Monthly Repository*, this titular emphasis upon the metropolitan origins of the publication and the publication's pretensions toward a physical location of accumulation and display declare an unprecedented aesthetic value and material reality for its literary contents.

Of course, the term "magazine" was hardly unknown in the eighteenth century. The *London Magazine*, a widely admired Whig monthly with which I will begin the first chapter, borrowed the name of an eighteenth-century predecessor and clearly tried to assert its continuities with the past. Rather, by calling attention to the physical and exhibitionary implications of the term, I am merely trying to suggest a new importance that the rubric acquired in those years of economic and territorial expansion that the periodicals documented and upheld. In addition to the physical connotations of collecting suggested by Pascoe, the magazine rubric also bore associations with the military might inextricable with territorial conquest, a conceit that clearly illustrates contemporary associations between periodicals and empire. The very term "magazine," for example, is itself a dead metaphor deriving from the warehouses or storehouses of military munitions, and no doubt stems from the reports on shipping and naval activity that comprised the contents of some of the first periodicals. These etymological origins in military might and conflict cast a substantially different light on the many periodicals that launched in the post-Napoleonic years of global conquest and expansion. As Hilary Fraser, Stephanie Green, and Judith Johnston note, the military rhetoric was "one of the most common metaphors used of the periodical press and the journalism in the nineteenth century" and existed as a "trope to express ideas (and anxieties) about authority."[23] Thus, although the magazine rubric was already common in the eighteenth century, and those early periodicals included coverage of far-flung global regions, the different stake of geopolitical expansion in the nineteenth century must have exerted a new resonance in their titular emphasis on collecting and display. In the context of contemporary imperial expansion—which, Jasanoff notes, is itself another form of collecting[24]—the daily developments of global expansion reported in their very pages must have raised additional, highly topical metaphors of imperial accumulation and exhibition.

We see elements of this conceit, and their use for the individual author, in the *Athenaeum,* the monthly review later famed for its rigidly enforced practices of objective criticism, and which launched in 1828. The very title of the magazine epitomizes the metaphors of materiality pervading periodicals during this era. Although its obvious reference is to the temple of learning associated with ancient Greece, the architectural classicism implied by the magazine's title also has a more contemporary embodiment in places such as the British Museum, and lends that architectural structure a specifically topical and imperial cast. The value of this imperial context for individual authors is further detailed in the article that headlined the magazine's first issue. A common attribute in many periodicals of this era, given the rapid proliferation of new periodicals and the pressure for product differentiation imposed by intensified market competition, is a metacritical editorial commentary that initiates readers into the attributes and concerns of that particular publication, often in a prospectus or first edition of the journal. In the *Athenaeum,* this prefatory introduction begins by celebrating the permanence of books, which are "made to endure for ever," but then goes on to lament the dwindling number of good books that characterize "the present state of English literature" at this time. The magazine uses this observation as grounds for its own establishment as a periodical, whose greater frequency of appearance serves the "production" and "demand" of the modern age but still is capable of maintaining the quality—and hence the permanence—of its bound predecessors.[25] As the magazine announces, explicitly articulating the premises of collecting and display that would characterize the respected series:

> We shall endeavour . . . first to lay a foundation of solid and useful knowledge, and on this to erect a superstructure of as much harmony, ornament, and beauty, as our own powers . . . will enable us to construct. If the edifice, so reared, be worthy of the name we have chosen for it, and, like the ATHENAEUM of antiquity, should become the resort of the most distinguished philosophers, historians, orators, and poets of our day,—we shall endeavour so to arrange and illustrate their several compositions, that they may themselves be proud of the records of their fame, and that their admirers may deem them worthy of preservation among the permanent memorials of their times.[26]

The *Athenaeum,* the editors claim, is a physical "edifice," founded upon "knowledge" and ornamented with "beauty." Like its nominal predecessor, "the Athenaeum of antiquity," the modern literary magazine is a showcase or meeting hall for the luminaries and monuments of contemporary culture, which houses "the most distinguished philosophers, historians, orators, and poets of our day," and arranges and exhibits their compositions in such a way that they are appreciated as triumphs of Romantic posterity—objects clearly "worthy of preservation among the permanent memorials of their times."

What is particularly valuable for individual authors about this museological conceit is that the conceit operates independent of any claims about the structural similarities between empire and periodicals, the very premise that might otherwise seem to be the underlying motivation of the geographical motifs within contemporary periodicals, and which indeed is a notable aspect of post-Napoleonic periodicals. Magazines share with empire a number of structural similarities in operation and industrial practice. Both processes of territorial conquest and dominion that rely upon capitalism, magazines and empire alike institutionalize rationalization and massification as primary methods of production. In periodicals, for example, the common practices of anonymity and pseudonymity that are so commonly associated with the early-nineteenth-century periodical press have their analogies in the atomized offices and de-skilling upon which the imperial system is based. Contemporary periodicals even answer to a rhetoric of reference that replaced these displaced individuals with corporate personality in the same manner as empire. Thus, where the countless imperial servants and officials that comprised the East India Company were collectively personified through the singular sobriquet of "John Company," the many authors and contributors affiliated with a periodical were similarly absorbed into contemporary tendencies to personify the magazine as a whole, as occurred in references to "Maga" (*Blackwood's Magazine*) or "Maggy Scot," the "old lady" (the *Scots Quarterly*).

Such points of comparison are important and underlie the commentary and imperial critique that periodical collaborators often use to conceptualize their critique of magazine print capitalism, but they take a backseat to the museological conceits of collecting whose power lay in the fact that its metaphorical rhetoric is wholly self-generated and autonomous. With their implicit, *Athenaeum*-like claims to presenting the "permanent memorials of our time," periodicals offered authors a shortcut to renown and posterity. Astute authors enhanced these claims for status by deploying geographical motifs resonant with contemporary imperial culture, and further enriched their claims for cultural capital when their periodical-published works specifically invoked tangible objects of empire such as foreign artifacts and commodities. To put it another way, precisely because to "enter the empire of signs as critic and interlocutor means to demystify all those signs" in which one appears, astute individual authors played up empire itself, a topical trope of considerable symbolic importance and the very master sign underlying the contemporary periodical format.[27] The rewards of this rhetorical system are profound. A striking aspect of the *Athenaeum*'s claims to preserving the era's "permanent memorials" is that it overcomes the obsolescence implied by seriality, and thereby converts the contents of periodicals into a perdurable form that is the antithesis of the very attribute that gives the form of publication its name.

To cite a very specific example of the utility of empire as a framework for conceptualizing the symbiotic power of periodicals, the interaction of Keats's poems on Greek artifacts within the *Annals of the Fine Arts* illustrates how the context of their periodical publication heightened qualities within the individual poems, and how a maturing poet increasingly sensitive to these attributes could capitalize on that symbiosis by further enhancing elements within the poems themselves. The Elgin Marbles sonnets are some of Keats's earliest works, and they exhibit the anxieties and insecurities of an ambitious but still largely unknown artist. The poems, composed after Keats viewed the magnificent remnants from the Parthenon frieze, which along with Memnon's Head had been some of the imperial trophies precipitating the building of the new British Museum, are notable for the profound degree of handicap and inadequacy they express. Where other contemporary artists and cultural figures, including Benjamin Robert Haydon, the painter and friend who insisted that Keats view the monuments, reacted with excitement and inspiration, for Keats his encounter with what Haydon praised as the "finest form that man ever imagined" only causes the poet to confess his lyric incapacity.[28] Unfavorably comparing his "weak" spirit and the "dim-conceived glories of the brain" with the Marbles' "Grecian grandeur," as he says in the first sonnet, Keats, in the second sonnet, "cannot speak / Definitively on these mighty things."[29] In a poignant contrast that suggests that even in their ruined state, the Elgin fragments still surpass Keats in artistic achievement, the two sonnets record the young poet's debilitating sense of artistic inadequacy.

Notably, in the sonnets the imperial provenance of the artifacts is invoked by Keats only to trope his inadequacy. While the Marbles, which had been acquired by Lord Elgin when the diplomat and collector represented Britain in Ottoman-occupied Greece, epitomize imperial plundering of local cultures (and indeed, remain—along with the British Museum's Egyptian artifacts—some of the most prominent objects in the current contest to return cultural patrimony to their homeland[30]), in his sonnets Keats's references to himself as a "sick eagle" invert the triumphal associations of a bird often symbolically associated with Napoleon.[31] A similar upending of conventional images of imperial triumph also occurs in the sonnets through their implied emphasis on the physical contrast between the monumental marble fragments and the sonnets' miniature shape. The "dizzy" confusion and vertiginous daze that Keats experiences upon seeing the Marbles are the opposite of the prospect view that conventionally figures empire—such as occurs elsewhere in Keats's reference to "stout Cortez . . . with eagle eyes . . . / . . . / upon a peak," and which Mary Louise Pratt has described as the trope of being "monarch-of-all-I-survey."[32] By thus inverting a customary device of imperial representation, Keats underscores the physical discrepancies between the monumental fragments and his miniature, purportedly inadequate sonnets. His poems seem to use the imagery of contemporary empire only to portray his artistic limitations, suggesting an indifference to the triumphalism in which those trophies of imperial might and icons of British power were then imbued. (As Lord Elgin had repeatedly emphasized in his efforts to sell the Marbles to the nation, the artifacts originating from the temple crowning the first democracy would be the perfect trophy for a nation currently unsurpassed in its culture and progress.[33])

In a peculiar twist upon the sonnets' actual content, however, the *Annals of the Fine Arts* reversed Keats's confessed inadequacy, and indeed restored a triumphal promotion of Keats's artistic power in a manner consistent with the iconic imperial potency with which the Elgin Marbles were by then typically perceived. One of the many specialized journals that originated in the post-Napoleonic era, the *Annals of the Fine Arts* was the first British quarterly to be entirely devoted to the visual arts.

The journal, which ran from 1816 to 1820, exactly concurrent with Keats's career, was targeted at artists, connoisseurs, and other cultural figures, and it made the nation's artistic patrimony a specific issue of concern. Citing the deplorable lack of exhibition space for local artists, the *Annals* agitated for government support that could acquire and endow such a location. Their efforts, which epitomize the strong identification of a literary magazine with the mission of physical museums common in the post-Napoleonic era, resulted in significant achievements. The magazine was instrumental in the founding of the British Institution—later developed as the National Gallery—and would be closely involved with the efforts to persuade Parliament to purchase the Marbles.[34] (Significantly, the *Annals* also praised the arrival of Memnon's Head.[35]) In fact, the magazine's admiration of the Marbles and advocacy for their purchase was such a repeated subject within its pages that it is all but impossible to find an issue that makes no mention of the subject. After all, the first volume of the *Annals* was dedicated to the Parliamentary Select Committee that ultimately recommended the nation's purchase of the antiquities, and the magazine's ability to overcome initial resistance to the incomplete and deteriorating fragments (by declaring their fragmentation to be integral to their beauty) voiced a canonical precept of Romantic aesthetics.

In terms of Keats's appearance amid the *Annals,* the sentiments of inadequacy actually stated in the sonnets were eclipsed in the larger context of the magazine's interest in the poems' visual subject. Conveniently coinciding with a major issue on the magazine's agenda, Keats's poems were only his second publication, and no doubt were selected by the journal for publication largely for their topical relevance, as Keats himself was still then a largely unknown poet. (In this he was aided by Haydon, who having already introduced the poet to the Marbles, also brought Keats to the attention of the *Annals'* editor, whom Haydon knew.) This incidental promotion of the young poet as occurred in the mere fact of publication would be further magnified by the magazine's other contents and their contextual effect upon the apposite poems. A tenet of critical study of periodicals is how the miscellaneous and multiple nature of most periodicals generates intertextual meanings that may not be present in an individual work itself.[36] As Mark Parker describes it, this "dynamic relationship among contributions" is one where "essay or poem is to magazine as figure is to ground in the plastic arts."[37]

In its echoes of the physical rhetoric of exhibition that pervades so many contemporary magazines, and in sculptural terms particularly pertinent to the *Annals of the Fine Arts,* Parker's comment wonderfully articulates the effect that the journal exerted upon an individual author. The *Annals* tended to place poetry at the end of each issue, which usually put it immediately after the "Notices of Works in Hand," a regular column in the magazine that cataloged notable recent artistic productions. Lawrence, Wilkie, Fuseli, West, and Landseer are but some of the august painters and sculptors who precede Keats in the March 1817 issue.[38] Like the "Notices of Living Artists," another regular feature in the *Annals* that championed promising new artists (Haydon was one of its protégés), the "Notices of Works in Hand" imparts upon Keats's poems its influence and agenda and suggests, through the "dynamic relationship among contributions," that the poet's literary artifacts are themselves as deserving of national admiration as those visual and plastic works of art that the previous column details and intends to promote. (Indeed, if the visual artists whom Keats accompanies were not sufficient proof of his promise, this was also secured by the other poets who preceded Keats in previous issues. An earlier installment of the *Annals'* poetry section featured Wordsworth.[39]) The implicit or inferred effect of this symbiotic dynamic is an unequivocal sponsorship of the individual author who appears under its aegis. In almost the same way that the admiration of the Marbles advocated in the *Annals* overcame and re-presented the fragments' aged and incomplete state, the magazine also rehabilitated the inadequacies confessed in Keats's sonnets. Just as the "Notices on Living Artists" column championed rising stars in the visual arts, the *Annals'* inclusion of his poems similarly makes Keats its protégé and beneficiary.

Of course, it is a tremendous irony that the poet whose resolution to never "Mortgage my Brain to Blackwood" should benefit so spectacularly from the magazine format that he disavowed, but it only reiterates the extraordinary authority that periodicals exerted in the development of late Romantic careers. By the time of his "great year," however, Keats was more cognizant of these advantages and had developed a poetic style increasingly oriented toward the kinds of aesthetic judgment leveled in periodical reviews.[40] Not surprisingly, in a later (and sadly final) contribution to the *Annals,* the poet's lyric about a foreign artifact deliberately plays up the visual and material qualities that had already benefited him in the Elgin Marbles sonnets.[41] The incomparable "Ode on a Grecian Urn," perhaps the single best-known ekphrasis of a foreign object within the English language, shares with the sonnets their topical attention to a visual artifact of Greek origin, but it also differs notably from the earlier poems by inverting the imperial imagery and other topical conventions by which Keats in the sonnets had diminished his poetic capacity. As an ode, the later poem adopts a traditionally elevated and expansive form whose greater length and implied ambition already assert a marked distinction from the miniature sonnets. The ode further amplifies this escalation in aspirations through the contrast between its size and the material object it describes, which as an urn belongs to the domestic and even minor arts. Thus, while the earlier sonnets had adversely compared the limited achievement of Keats's small poems to the fragments' still monumental size, the Grecian Urn ode reverses that relationship by applying its longer and elevated form to a smaller and more banal art object. In so doing, the ode's restored prospect view revives the imperial triumphalism conventionally associated with exotic artifacts during this era.

Keats's several poems on Greek artifacts therefore illustrate a particularly effective synthesis of Romantic ambition with contemporary periodicals, and in their visual, highly material enactment of Keats's philhellenism, the iconic emblems at the heart of the three poems all demonstrate the particular advantages available to periodical contributors when their works use an explicitly visual or accessible icon of contemporary imperial culture to anchor the triumphal self-promotion of their periodical collaboration. With its close identification with the visual arts and its actual involvement in contemporary imperial collecting and museological display, the *Annals of the Fine Arts* is a particularly lucid example of the utility of periodicals in augmenting the tropes of imperial triumph implicit in late Romantic invocations of geographical exoticism, but it is equally important to note that the symbiosis of miscellany with individual form that occurs in these collaborations remains true even in those periodicals where visual or imperial tropes were less readily apparent. Both the Elgin Marbles sonnets and the "Ode on a Grecian Urn" were also published in the *Examiner,* the liberal weekly behind "Ozymandias" that also printed a number of Keats's other poems. It is the *Examiner,* in fact, that is usually credited by scholarship as the periodical most closely affiliated with Keats's sponsorship and gradual rise to acclaim.

Yet even if the *Examiner*, with its more diffuse interests, politically engaged commentary, and titular harking back to general notions of periodicals as a reflective mirror upon society, lacks the artistic and explicitly acquisitive focus of the *Annals*, Keats's poetry is still able to invoke the artifactual and museological conceits instrumental to era's prevailing tropes of empire within the periodicals. Very generally, this occurs in the *Examiner*'s "Young Poets" column, where Keats appeared alongside Shelley, and whose reports on rising new authors resemble the "Notices of Living Artists" column in the *Annals*. More specifically, though, Keats himself enacts the visual and physical emphasis of his poetry by using, in the Grecian Urn ode, his poem's odal structure, and particularly a variable rhyme scheme in the second half of each stanza, to convey the palpable roundness and shape of an urn. The poem, which is often compared to the opening stanza of the "Ode on Indolence," in which Keats describes how "figures on a marble urn, / When shifted round to see the other side; / . . . came again," has a fluctuating rhyme scheme where the last three lines of each stanza scramble the pattern employed in the previous three lines.[42] (Thus, in lines 5–7 of each stanza, a rhyme scheme of *dce* in the first shifts to *ced* in the second; to *cde* in the third and fourth stanzas; and finally returns to *dce* in the fifth and final stanza.) While these variations in rhyme scheme are too subtle for the ear, they inscribe a physicality that the *Examiner*'s underdeveloped exhibitionary function could not confer. As the stanzas of the ode pass, like the figures on the urn in "Indolence," through their silent but nevertheless visible movement, the poem conveys a distinct lyric progress that suggests the cylindrical shape of the urn.[43]

In this perfect symbiosis of periodical and contribution—or, as Mark Parker appropriately puts it, figure and ground—Keats's poetic "Urn" revolves before readers like those mechanized displays in modern museums, designed to show viewers all sides of an artifact. In the specific context of Keats's lifelong literary love affair with Greek antiquities, such palpable artistry within the ode reclaims the lyricism that the Elgin Marbles had challenged, and indeed achieves the poetic triumph over physical monuments that Shelley asserts in "Ozymandias." And in the more general context of Keats's authorial advantages from periodicals—

the same kind of imperial conquest of readers and audience that Shelley's poem gains through allusion and dissemination—this physical quality within the ode has the further advantage of inviting the exhibitionary context that less self-consciously imperial magazines such as the *Examiner* lacked. The quintessential "well-wrought urn," Keats's poem demonstrates through its contextual history within a periodical magazine the conceptual space of exhibition that so many post-Napoleonic periodicals, such as the *Annals of the Fine Arts,* presented themselves as and were thought to be.

Of course, many late Romantic writers were far more self-conscious in their periodical collaborations than Keats, and not all of the geographical motifs invoked by these authors were as explicitly iconic of empire as the Greek or Egyptian antiquities adopted by Keats and Shelley. Accordingly, the body of this book focuses on four authors whose periodical involvement capitalizes upon those attributes more specifically associated with periodicals, such as their serial publication or the multi-author format of the corporate form. I begin in the first chapter with Charles Lamb, whose prominent contributions to the *London Magazine* are the archetypal example of an enthusiastic collaboration with post-Napoleonic periodicals that is conceived in expressly imperial terms. The essays that he first published in the *London Magazine*—later collected as the *Essays* and *Last Essays of Elia*—are loosely autobiographical works that play upon the facts of Lamb's concurrent employment in the East India House to suggest a literary profession directly modeled upon his imperial career. In the prominent role of economic improvement within his essays, the Elia series both reflects a general endorsement of imperial expansion that characterized the Whig magazine and uses that depiction of class mobility to figure Lamb's achievement of literary prestige. The most obvious instance of this profoundly material sensibility within the essays is a recurring theme of consumption and consumerism, which culminates in Elia's effusive depiction of oriental porcelain in the series' final installment, "Old China." In notable contrast to Keats's Grecian Urn ode, Lamb's essay about a Chinese teacup displays an economic sophistication whose explicitly material theory of status emulation through commodity consumption far surpasses Keats in its invocation of empire as a metaphor for prestige. Lamb's triumphal depiction of empire as a metaphor for the authorial benefits and advantages of periodical collaboration is the case by which all other late Romantic engagements with the post-Napoleonic periodicals are measured.

By contrast, James Hogg's ill-fated affiliation with *Blackwood's Edinburgh Magazine* is just such an example of an antithetical experience with contemporary periodicals. Although the rustic Scottish author became a household name largely because of his association with the urbane literati affiliated with the popular Tory monthly, the means of this celebrity were hardly favorable, as a comic series in the magazine—the mischievous "Noctes Ambrosianae"—lampooned Hogg in parodic caricatures that grossly undermined his small and hard-won literary reputation. The second chapter of this book therefore examines Hogg as an antithetical case of post-Napoleonic periodical collaboration, whose adverse relationship with a monthly magazine is evident in his representational identification with an imperial system opposed to the British triumphalism celebrated by Lamb. Napoleon, and specifically the fashion for Egyptian archeology that the French general precipitated with his North African campaigns, is a figure that pervades Hogg's most intriguing portraits of his relationship with *Blackwood's*. Both the "Translation from an Ancient Chaldee Manuscript," Hogg's first important contribution to the magazine, and *The Private Memoirs and Confessions of a Justified Sinner*, the allegorical novel about Hogg's relations with *Blackwood's* that remains his best-known work, allude to the Rosetta Stone, the hieroglyphic tablet unearthed in Egypt by Napoleon's savants, and which—along with Memnon's Head—was among the most prominent trophies of Napoleon's Egyptian campaigns to be requisitioned by the British upon their defeat of the French. By tracking the changes in Hogg's topical treatment of the stone—which first appears in the earlier "Translation" as a British trophy emblematic of Hogg's desire to affiliate with the corporate magazine, but which later resurfaces as the model for the mystical obscurantism of Hogg's famously complex and indeterminate novel—I show how Hogg capitalized upon the stone's translation to equate authorial genius with solitary production. Such a depiction, which reaffirms Romantic values for the individual imagination, functions in Hogg's novel to signify his post-*Blackwood's* disillusionment with periodical collaboration.

The mutual use of empire that occurs in both Hogg and Lamb, despite the vast differences in their relationships with the magazines with which they were involved, demonstrates the ubiquity of empire as a paradigm for conceptualizing periodical collaboration during the post-Napoleonic era. Despite their oppositional positions on empire and their respective involvement with monthly magazines at different sides of the political spectrum, Hogg and Lamb exemplify the contemporary use of empire as a professional model, through their identification with key spaces of recent territorial conquest, by their involvement with exemplary monthly magazines, and especially in the explicit organization of their imperial rhetoric around accessibly visual, material conceits. It is also significant that both these exemplary cases of post-Napoleonic collaborations with periodicals are authors commonly categorized as marginal or "minor" figures outside of the traditional Romantic canon, whose perceived sense of imaginative inadequacy is obvious in their frequent self-comparison of themselves to certain admired peers (Coleridge for Lamb, Scott for Hogg). Significantly, both case studies show that the authors overcome these perceived comparisons through their periodical involvement; indeed, this will also be true for Letitia Landon, discussed in the following case study, whose periodical involvement builds upon techniques she adapts from Madame de Staël. As with the use of imperial material culture as tangible forms of cultural capital instrumental to social mobility described by Maya Jasanoff, Lamb and Hogg suggest the particular value of these visual and imperial motifs for minor and marginalized authors who might most obviously benefit from the auspices of a periodical magazine. Indeed, like the countless Scots and Irish who discovered in imperial service a greater social and class status than they might ever have attained at home, the cases of Lamb and Hogg—a failed dramatist and a provincial autodidact—illustrate how the socially promotional qualities of empire were simulated in the massified, rationalized, and corporate nature of the periodical magazine.

But what of authors not involved with such exemplary forms of periodicals, or whose chosen geographical motif was not as visually accessible, or even of such explicitly imperial topicality as Greece, China, and Egypt? Part of the remarkable ubiquity of empire as a paradigm for conceptualizing periodical collaboration is that it prevails even among authors whose affiliation with periodicals is more subtle than Hogg's or Lamb's. Accordingly, the second half of this book focuses on a pair of writers whose periodical affiliation is as exceptional as Lamb's and Hogg's are exemplary. In the third chapter of this study, I examine the poetical work of Letitia Landon, the prolific poetess and former prodigy best known for her work with the giftbooks and annuals, but also an author distinguished for a repeated identification with *Corinne; or, Italy,* Madame de Staël's best-selling novel set in Napoleonic Italy. By exploring the mutual use Landon made of a poetics of derivative emulation within both of these veins of her literary production, I show how Landon's later work in the periodical giftbooks found a stylistic precedent in her adaptation of *Corinne,* particularly a depoliticizing take on the novel's Italian setting that Landon introduces to *The Improvisatrice,* one of her earliest and most important *Corinne* imitations. Such reductive engagement with empire—where empire is reduced to a mere figure for a formal device—marks an extreme variation upon post-Napoleonic engagements with empire among the periodicals, and indeed typifies a cultural trend that Byron works against. But at the same time, by working in the giftbooks and annuals—a format not usually considered a periodical publication comparable to a monthly or quarterly magazine—and by adapting elements of Staël's Napoleonic novel into a poetics suited for a post-Napoleonic periodical form, Landon's career testifies to the variety of imperial engagements within periodicals during this era.

Similarly, in the final chapter, on Byron, I examine a symbiosis of empire and the periodical press that contrasts with Landon's, and indeed all the previous cases of periodical engagements, in the purpose and degree of involvement to which empire is put. Where the previous writers employ empire as a paradigm to portray their professional relationship with the periodical press, Byron cultivates an explicitly political dimension to his periodical collaboration, where the form is instrumental to combating contemporary British imperial culture. In his role as cofounder of the *Liberal,* a short-lived but much discussed journal that Byron launched with Shelley and Leigh Hunt while the three were in Italy, and especially in works such as *The Island,* a fictionalized depiction of the notorious mutiny on the *Bounty* that Byron wrote with the *Liberal* in mind, the poet harnesses periodicals' very imperial qualities of territorial coverage and temporal continuity to recruit sympathy for a politically radical and often explicitly anti-imperial position. This project hinges upon Byron's use of poem and periodical to carve an alternative political and psychic space, whose symbolic model is the Tahitian island where the *Bounty* sailors hoped to remain, and whose political symbolism is obviously an antithesis to the imperial isle of England. Such involvement by the era's leading author and personality only demonstrates the omnipotence of the periodical format within the literary culture of the post-Napoleonic era, and in its radical, subversive, and oppositional use of periodicals to combat empire itself, is of course consistent with Byron's revolutionary politics. As the final chapter explores the difference between Byron's original intention to publish the *Island* within the *Liberal*, and the poem's eventual appearance as an independent publication, Byron's unique involvement with periodicals serves as a poignantly compelling case of both the attractions and the limitations of periodical involvement within the late Romantic, post-Napoleonic era.

The three minor writers and one major author who comprise the main part of this study therefore encompass a variety of positions and placements within the era's diverse periodical press. In their respective involvements with a Whig or Tory magazine, books targeted for young women, or an English magazine originating from Italy, the different periodical involvements explored in these chapters run the gamut of partisan reading, mass culture, and radical publication that comprise the various audiences of nineteenth-century periodicals. Indeed, like the different audiences and social bodies examined by Jon Klancher, Kevin Gilmartin, Ian Heywood, and Hilary Fraser, Stephanie Green, Judith Johnston, and others, the different cases examined in this study collectively portray, in microcosm, the variety and range of periodical involvement possible within the post-Napoleonic era.[44] Similarly, the distinct identities of the authors themselves also provide different veins of significance within the contemporary literary landscape. As the chapters move from Lamb's economic optimism as a member of imperial industry, Hogg's social marginalization by Edinburgh's urbane literati, and Landon's pragmatic manipulation of sentimental conventions, to Byron's revolutionary turn to the format for the purposes of subversive agitation, this book explores periodical involvement as it is refracted through the different allegiances and subjectivities of class, nationality, gender, and political ideology.

Indeed, Lamb, Hogg, Landon, and Byron may seem to have little in common other than the fact of periodical collaboration, but it is appropriate that their place in this study is unified, as it would be in a periodical, by the synchronicity of their publication. "Old China" and *The Island* both appeared in 1823, and *The Improvisatice* and *The Private Memoirs and Confessions of a Justified Sinner* are both publications from 1824. Thus, in the same way that the variety of contents within a periodical magazine provide a cross-section of contemporary literary culture within a specific moment in time, the works examined in these chapters all cluster around a very limited chronology, and resemble the miscellany of the very format that this book examines. (In fact, in the geographical variety encompassed in these chapters, these case studies recall the globe-trotting coverage cited in the *Examiner* number containing "Ozymandias.") Moreover, this collection also records thematic similarities that override initial differences to produce surprising cross-connections. For example, although Keats, Lamb, Hogg, and Landon are all minor or marginalized authors for whom periodicals were instrumental to their literary-professional advancement, the case of my last author, Byron, shows how the power of periodicals in the post-Napoleonic era was so extensive as to put even that major author—whose increasing radicalism placed him in the curious position of competing with his own, more commercially popular self—within need of the format. And although I have previously contrasted Lamb's and Hogg's exemplary periodical collaborations with the exceptional contributions of Landon and Byron, the pairs also suggest cross-relationships, where Lamb and Landon are similar in their enthusiasm for empire and periodicals, and Hogg and Byron similarly implicate periodicals in imperial critique.

But in outlining the comprehensiveness implied by these positive and negative collaborations with periodicals, it should also be noted what this book omits. Any study of empire within early-nineteenth-century periodicals might be expected to address India, the crowning jewel of the expanding reign, and might be likely to examine Macaulay, a former Indian administrator and the author of essays on Clive and Hastings for the *Edinburgh Review,* or De Quincey, whose rabidly imperial writings on China and India chronicle a literary career rife with periodical publications.[45] This book, however, does not limit itself to these journalistic and more explicitly political and topical writings—in the case of De Quincey, already brilliantly analyzed elsewhere[46]—in favor of the more oblique representations of empire that occurred in what used to be called the belle lettres. This is precisely why literary monthlies such as the *London* and *Blackwood's* figure more centrally than political quarterlies such as the *Edinburgh Review.* In these publications, such allusions to empire may occur in geographic references that use topical exoticism generally to suggest the expanded global consciousness associated with empire, and are a primarily metaphoric (if often highly detailed and sophisticated) use by these authors to conceptualize both Romantic ambition and the particular theater of publication in which their aspirations would take place. Indeed, the impact of periodicals for these late Romantic writers was so great that the ubiquity with which they use empire to characterize that experience also defines the periodicals themselves. Accordingly, although this book examines the collaborations of individual authors with distinct periodical series, it does so often to trace the continuing influence of periodical culture in works that were published outside of the format, but that still display traits clearly suggestive of the periodical culture in which they were developed.

I began this introduction by describing a curious synthesis of materialism and idealism in late Romantic writing, where the abstract ideals and sublime aesthetics commonly associated with romanticism found, in the economic and territorial expansion of the post-Napoleonic period, a powerful paradigm by which to conceptualize literary ambition. The periodical publication is a literary commodity whose qualities of corporate production and commercial expansion provided authors with a convenient analogue for the capitalist vectors of empire, and astute authors in turn exploited the format by propagating exotic geographical motifs suggestive of the expanding horizon of the imperial world. I would like to conclude, however, by returning to some of the larger implications of these moments of intersection between nineteenth-century materialism and Romantic idealism. Perhaps the most obvious issue at stake in this topic is orientalism, the deliberate deployment of "dreams, images, and vocabularies" used to "provoke a writer to his vision," and which, since Said's groundbreaking articulation of the concept, is inextricable from its complicity in imperial power.[47] With their deliberate mobilization of geographical exoticism as a vehicle for their literary-professional progress, Keats, Lamb, Hogg, Landon, and Byron all unquestionably participate in that practice. Indeed, in the case of the first three authors, with their rhetorical investment in specifically visual and material icons of contemporary empire, Hogg, Lamb, and Keats might be compared to the plunderers and profiteers whose pillaging of cultural patrimony is a particularly vivid example of the violence underlying orientalism (and whose consequences the twenty-first century continues to undo[48]). But from another perspective such moments of exoticism within late Romantic writing are vastly different from the kind of deliberate assertion of racial difference that underlies imperial and colonial power, a fact that may reflect their position in the first stirrings of nineteenth-century imperialism, before the bloodshed of transformative events such as the 1857 Indian Mutiny.

One version of such an alternative paradigm to imperial orientalism is "ornamentalism," the mitigated, less binaristic mind-set that David Cannadine claims characterized most imperial servants. In this controversial revision of Said's analyses of imperial power, Cannadine argues that visual and rhetorical modes of self-representation by imperial subjects were directed primarily at heightening internal class distinctions rather than enforcing racial difference between native and colonizer. "The 'really important category' was not race," Cannadine asserts, "it was status."[49] Such an insight may seem an appropriate model for the literary strategies of prestige apparent in late Romantic writing among the periodicals. Like the British viceroys and proconsuls who embellished their office with sartorial details (such as headdresses, regalia, and other imperial insignia), or the English aristocrats who sought equality with Indian rajahs, writers during the post-Napoleonic period invoke iconic emblems in their own versions of the "concept of hierarchy as social prestige."[50] Their uses of the exotic at such times depend upon empire's pomp and circumstance, but in their recurrent professional focus upon periodical collaboration, they may have little investment in the policies and power differentials of empire itself.

Another, more obviously literary analogue to the self-interested orientalism described by Cannadine may be *The History of British India,* James Mill's seminal tome of British policy that became required reading for imperial servants immediately upon its publication in 1817, despite the fact that Mill knew nothing of Indian languages nor had even visited the subcontinent. As Javed Majeed has argued, Mill's book is less relevant for its insight into Indian customs and manners than the ways in which its positions in contemporary colonial policy encoded a fierce attack upon British expansionism and the romantically paternalist, largely aristocratic impulses that Mill believed to be bankrupting British power.[51] In this displaced critique of the excesses of imperial expansion, Mill's use of empire anticipates the orientalism of his more literary contemporaries in the periodicals. In the same way that Mill's imperial critique really focuses on the nation at home, empire functions for late Romantic collaborators with periodicals primarily as a paradigm by which authors consider the more specifically professional conditions of the periodical industry in which they labored.

To accept such a nonviolent and aconsequential account to the imperial machinations of late Romantic writers is, however, profoundly naïve, but not only because it underestimates the complicity of authors among imperial culture. Rather, such an assertion does tremendous injustice to the sophisticated insight into imperial power that Romantic contributors to the periodicals demonstrate, and which they garnered from their collaboration with the literary analogue of imperial ambition and structure. Nigel Leask and Saree Makdisi have already documented how many Romantics were troubled by territorial expansion even as they grew proficient in its literary representation;[52] what needs also to be recognized is how the literary format so closely associated with empire reinforced that topical consciousness. Late Romantic authors closely affiliated with periodicals were deeply familiar with the adverse effects upon autonomy and personal integrity that empire entailed, precisely because of the way that the periodical practices of anonymity and pseudonymity, as well as the ability of a mass publication to manufacture reality, loosely resembled empires in their corporate practice and use of commodification to conquer vast populations. As a consequence, reference to empire among late Romantic writing in periodicals may have been a means of obliquely commenting upon the periodical industry itself, but it also was, increasingly, something more, as some periodical authors grew critical of empire and capitalized upon their familiarity with the periodical form to launch a concomitant critique of empire itself. Lamb and Byron, for example, the opening and closing case studies in this book, delineate the two extremes of post-Napoleonic positions upon empire. In their respective enthusiasm for periodical publication and oppositional use of periodicals to disseminate anti-imperial feeling, the periodical collaborations of the two authors illustrate alternate positions on empire—that is, to exalt or combat it.

By calling attention to the imperial critique embedded in their writing upon periodical collaboration, I want to show how late Romantic writers within the periodicals were far more revolutionary than has conventionally been recognized. An entrenched theme of Romantic history is the apostasy and domesticization of the revolutionary impulses of high romanticism. Whether described as the "Biedermeier" romanticism identified by Virgil Nemoianu, in an allusion to the focus on visual artifacts and commodities that fills much late Romantic writing, or "Romantic Victorians," Richard Cronin's recent account of the last years of Romanticism as an intriguing forecast of the prevailing concerns of the Victorian era, the years in which periodicals proliferated are not usually seen as a continuation of the revolutionary transformations of prior years.[53] This is in part because empire succeeded revolution as the era's dominant historical process, and introduced a different paradigm of expansion, consolidation, and bureaucratization whose literary parallels are thought to be apparent in the commercial predominance of sentimentalism. By contrast, by focusing on periodicals as the transformative historical process to which late Romantic authors responded, this account emphasizes how these authors manipulated and exploited those conditions to their own individual benefit. Indeed, the overtly visual and material motifs in their writing are integral to their literary strategies. The most obvious instance of the "signs" invoked by these authors, these motifs are indicative of the technique and sophistication with which these strategies are deployed. It is worth noting that both of these propensities toward commerce and visuality are attributes often portrayed as antithetical to the idealism of high Romantic aesthetics;[54] by embracing the conditions from which their immediate forebears recoiled, these late Romantic authors assert their artistic innovations and achievements.

Such innovations and achievements on the part of the late Romantics are perhaps most obvious in their unusual take on the place of the imperial and colonial culture within literary history. In *The World Republic of Letters*—a study whose title references a trope commonly assigned to periodical culture[55]—Pascale Casanova identifies an international literary space whose cosmopolitanism paradoxically elides the local or regional markers by which access to prestige is truly determined. (Thus, as Casanova describes it, authors in "small languages" are inevitably ghettoized by the limits of translatability, while authors from small nations but writing in major tongues conversely can transcend their citizenship to make claims for metropolitan appeal.[56]) Although the British Romantics who are the subject of this study may at first seem far afield from Casanova's interest, her model of an "international literary sphere" is valuable in that it provides an analogous instance of how those authors used geography to map literary prestige. "Literary relations of power are forms of political relations of power," Casanova asserts, stating one principle of a global literary sphere that also applies to the imperial motifs adopted by late Romantic writers; and in a further description of the principles of this representational sphere, which might also describe the specificity of distinct geographic spaces each Romantic author evokes, Casanova notes that "every project must be put in relation to the totality of rival projects within the same literary space."[57] Here Casanova recalls Bourdieu in her description of literary culture as a "network of objective relations" between agents, but Casanova's paradigm is particularly valuable for its inventive application of imperial and postcolonial history to literary study.[58] Instead of simply subjecting literature to ethical assessment, as have so many prior applications of literature to imperial history and postcolonial scholarship, Casanova reveals how political and historical conditions have and continue to structure literary production and reception.

The latter observation is particularly apparent in the comprehensive and cumulatively global range of geographic locations invoked by the authors examined in this study. Moving from Greece, China, Egypt, Italy, and Tahiti, the individual case studies in this book encompass a global diversity that simulates the circumference of the world itself. Such interdependent representational schema provides crucial insight into how their imperial tropes work. Because the specific location that each author adopts invokes a correlative in real-world politics—what Casanova calls "the extreme particularism of a literary project"[59]—the alternately abject or triumphal position of that place within nineteenth-century imperialism is a precise and highly detailed method by which the late Romantics portray their own, perceived autonomy within the corporate capitalism of contemporary periodicals. (Thus, Lamb aligns his authorial ascendance with the British opening of China, and Hogg portrays his changing position upon periodicals by his alternate identifications of Egypt with French and British occupation.) More generally, the real global positioning of each of these psychic spaces telegraphs in brief the author's immersion within contemporary periodical culture. This is most obvious in the final chapter, where Byron's identification with the remote South Seas emblematizes both his imperial opposition and his mounting disillusionment with the periodical press.

In summary, then, one of the greatest insights to be gained from applying imperial and postcolonial scholarship to early-nineteenth-century periodicals is the major reconceptualization of the periodical form that those insights prompt. We tend to think the defining attribute of periodical publications to be time, as implied by the rubric for which the format is most commonly known, but the prominence of imperial and geographic metaphors throughout writing developed around the early-nineteenth-century periodical press suggests, instead, that the format is as dependent upon space. A synchronic attribute that works in complement with the periodical's recognized diachronic quality of time, space manifests in periodicals in multiple ways. It exists in the physical space of their pages, whose contents report on a variety of spaces within Britain and around the globe, and is further charted by the dissemination of the publications themselves, whose centripetal journeys from the metropolis to the provinces map the communities that comprise a nation. Some periodicals further augmented these allusions to space by titular and institutional identifications with the nation's capital cities or ministerial centers, such as in the *London, Edinburgh,* and *Westminster* reviews. Indeed, if many contemporary periodicals proclaimed themselves the literary equivalent of the nation's capital, some periodicals went one further by evoking the physical sites for collection and display that crowned those metropolitan centers, and thereby enabled astute contributors to capitalize upon that conceit by likening their writing to the precious icon or artifact those sites displayed.

Most important, by systematically cultivating imperial and geographical motifs in their writing developed amid the periodicals, some late Romantic authors were able to effect a literary simulacrum, in which rhetorical allusion to contemporary world spaces figured their ambitions within the British literary sphere. To return to Benedict Anderson, it is the format's double ability both to jump massive distances in space through the collapsed time of its juxtaposed contents, and to use its perpetual production and vast distribution to conquer space, that makes the periodical publication such an effective vehicle for literary ambition. It explains why empire is such a compelling figure for that ambition. I will return to this subject again in the conclusion, but for now suffice it to say that some late Romantics were uniquely proficient in cultivating these attributes as opportunities for their own professional advantage. Even when their personal politics and professional perspective upon periodicals were critical of one or both of these elements, all of the authors explored in this study portray the power of periodicals as comparable to empire itself. The rich geographic variety of their writing amid post-Napoleonic periodicals is an intriguing early version of the "world republic of letters" described by Casanova, and a vivid, compelling glimpse into the nineteenth century's vibrant intersection between empire, periodicals, and literary ambition.

One

China for Sale

Porcelain Economy in Lamb's *Essays of Elia*

Few studies of Charles Lamb give sufficient attention to the impact of magazines on the development of his style and literary reputation. The occasionally obscure but often beloved essayist is known for the baroque and whimsical voice he unveiled in the series of essays he published from 1820 to 1824 in the *London Magazine,* and later collected as *The Essays of Elia* and *The Last Essays of Elia,* but most studies of Lamb tend to focus on his personal biography, particularly his lifelong friendship with Coleridge or his sister Mary's 1796 murder of their mother in a fit of insanity. In such psychobiographically driven approaches, the coy and quaint voice of the *London* essays invariably is explained as an escapist swerve or displacement from artistic inadequacy or an unthinkable past, such that the essays only make sense by association with those other figures.[1] The consequences of this widespread disregard for the magazine context of the Elia essays have been detrimental to Lamb. In their regressive emphasis upon authors and events of the 1790s, such accounts uphold the long-standing status of Lamb as a minor writer, apprehensible only in unfavorable comparison to figures such as Wordsworth and Coleridge, whom Lamb knew when they were at their height and when Lamb himself had achieved only the occasional poetry, a relatively unnoticed novel, and the failed play that constituted the extent of his literary production prior to his collaboration with the *London.*[2]

The magazine series in which the Elia essays first appeared, however, should give a very different background to the publications, one that substantially revises these long-standing notions of Lamb's authorship and reputation. As one of the many new magazines to launch during the periodical explosion of the post-Napoleonic years, and as a publication whose metropolitan title expressly identified itself with the national capital, the *London Magazine* was a periodical steeped in the contemporary culture of post-Napoleonic expansion. This aspect of the magazine's contents suggests a topical relevance to the Elia essays that contests past critical emphases upon Lamb's earlier decades, and it further expands scholarly accounts of Lamb by presenting, in the form of the corporate production of magazines, a vastly different kind of collaborative context to his authorship. The sum of these various elements is a dramatically different vision of Lamb as an author greatly advantaged by his fruitful collaboration with periodicals, a point previously made by Hazlitt in *The Spirit of the Age.* "Mr. Lamb," Hazlitt observes, "would probably never have made his way by . . . independent efforts; but, fortunately for himself and others, he has taken advantage of the Periodical Press, where he has been stuck into notice; and the texture of his compositions is assuredly fine enough to bear the broadest glare of popularity that has hitherto shone upon them."[3] In this celebratory account of Lamb's collaboration with magazines, Hazlitt acknowledges the format's capacity to provide the public exposure that hitherto had escaped Lamb. In a dramatic revision of the common critical accounts of Lamb's minor place in the Romantic canon, Hazlitt's description suggests the triumphal rather than tragic contours of Lamb's late career, points to the role of the *London* in enacting that rehabilitative process, and therefore suggests the importance of understanding the Elia essays in the context of the periodical in which they first appeared.

Accordingly, this first chapter examines Lamb as an exemplary instance of late Romantic collaboration with the post-Napoleonic periodicals, both in the general sense of the advantages gained from his periodical collaboration and the more specific fact that Lamb portrayed that success by explicitly identifying periodical authorship with the contemporary imperial project. The essays that Lamb composed for the monthly in the first four years of its establishment are loosely autobiographical. Although the continuity of Lamb with his fictional surrogate is perhaps most evident in details such as Elia's love of theater and prints (an aspect of Lamb already familiar to contemporary magazine readers through his essays on Shakespeare and Hogarth in the *Reflector*) or the character of "Bridget," Elia's spinster cousin and housemate, and a personality clearly based on Mary Lamb, the essays also reference Lamb's thirty-year career in the East India House. Far more so than Lamb's personal life, Lamb's professional affiliation with the era's prevailing engine of contemporary expansion is an intriguing analogue to the authorial conditions of periodical involvement, and as the organizing principle of the Elia essays, this parallel is secured by an ingeniously convenient pun. At the India House, Lamb was a clerk or "writer," a copyist whose job was to manually replicate the countless invoices and correspondence that documented the daily business of imperial trade.

This explicit identification of writing with imperial employment is most apparent in "Old China," a late essay whose allusion to the kinds of imperial objects and commodities that would have been the basis of Lamb's imperial labor anchors a complex analogy in which the upward mobility acquired through imperial service is equated with literary genius. For Lamb, the essay's subject of oriental porcelain will be particularly convenient because of its reference to Coleridge, but it also underscores Lamb as the most archetypal collaborator with the late Romantic, post-Napoleonic periodicals, whose sustained participation with the *London* far exceeds Keats in both the sophistication and the success to which empire is used as a metaphor to conceptualize his periodical contributions. Unlike Keats, Lamb was from the outset an enthusiastic magazine contributor, and his turn to an exotic artifact or commodity recalls Keats; but in a further distinction of himself from Keats, the specific emblem evoked by Lamb exerts an economic fungibility whose capacity for upward mobility is more demonstrable than Keats's urn. This capacity to convert economic determinism into a paradigm for authorial self-promotion that Lamb exerts in the Elia essays exemplifies the late Romantic fusion of idealism and materialism that is the larger interest of this study, and is also apparent, more specifically, in the triumphal imperial metaphors deployed by Lamb that differ drastically from Keats's images of lyric inadequacy. Indeed, in his productive collaboration with late Romantic, post-Napoleonic periodicals, Charles Lamb embodies the era's archetypal periodical engagement, and his collaboration with the *London Magazine*, long recognized as "one of the most important journals of the nineteenth century," constitutes an exemplary case study against which all subsequent collaborations must be compared.[4]

A Tempest over a Teacup

Founded in 1820 with the same name as a magazine popular a century earlier, the new, nineteenth-century *London Magazine* was a progressive journal that embodied all the postwar optimism of the post-Napoleonic period. As the prospectus announcing its formation proclaimed, "One of the principal objects of the LONDON MAGAZINE will be to convey the very 'image, form, and pressure' of that *'mighty heart,'* whose vast pulsations circulate life, strength, and spirits, throughout this great Empire."[5] Such direct connection between empire and the capital as the prospectus proclaimed uses the journal's metropolitan identity as an emblem of contemporary imperial expansion, reflecting the fact that the centripetal expansion of imperial interest beyond its national borders produces a corresponding centrifugal concentration of power in the metropolitan core. Thus, like the journal's eighteenth-century antecedent, which began in 1731 and was contemporary to the *Tatler, Spectator,* and *Gentleman's Magazine,* the new *London Magazine* made metropolitan culture a symbol of its modernity, and blended its metropolitan themes with avowedly outward-looking concerns. Most of its contributors were London residents, including its most prominent authors, such as George Darley, William Hazlitt, Thomas Hood, and Thomas Griffiths Wainwright, and urban identity also was an important attribute of the fictional personae the *London* authors occasionally adopted. In addition to the City worker Elia, for example, the *London* also hosted "Janus Weathercock," Wainwright's persona, a genial, dilatory commentator on all things in local, contemporary culture, and a figure whose urbane style was an obvious continuation of the periodical personas of the previous century, such as Mr. Spectator and "Sylvanus Urban," the personality of the *Gentleman's Magazine.* The contents of the new *London Magazine* also included features that emphasized either the exotic or the urban. The journal, closely identified with Whig interests and founded in opposition to the Tory *Blackwood's,* contained the greatest coverage of foreign topics among all contemporary magazines. It also included explicitly city-identified features such as the "Literary Police," a regular "intelligencer" column that reported on literature and the arts by parodying the police reports common in other periodicals, particularly since the establishment of the new metropolitan police with Peel's Police Act of 1819.

One particularly telling example of the *London*'s synthesis of urban and foreign was symbolized in Waterloo Bridge, an urban landmark with which the magazine was closely identified. The structure, originally known as Strand Bridge, but renamed in 1817 upon the second anniversary of Waterloo, was a monument of postwar British power that used urban markers to metonymize recent Napoleonic history. The *London* declared its affiliation with this simultaneously imperial and metropolitan symbol by locating its offices near the bridge and even printed an illustration of it on the cover of at least one issue (June 1822). Some *London* contributors further built upon the magazine's conflation of urban geography with post-Napoleonic expansion by referencing the bridge in their publications. In November 1821, for example, Thomas Hood provided the magazine with "A Sentimental Journey, from Islington to Waterloo Bridge," an essay whose topic seemed to dramatize the circulation of life throughout city and empire that the magazine's prospectus promised. In its reprise of the magazine's symbolic identification with Waterloo Bridge, Hood's memoir offers another instance of the kind of sentimental prose amid topical representations of empire that would also characterize the Elia essays.

So consistent, in fact, was the *London* in upholding a contemporary culture of modernization that the magazine's organization and business practices were similarly progressive, further revealing the journal's affinities with imperial enterprise. Like the *Edinburgh Review,* which famously professionalized journalism by introducing a regular standard of pay, the nineteenth-century *London* employed a stable of regular contributors who were paid at standardized rates, thereby constituting a rationalized collection of professional laborers. Moreover, these institutional practices were conceived in suggestively democratic terms. In her valuable history of the magazine, Josephine Bauer notes that in this era of fiercely partisan journalism, the *London* was known to be one of the most fair-minded of contemporary periodicals.[6] The reactionary politics of the Tory *Blackwood's Magazine,* against which the *London* developed in self-conscious alternative, will be discussed in the next chapter, but the comparatively nonpartisan culture of equality for which the *London* was known is apparent in the rhetoric by which contemporaries described the periodical. Francis Jeffrey had once characterized his editorship of the *Edinburgh* as that of a "feudal monarch who really had but slender control over his barons."[7] If Jeffrey's metaphor hints at the changing nature of contemporary journalism, the *London* embraced it, as Thomas

Noon Talfourd observed of the magazine that its editor, John Scott, "was more fit to preside over a little commonwealth of authors than to hold a despotic rule over subject contributors."[8] With his metaphorical comparison of the *London* circle to a "commonwealth," Talfourd's comment illustrates contemporary conceptualization of periodicals in political, if not imperial, terms.

With such evident embodiment of progressive ideology, the *London Magazine* could be considered a literary microcosm of contemporary imperial culture. But although these aspects of the magazine's institutional culture encouraged certain themes or topics within the publication, such as the *London*'s coverage of foreign literature, the power of such themes was so significant that they could encourage meanings even when not intended. Mark Schoenfeld, for example, has suggested that in the *London* "seemingly apolitical, subjective articles positioned next to highly political . . . accounts are transformed," and thus that "a Charles Lamb essay is affected by a Hazlitt piece published in the same issue."[9] Perhaps even more intriguing is how institutional interests could effect unlikely collaborations between a journal and contributors who might otherwise be less predisposed to the organ. A point often made about early-nineteenth-century magazines is the diversity and dissonance within individual numbers and series, such that despite the oft-noted partisanship of the era, many periodicals include contributions from authors at opposite ends of the ideological spectrum.[10] De Quincey's famous *Confessions of an English Opium-Eater* is a case in point. The memoir was first printed in the *London* as a two-part essay series in the September and October issues of 1821 (which included two Elia essays, "The Old Benchers at the Inner Temple" and "Witches, and other Night-Fears"), and came at the initiative of Lamb, who had met the younger author at the East India House.[11] Although De Quincey was a Tory, and already involved with *Blackwood's,* the *Confessions* had a general relevance for the *London*'s interest in the foreign, and thus, like Keats's Elgin Marbles sonnets, presumably were accepted for publication based on their thematic appeal.[12]

Indeed, this theme of exotic consumption within De Quincey's *Confessions* was a point of connection with the Elia essays that shared the *London*'s pages. Although, as Klancher points out, commodity culture and an ethos of consumption were often integral to the nineteenth-century magazine form, Lamb's essays for the *London* were a particularly overt instance of this tendency through their identification with mercantile trade. The first essay in the *London* series, "Recollections of the South Sea House," which appeared in August 1820, introduces the character of Elia by establishing his long history within imperial industry. As Elia calculates, it began "forty years ago, when I knew [the South Sea House]."[13] This detail about Elia establishes the autobiographical continuity between the character and Lamb himself, who also experienced a brief stint at the famed trading firm of the preceding century. In 1789, upon his graduation from Christ's Hospital, the charity school that Lamb had attended and where he and Coleridge became lifelong friends, Lamb had entered the burgeoning imperial industry by first working, for a few months, at the South Sea House, where his older brother was already employed. A few years later, in 1792, Lamb settled at the East India Company, the preeminent engine of the era's mercantile capitalism, and where Lamb would work for the next thirty-three years—the whole of his working life. Together the two experiences had an influence that always defined Lamb for himself as well as for his friends and peers. In the 1800 publication of Coleridge's poem "This Lime-Tree Bower My Prison," for example, the work is "Addressed to Charles Lamb, of the India House, London."

With Elia's imperial identity firmly established in the *London* series, Lamb's essays grew more explicit on the link between literary and imperial writing. In the second essay in the series, "Oxford in the Vacation," Elia describes how "the very parings of a counting-house are . . . the settings up of an author."[14] He claims, for example, that the long stretches of purely reproductive writing he performs during the day give him renewed inspiration to write at night when, instead of copying, his "enfranchised quill" can move for creative purposes. And, more practically, Elia's day job provides resources that serve one occupation as well as the other, as remaindered paper from the India Office, such as "outside sheets, and waste wrappers of foolscap, do receive into them, the impression of sonnets, epigrams, *essays*." Such economical recycling of "the many commodities incidental to the life of a public office" was, in fact, practiced by Lamb. At least one personal letter written on East India House stationary in Lamb's correspondence shows that he was not above filching from his employer for his personal writing.[15] Although Elia's discussion here is mercantile rather than imperial, and might describe privileges available to any clerk, the specific context of Elia's and

Lamb's imperial employment makes that representation of commerce inextricable with imperial logic. Indeed, in dramatic depiction of a Keats-like investment in exotic objects, Elia also turns those imperial imports into opportunities for Romantic wonder. Thus, although it is true, Elia admits, that he is "a votary of the desk . . . [,] one that sucks his sustenance . . . through a quill," the same imported merchandise that his quill daily counts also inspires his imagination. Thus Elia remarks in the same essay, with a longing, aesthetic sensitivity that would be recognized, as the series grew, as a distinct attribute of Lamb's style, that "I confess that it is my honour, my fancy . . . to while away . . . my time in the contemplation of indigos, cottons, raw silks, [and] piece-goods" (365).

The culminating account of Elia's enthusiasm for exotic or foreign commodities is "Old China," a late essay that Lamb produced for the *London* after a hiatus and only as a favor to the editors, but which remains one of the best-known installments in the series and is an essay often anthologized as one of the finest examples of Lamb's work.[16] The essay is a paean to Chinese porcelain occasioned by Elia's purchase of a china teacup, and begins, in Elia's characteristically nostalgic aesthetic sensibility, by recounting the powerful spell that oriental ceramics hold upon Elia's imagination:

> I have an almost feminine partiality for old china. When I go to see any great house, I inquire for the china-closet, and next for the picture gallery. I cannot defend the order of preference, but by saying, that we have all some taste or other, of too ancient a date to admit of our remembering distinctly it was an acquired one. I can call to mind the first play, and the first exhibition, that I was taken to; but I am not conscious of a time when china jars and saucers were introduced into my imagination. (269)

Here Elia's remarks illustrate the late Romantic mingling of idealism and materialism that characterizes so much writing in the post-Napoleonic periodicals. By yoking commodity culture with imagination, Lamb renders aesthetic sensibility as something measurable by commercial indices. Such aesthetic interest in a foreign object may be consistent with the *London*, but it is most important for the insights it reveals about Lamb. By including porcelain among more familiar Romantic pleasures of drama and painting, Lamb makes a strong claim for the aesthetic and cultural significance of porcelain, a household item usually trivialized as a decorative—and therefore minor—art. Indeed, Elia does not merely equate china with these subjects, but in fact hierarchizes and prioritizes porcelain. When presented with a chance to see the prized collections of the nation's great houses, Elia first visits the china closets before the picture gallery. He even acknowledges that his love of these items precedes other aesthetic pleasures, having inhabited him for so long that Elia cannot remember a time before porcelain was part of his imagination. Such association of porcelain with "imagination," the key term of Romanticism, encapsulates a variety of radical gestures characteristic of the imperial romanticism of second-generation, post-Napoleonic writing. It naturalizes foreign among domestic, elevates minor above major in a leveling of the traditional aesthetic hierarchies, and allies commodity culture with the traditionally transcendent concerns of Romantic imagination.

Importantly, however, and perhaps in keeping with the *London,* this extraordinary aesthetic enthusiasm for porcelain with which Elia opens "Old China" is immediately succeeded in the essay by a sophisticated economic discussion, which occurs in a debate between Elia and his cousin Bridget, who is dismayed by Elia's purchase of the china teacup. This debate, which comprises five of the six magazine columns devoted to the essay, might be an informal version of the essays on political economy that a contemporary magazine reader might expect from De Quincey, and illustrates the sophisticated contemporary consciousness with which imperial commodities are treated by Lamb in the *London.* Bridget, who is older than Elia, objects to the teacup, apparently because her economic understanding is based on scarcity and privation. She remembers a time when picnics and playgoing had "relish" "in proportion to the infrequency" (271), and believes that a "thing was worth buying [only] when we felt the money that we had paid for it" (270). Consistent with this economic philosophy of virtuous austerity, then, Bridget cherishes her memories of how they suffered for each individual acquisition, and she heightens the emotional sensations of purchasing by compounding the pleasure with guilt ("pleasure was the better for a little shame" [271]). In the various anecdotes Bridget recounts, such as how Elia wore an embarrassingly threadbare coat in order to save up for another item they hoped to buy, Bridget shows that she values sacrifice more than the object it obtains. Such consumer trepidation avoids moral hazard by always seeking to spend as little as possible. Indeed, Bridget is acutely sensitive to cost, as her memories are always careful to include the exact price of items ("half," "twice," "single share"; "a less number of shillings," "the one-shilling gallery," "fifteen—or sixteen shillings was it?" [270–71]). In such nervous anxiety over consumption, it is not surprising that Bridget overstates economic status and the cost of commercial transactions. Thus, despite her proclaimed desire for a "middle state" (270), in fact her economic perspective is too polarized to permit such a condition. Claiming that "it is the very little more that we allow ourselves beyond what the actual poor can get at, that makes what I call a treat," Bridget exaggeratedly describes herself and Elia as "rich" (271).

Both the anxieties she suffers over consumption and the language by which Bridget exhibits them reflect what John Sekora has called the "classical" view of luxury. As Sekora explains, Puritan suspicions of self-indulgence and aristocratic excess grew so pervasive that in the eighteenth century, pronouncements against luxury were so common as to constitute a distinct literary mode.[17] With her biological seniority and economic conservatism, the portions of "Old China" written in Bridget's voice clearly belong to this antecedent literary tradition. Indeed, Bridget exhibits her cultural archaism in both the language and the imagery that she invokes and in the overly emotional way in which she responds. Rejecting their current situation, when "a purchase is but a purchase," and wistfully longing for a bygone time when "it used to be a triumph," Bridget betrays the fact that the "good old times" for which she yearns for are romantic poverty (270). In this curious fusion of *ubi sunt* sentiment with economic policy, twice she rebukes Elia with the question "Was there no pleasure in being a poor man?" (270, 271). And, clearly favoring an earlier moment in economic history, Bridget idealizes an idyllic England before industrial development, as she dwells on the literature and drama of the previous centuries (Shakespeare, Walton, and Beaumont and Fletcher) and recounts anecdotes that feature small business, in which transactions are handled by a single proprietor (the innkeeper, the bookshop owner). Ironically, though, Bridget herself is the only person affected by her longing, and the affect she registers is profound. Consumed by her feelings about consumption, Bridget disgorges a relentless flow of memories, which follow upon each other in such swift succession that a single period constitutes a whole paragraph, and thereby betrays a consumer so little jaded by experience that she is all but overcome with excitement.

Elia, by contrast, is wholly at ease with luxuries. He has no guilt over his teacup, and is no more apologetic of it than of the "luxurious" sofa upon which he and Bridget then sit (272). His comments to Bridget brush away her reminiscences ("they are dreams now"), argue that the "resisting power" has "long since passed away," and justify their improvements in lifestyle as necessities due their age ("Competence to age is supplemental youth. . . . We must [now] . . . live better, and lie softer") (272). In stark contrast to Bridget's protracted and almost hysterical response, Elia's allusion to his teacup is so minimal as to pass parenthetically: "(a recent purchase)" (270). Similarly, his sense of value lacks the precision of Bridget's memory for prices but is more balanced in his sense of proportion. Proving himself to have a better idea of a "middle state" than Bridget, Elia clarifies that though they now have "a clear income of poor —— hundred pounds of year" (272), they are still far from being "rich."

Elia's refusal in the previous quote to specify the exact sum of their income is of course a further point of distinction between his pleasures and Bridget's obsessive interest in prices. In the long context of the Elia series, which by the time of "Old China" had appeared in nearly fifty essays over the course of five years, this extended insight into Bridget's perspective—the single longest depiction of the character in the series—merely reiterates the charming revelation of personality that infused nineteenth-century periodicals and with which the Elia series was replete. But in the more specific concerns of the *London* and Lamb's interests in particular, "Old China" offers a glimpse into the benefits of imperial expansion, particularly how they are experienced by individual citizens. The china teacup that occasions the essay is explicitly a component of imperial economy, along with the tea that it held and which Bridget and Elia drink. Indeed, the East India Company was the era's leading importer of porcelain, and hence the teacup upon which Elia discourses is exactly the kind of item that Lamb daily tabulated at his imperial employment. The teacup's significance as a luxury symbolic of the upward mobility possible through imperial expansion is doubly true for Lamb because of his income from imperial service. A former bluecoat boy and child and grandchild of servants, Lamb would not otherwise have been able to describe himself as "rich." That his fictional surrogate does is because of the "favourable circumstances" (270) that Elia references in the essay—clearly a reference to the imperial economy that both has brought foreign goods like porcelain to British consumers and, in Lamb's case, that also provides the disposable income to acquire those artifacts.

In keeping with the *London*'s progressive economics, then, Elia voices a distinctly modern consumer philosophy. In his allusion to being "introduced" to porcelain, Elia arguably references the new strategies of advertising that marketers developed to vend industrial and imperial abundance, and in his gleeful ability to "love" one pattern of china, and love another, "still more" (270), Elia expresses a consumer insatiability that would be a retailer's dream.[18] That the essay "Old China" consists overwhelmingly of Bridget rather than Elia does not obscure his role as the true heart of the essay. The sociologist Colin Campbell has argued that Romantic capacities for nostalgia and aestheticism were instrumental in neutralizing the proscriptions against luxury consumption once common in Puritanism. Building upon the insights of Harold Bloom, but showing those precepts operating in economic decisions as well, Campbell shows how the Romantic capacity for double-consciousness was instrumental to the emergence of modern consumer culture.[19] Such insight into modern consumer economics illuminates the double-voiced structure of "Old China," which is not unique among the Elia essays, but which certainly develops that device to an unusual degree. In his good-natured audience to Bridget's monologue, Elia indulgently allows Bridget to state her objections, without really responding to or even acknowledging them. Indeed, in the very pattern that Campbell describes of including nostalgic commentary only to contain it, Elia's sole response to Bridget's anxieties is to return her attention to the teacup. Urging her to "just look" (272) upon the cup, Elia assumes that visual pleasure can resolve moral resistance and economic reservations, exhibiting a typically modern consumer sensibility that believes that an object itself legitimates its purchase.

But if "Old China" presents a modern consumer sensibility consistent with the *London*'s progressive economics, what is the significance of the specific luxury item that provokes Bridget's and Elia's debate? A century earlier, oriental porcelain had been at the center of a consumer craze known as "chinamania."[20] Like "tulipmania," the frenzy for tulip bulbs in seventeenth-century Amsterdam that caused a massive economic collapse, this mania for porcelain china in eighteenth-century Britain was the subject of considerable moral and political concern. William Gay's 1725 poem "To a Lady, on her Passion for Porcelain China," for example, gently chastises a woman for her bankrupting predilections for these items of fashion, and specifically illustrates the fact that female consumers were popularly figured as the source of this consumer craze.[21] Similarly, "Old China" alludes to this gendered history of chinamania in both Elia's allusion to his "almost feminine" love of porcelain and Bridget's defensive concern. Another factor of anxiety in the history of chinamania was the fact of foreign profit that consumer craze entailed. In 1730 Henry Fielding remarked of the frenzy that "the mud of one Indies runs away with the gold of another."[22] In effect, Fielding points out, the purchase of these exotic items squanders the very profits just earned through foreign expansion. These comments from the history of chinamania point to another reason for porcelain's significance in Lamb's essay, as well as for the *London* magazine and the *Elia* series at large. If essay, magazine, and series all testify to the transformative importance of empire in the daily life of British citizens, they do so in explicit acknowledgment of their difference from the same topic a century ago. Indeed, as an essay on porcelain china published in an urbane cultural magazine explicitly titled after an eighteenth-century predecessor, "Old China" also has more obvious literary antecedents in the several essays about porcelain consumption by Addison and Steele that appeared in the *Tatler* and the *Spectator,* and which, like Gay's poem, cautioned against the moral hazards of excessive enthusiasm in oriental porcelain.[23] Yet although Lamb's essay clearly emulates its predecessors in subject as well as style, "Old China" asserts—as did the new *London* in comparison to its eighteenth-century forebear—an explicitly modern consumer ease with this potentially scandalous luxury object.

The specific means by which porcelain attained this newly unproblematic status in the early nineteenth century should of course be an issue of inquiry, as well as why porcelain sparked such remarkable consumer desire, but it is worth first exploring how "Old China" relates, more generally, to the visual object at the center of the essay. Lamb's essay is often compared to Keats's "Ode on a Grecian Urn," an observation that highlights the works' shared interest in an exotic artifact, as well as a mutual tendency in both literary works to verbally emulate the visual item at its subject. In "Old China," this tendency is implicit in the charm and apparent triviality of Lamb's distinct form of the familiar essay, a prose genre whose personal tone and domestic subject have obvious affinity with the "minor art" of household porcelain. It is also apparent in Lamb's typically ingenious plays upon words and imagery. "Here is a . . . Mandarin, handing tea to a lady," Elia remarks in an ekphrastic description of the cup. As he notes "how distance seems to set off respect," he puns upon his own status as a servant or "mandarin" of imperial bureaucracy, and points out how the images on the china cup replicate his and Bridget's debate (270). These similarities in subject and achievement between Lamb's essay and Keats's poem have not gone unnoticed in criticism. In a characteristic statement of his aestheticism, Walter Pater once praised "Old China" for "realis[ing] the principle of art for its own sake, as completely as Keats."[24] And in a more specific description of the essay's likeness to its visual emblem, Richard Haven contrasts the intensity of feeling in Bridget's monologue to the equanimity of Elia's framing remarks, arguing that their debate—an alloy of sentimentality tempered by irony—evokes the teacup's hollow structure and cool porcelain glaze. "At the end," Haven claims, by reading the essay, "it is, so to speak, the tea cup which we hold in our hands."[25]

The problem with such formal approaches to Lamb's essay, however, is that they overlook the material pragmatism underlying "Old China," which distinguishes Lamb's periodical contribution from less self-conscious collaborations such as Keats's. In particular, such interpretations that attend to only the verbal-visual relationship overlook the crucial fact that Elia's teacup differs from Keats's urn in being a commodity, an item of commercial transaction, which is not necessarily true of the Grecian urn. Keats's urn, for example, is only the object of Keats's gaze and contemplation, and is not described as being acquired or fungible. This inert and priceless quality of the urn is exactly how the ode cultivates the conditions of museum display that make the poem such an apt contribution to the museological *Annals of the Fine Arts.* By contrast, price is everything about Elia's teacup, as Bridget's disquisition on the item demonstrates, and her protracted discussion of their past purchases and the other items they forwent in order to acquire them uses the economic concept of opportunity cost to emphasize the commodity's fungibility. These attributes of accessibility and fungibility assert a dynamic quality to the china teacup that far exceeds the urn, and they will be crucial in

Lamb's ability to use his magazine collaboration to advance his authorial stature. In playing upon the teacup's representativeness for historical change, and by further enhancing that mobility by its place in the progressive *London* and especially in the essay series modeled upon imperial service, Lamb uses the item's economic mobility as a figure for his own authorial self-advancement.

Marx's classic analysis of the commodity form thus provides an illustrative paradigm by which to understand the significance of Elia's teacup and the essay that Lamb builds in emulation of that artifact. In *Capital,* Marx notes that a commodity "appears at first sight an extremely obvious, trivial thing," but "analysis brings out that it is in reality a very strange thing, abounding in metaphysical subtleties and theological niceties."[26] This recognition of the commodity's seemingly trivial but actually complex nature echoes the "subtleties" and sophisticated resonances that underlie Lamb's apparently trivial familiar essay, and suggests as yet untapped significances to "Old China." One of the most important aspects of these connotations is the specific foreign location with which the "china" teacup is associated, and which is linked in Lamb's mind with romantic posterity. "I should like to have my name talked of in **China**," confessed Lamb once in a letter to Thomas Manning, a friend and fellow India House employee who would be the first Englishman to meet the Dalai Lama.[27] His remark hints at a link between China and fame that runs throughout the Elia essays, and which culminate in "Old China" through an immensely strategic allusion to Coleridgean genius.

Made in China

For Marx, the foreign is often integral to commodities, and indeed is an element crucial to the commodity's transformation into a "thing which transcends sensuousness."[28] His own reference to commodities as a "fetish" borrows the term for African objects of worship, and uses the word to claim exoticism as a value-added attribute that inflates a commodity's exchange value. These issues of foreignness are clearly at stake in "Old China." In the essay, Bridget's objections to the teacup notably emphasize local produce (lamb, strawberries, and peas) as more seemly alternative purchases, therefore suggesting their consumer debate as one between economic isolationism and geopolitical expansion. (Bridget, one might say, occupies the position that De Quincey would later advocate in *Blackwood's*, and enfolds into the essay's competing economic philosophies a market differentiation between the two magazines.) Indeed, in further distinction from De Quincey, Elia shows a singularly undistracted interest in China. In sharp contrast to the syncretic mix of Chinese objects that mingle with Egyptian crocodiles in De Quincey's essays on opium, as well as the jumble of Japanese lacquer and Arabian or South American coffee that occurs in Pope's "Rape of the Lock," to cite one well-known literary depiction of porcelain, Elia exemplifies the topographical precision that distinguishes the expanding imperial consciousness of post-Napoleonic Britain.[29] In "Old China," Elia drinks his Hyson tea "unmixed" (270), in the Chinese fashion, refusing even to add the sugar that was another staple of British imperial trade. His sinophilic dedication to experiencing the exotic as exotic is further corroborated by the consistent interest in Chinese artifacts that Elia displays in other essays. Some forty essays before "Old China," in February 1821, Chinese commodities first appear in "Mrs. Battle's Opinion on Whist," in which Elia remarks upon "delicately-turned ivory markers [the] work of Chinese artist" (163); and in "A Dissertation upon Roast Pig," a later essay whose title recalls an influential volume of eighteenth-century chinoiserie, William Chambers's 1772 *Dissertation on Oriental Gardening*, Elia's enthusiasm for Chinese commodities is directed toward a Chinese recipe.[30]

Elia's interest in porcelain thus exists because he is interested, more specifically, in China, reflecting a common association by European consumers of the commodity with its county of origin. After all, the colloquial name, "china," explicitly asserts this metonymic relationship and derives from the item's material relation to the country. Like pottery, porcelain's less refined cousin, porcelain ceramics are made by firing clay, usually mixed from local soil. With this commodity being formed from the very Chinese earth, every piece of Chinese porcelain was a tangible remnant of the remote land from which it originated. "Old China" plays upon this connection of country and commodity in a number of ways. The very title of the essay invites this conflation, as the label could just as well signal the geographic location, particularly before the visual and economic discussion within the essay begins. More imaginatively, in "Old China," the indexical relationship of commodity to country is further developed through the ekphrastic pleasure Elia takes in his teacup, as he gazes upon its ornamental decoration as if it were a telescopic window into China itself. The vignette painted on Elia's teacup, of two figures and a small stream topped by a bridge and surrounded by trees, contains just enough detail to comprise a miniature world. The pattern identifies it as the blue and white "willow-ware" pattern characteristic of Ming dynasty porcelain, which was the most popular china pattern in Britain throughout the eighteenth and nineteenth centuries and, by the time of Lamb's essay, was also known as "old blue china" or—as Elia calls it in the essay—"old blue" (270).[31] For Elia, part of the fascination of "old china" is the glimpse it provides into this curious world. Thus, although in the nineteenth century both terms to describe ceramics were used interchangeably, in Lamb's idiosyncratic locution, the synonym "porcelain" never appears. Moreover, in further insistence upon the commodity as a glimpse into remote China itself, Elia cites the gravity-defying imagery on the teacup. Charmed by the "little, lawless, azure-tinctured grotesques, that . . . float about, uncircumscribed by any element," Elia uses the contrast between "our optics" and "that world before perspective" to juxtapose the countries of Britain and China (269–70). Like a new planet that swims into ken, the teacup causes Elia to confuse and conflate its porcelain glaze for the "lucid atmosphere of fine Cathay" (270).

Such an impulse to see commodity as country was encouraged by the limited knowledge of China then available in the West. Throughout the eighteenth century, China was closed to Western contact, as trade with the country was handled entirely by the few Dutch and Portuguese compradors who had been located there for centuries. (It was Portuguese traders, in fact, who supplied the Chinese porcelain presented in the marriage of Catherine of Braganza to Charles II in 1662, and who first introduced the material to the British.) In 1793 and 1794 Lord Macartney failed in missions funded by the East India Company to persuade the Chinese emperor to lessen strictures against British trade, and as late as 1816, a similar mission by Lord Amherst also failed. This gross imbalance in familiarity with China then endured by the West resulted in an interesting set of conventions about China, which often figured the impregnable and clearly advanced country as something verging on the sublime. As Arthur Lovejoy and others have shown, aside from vague notions about the remote country's vast size and population, China was largely known in Western imagination for the luxury items, such as silk, porcelain, and tea, that the country exported to enthusiastic British and European consumers, as well as the wondrous feats and charming accomplishments of their culture, such as the Great Wall or the vogue for oriental gardens that took hold of Europe in the middle of the eighteenth century.[32] For the British in particular, porcelain became an emblem of their relative economic weakness in comparison to China—a fact spurred by British demand for tea, but compounded by fierce trade protections on the part of the Chinese, who demanded all payment for exports in specie.

"Old China" alludes to some of these contemporary notions about China through Elia's remark that in china patterns, "likeness is identity" (270)—a claim that conflates the indiscriminate numerousness of that population to the ceaseless import of matching teacups. A more explicit glimpse into this distinctly eighteenth-century version of sublime China, however, can also be seen in "Kubla Khan," Coleridge's immortal "vision in a dream" about Xanadu, the fabled empire that Mongol rulers established in thirteenth-century China, and now a canonical Romantic poem that at the time of its composition was already much admired and envied by Lamb.[33] As described in its preface, the poem was composed by Coleridge in 1797—the year in which reports of the failed Macartney mission to China were published—and is based on an opium-induced dream the poet experienced when he fell asleep while reading *Purchas his Pilgrimage,* the widely known seventeenth-century travel narrative that includes passages based on the memoirs of Marco Polo. With this text, an exemplar of the eighteenth-century vision of sublime China, as the stimulus of Coleridge's slumbering imagination, the dream-vision in the poem is consistent with fantastic contemporary accounts of China as a place admired, desired, but largely unattainable by British citizens. In "Kubla Khan," the vast and mysterious country of China defies comprehension, with its "caverns measureless to man" (lines 4, 27), and the artful Chinese landscape—a quintessential genius loci—itself seems to produce more art, as it throws up a "mighty fountain," "huge fragments," "dancing rocks," a "sacred river," and an "incense-bearing tree" (lines 19, 21, 23, 24, 9). The Khan himself, who rules the country by autocratic fiat, is an extension or epitome of the wonders of the country. The Khan embodies Chinese luxury and the genius that creates it through the "stately pleasure-dome [that he] decree[s]" (line 2). With a wave of his hand he fashions things of physical impossibility, like the dome, "that miracle of rare device" that defies the laws of science ("A sunny pleasure-dome, with caves of ice!") (lines 35–36).

Interestingly, however, "Kubla Khan" invokes the Chinese setting as a metaphor for imagination, and like "Ozymandias," the poem uses oriental imagery primarily as a vehicle for authorial exaltation. Coleridge's poem is commonly understood as an allegory of Romantic genius, in which the Khan, who personifies the imaginative power of Chinese landscape, is only a transitional figure, apparent in the fact that the dream-vision includes a prophecy of monarchical succession: " 'mid this tumult Kubla heard from far / Ancestral voices prophesying war!" (lines 29–30). The claimant to the Khan's rule that the poem heralds is described in the final strophe, which warns of a mystical figure (he of the "flashing eyes, and floating hair" [line 50]). The allegorical implication of the poem is clear: Coleridge, the poet-dreamer who voices the vision, in incantatory verse that repeats Xanadu's convulsive creation of beauty, is the Khan's successor. "Could I revive within me / Her symphony and song," the speaker claims, "I would build that dome in air" (lines 42, 46). Conditional tenses notwithstanding, Coleridge's claim to "build in air" both describes the poetic act of verbal artistry and aurally puns on the genetic lineage from Mongal conqueror to Romantic poet, the Khan's heir. Coleridge may have used opium to get there, but it is he, the poem implies, who "on honey-dew hath fed, / And drunk the milk of paradise" (lines 53–54).

Such strong claim of poetic genius as Coleridge makes in "Kubla Khan" illuminates Lamb's similar thematic interest in China, which, apparently in keeping with long-standing accounts of the Romantic canon, portrays Lamb as only a minor writer distinguished primarily for emulating his peers. The standard critical version of Lamb's writings is that they are imitations of his more illustrious contemporaries, such as Wordsworth and especially Coleridge. In this hieratic reading, Lamb's familiar essays are a diversionary prose version of what he could not achieve in poetry, and merely a symbol of his imaginative limitations. Contemporary commentary on Lamb, for example, often stressed how his essays, which Lamb began after over twenty years of only modest success as a critic and playwright, were the first time he exhibited a unique voice.[34] Modern criticism for the most part continues this diminutive characterization of Lamb, emphasizing his collaborations, influences, and perceived inadequacies rather than exploring him as an independent and successful artist.[35] Even Thomas McFarland, for example, who argues that prose is as structurally accomplished a medium for Romantic expression as is poetry, repeatedly emphasizes Coleridge as the object of Lamb's anxiety of influence, and therefore seems to corroborate the very subordination of Lamb that he intends to interrogate.[36]

Indeed, Lamb himself initially seems to uphold these opinions, as he explicitly addresses his relationship to Coleridge in the earlier Elia essay "Witches, and Other Night Fears."[37] In the essay, which manipulates the same geographical symbolism in which China figures so prominently in "Old China," Elia confides how he envies Coleridge, who "at his will can conjure up icy domes, and pleasure houses for Kubla Khan," while he himself "cannot muster a fiddle . . . [or] raise up the ghost of a fish-wife." This description of Coleridge's creative powers clearly picks up on the generational allegory in "Kubla Khan," and even seems to admit Elia's inability to participate in that lineage. As Elia laments, "The poverty of my dreams mortifies me." Indeed, in further elaboration of the belatedness often attributed to Lamb, the "Witches" essay goes on to describe, à la "Kubla Khan," a dream-vision Elia had "that very night" after reading. Although the poet Elia mentions is Barry Cornwall, Elia's dream consists of a seaborne procession with himself as "the *leading god,*" and in this "marine spectra" recalls Coleridge's other classic of exotic imagery, his "Rime of the Ancient Mariner." Such an allusion to Coleridge would seem to affirm the character's apparently debilitating genius envy. Indeed, just as "Kubla Khan" was forever prevented from completion by the interruption of the man from Porlock, Lamb too is ignominiously cut short. Despite Elia's momentary vision of himself in triumphal parade, his thrill is abruptly truncated as the waters subside into the Thames, his exotic marine vision dissolves, and he is abruptly deposited, "inglorious, somewhere at the foot of Lambeth Palace" (387).

But if "Witches, and Other Night Fears" at first seems to uphold Lamb's belatedness to Coleridge, the essay also uses its allusions to revise this initially unfavorable comparison. As suggested in his allusion to the "poverty" of his dreams, Elia's self-comparison with Coleridge is a fundamentally class-based paradigm, in which Coleridge's access to exotic and imagination-inspiring locations such as Kubla's China and the allegorical sea of the "Rime of the Ancient Mariner" is contrasted with Elia's habitation in London, and hence to the bounds Elia experienced as one whose livelihood depends upon his employment as a City worker. (Similarly, elsewhere in the essay, Elia laments that he has no ability "to make out a shape, in any way whatever, of Helvellyn," reinforcing the country-city dichotomy often noted in Lamb scholarship as an example of his benighted self-perception [387].) Yet just as Elia assumes "recent favourable circumstances" to have rendered anachronistic the historical proscriptions against luxury consumption that Bridget raises in "Old China," "Witches, and Other Night Fears" also foregrounds the upward mobility experienced by recent historical change. Lambeth Palace, where Elia's dream ends, was a new residential area near Waterloo Bridge and the City of London to which Lamb had recently moved, and it featured significantly more comfortable housing than that available within the City itself. Just like the china teacup, then, Elia's residence at Lambeth Palace signifies the improved circumstances of the new class of clerical workers employed by imperial industry. The triumphal symbolism of the area is further suggested by its proximity to Waterloo Bridge, the imperial monument so important for the *London Magazine,* and exhibits the newfound benefits enjoyed by Londoners as imperial progress catapulted the national capital into new prominence as the world's capital, bringing its urban residents along with it.

Readers of Lamb are familiar with his unabashed love of London. In his correspondence with Wordsworth, despite his expressed envy of the poet's access to the Lakes, the proud Cockney also enthuses about the city's endless joys, and when Wordsworth visited the city in 1802, Lamb's enthusiastic tour of the city did much to correct Wordsworth's prejudices.[38] More important here, however, is how Lamb's use of urban geography within the "Witches" essay maps a psychic geography of Romantic privilege that equates genius with class, and hence how Lamb uses that class-based paradigm to show himself overcoming that structure and simulating the language associated with the very high Romantics whom he admired. In "Recollections of Christ's Hospital," for example, the third installment in the series and another of the best-known Elia essays, Lamb offers a protracted reminiscence of the charity school that he attended with Coleridge.[39] Interestingly, however, although the setting and subject might again seem to suggest the essay as an instance of Lamb's inadequacy, the "Christ's Hospital" essay surprisingly overturns that expectation, as Lamb writes part of the essay in the voice of Coleridge and portrays the future poet in notably unromantic terms (namely, as childishly envious of treats that Lamb receives from his family). Even more ambitiously, in "Blakesmoor, on H——shire," an essay from much later in the series, Elia visits the country estate where his grandmother had been in service as a housekeeper.[40] Yet despite its setting at a country house, an archetype of aristocratic privilege, in the essay Elia stages a subtle but remarkable assertion of his claim to that privilege, and does so in language and diction strongly associated with Wordsworth. Rejecting traditional aristocratic conventions of birthright and patrimony, Elia claims that sentimental love of the house causes his "own" blood to "answer" the "tedious genealogies" of the great house's previous tenants, and thereby produces his own "correspondent elevation" (227). Such a claim echoes the *Prelude*, particularly the passage where the "corresponding . . . creative breeze" causes Wordsworth to feel "the sweet breath of Heaven" (1.43, 41); and in an unmistakable echo of the passage in the *Prelude* referring to the Boy of Winander, which describes an "uncertain heaven, received / Into the bosom of the steady lake" (5.387–88), Elia goes on to claim that in his love of the country house "I received into myself Very Gentility" (227).

In their ventriloquizations of Wordsworth and Coleridge, these essays employ a version of the Romantic double-voicing that also underlies the formal structure of "Old China." Indeed, if, as Colin Campbell shows, such nostalgic embedding of older sensibilities into an explicitly modern aesthetic was instrumental in the naturalization of modern consumer desire, the double-voicing in these Elia essays works to enfold a similar economic concern, linking class privilege with Romantic genius to use Elia's changing economic circumstances to portray his developing authorial voice. In "Blakesmoor, on H——shire" and "Recollections of Christ's Hospital," this accession to Wordsworthian and Coleridgean language comes by way of overt examples of class status (a country house, a charity school), but in other essays Lamb portrays this social standing through more subtle but topically relevant motifs of urban and global geography. After all, as early as "Oxford in the Vacation," the early essay whose main subject is how the nongenteel Elia can attend university only during its recess, Lamb juxtaposes that exclusion with the "indigos, cottons, raw silks, [and] piece-goods" that he observes through his India House employment. The essay implies that imperial experience provides opportunities that compensate for exclusions suffered by his class. Similarly, in "Witches, and Other Night Fears," Lamb uses the alternatively exotic and "prosaic" imagery available to himself and Coleridge to assert his artistic equivalency. In "Witches," as in all the other essays, Elia may be rooted in London, but his daily access to the artifacts and commodities originating from exotic locations that he experiences through his imperial employment makes Elia's city experience reach outward—as does the magazine in which those essays appeared—toward a global geography that includes the visionary glimpse of Coleridgean China at the center of the late essay "Old China."

To return to "Old China," then, these discursive affinities between Coleridge's major poetry and Lamb's purportedly "minor" essays should raise questions about such hieratic rankings. "Old China" does not just obliquely address the same oriental subject of China within "Kubla Khan." It also contains many terms and images that mirror the language and imagery in Coleridge's poem. The "deep romantic chasm" (line 12) that in "Kubla Khan" yawns at the side of the hill reappears in "Old China" as the "chasm . . . impossible . . . to fill up" (271) should Bridget or Elia miss a word in a play. Coleridge's "caverns measureless to man" are recalled in the later essay by Elia's denial of a "fathom line that ever touched a descent so deep" (272), and the "shadow [that] . . . / Floated midway on the waves" (lines 31–32) in Coleridge's poem reappears in Lamb's essay as the "passing sentiment" that "overshade[s] the brows" of Bridget (270). Such lexical echoes and similarities in imagery, moreover, are mirrored by additional correspondences in form and tone. For example, the hyperventilated excitement that Bridget exhibits as she recounts her memories resembles the "fast thick pants" (line 18) with which the earth breathes in "Kubla Khan," and Elia's indulgent dismissal of Bridget, which "smil[es] at the phantom . . . which her . . . imagination had conjured up" (272), resembles the tone of Coleridge's preface to the poem, which similarly describes a powerfully transfixing image only to also narrate its abrupt dissolution.

In the agonistic account of Lamb's anxiety of influence regarding Coleridge, all these parallels between Lamb's essay and Coleridge's poem could be seen as evidence of Lamb's derivative imitation of Coleridge—as if Lamb's work as a clerk influenced his writing only by confusing creation with copying. Instead, though, the precision and extent to which Lamb reprises Coleridgean words and images demonstrate his brilliant appropriation of the sublime genius associated with Coleridge that he previously envied. Of paramount importance is the fact that Lamb's essay most notably compares with Coleridge's poem in the shared geographical origins and physical attributes of their visual emblems. Elia's teacup, also made in China, is round and hollow, like the Khan's pleasure-dome, and is described with similar physical attributes. Both items contain glimpses of an enchanting, geometry-defying topography, as the images painted on the sides of the teacup in the "speck of deeper blue" (270) reconstitute, in a slightly different hue, the "sunny spots of greenery" (line 11) with which the Khan's dome also is "girdled round" (line 7). Thus, a "*speciosa miracula*" (270), if not a "miracle of rare device," Elia's porcelain teacup bears cold and bright attributes similar to a "sunny pleasure-dome with caves of ice."

Of course, a teacup is only a dome in miniature and overturned, a physical distinction that elucidates how the relationship between the two texts, and their authors, ought to be understood. That is, the morphological similarity of dome to teacup (where "likeness is identity") claims Lamb's equivalency with Coleridge, while the diminution and upending of the cavernous dome into miniature cup symbolically inverts the sublime pretensions within Coleridge's dream-vision of China in "Kubla Khan." This radical gesture of miniaturization and inversion symbolizes Lamb's confident appropriation—and even transcendence—of Coleridgean genius. By adopting a purchasable emblem of China, instead of attempting to depict immense China itself, Lamb is able to triumph with a complete, rather than fragmented, work. "Kubla Khan," after all, is a poetic fragment, famously truncated when Coleridge was "unfortunately called out by a person on business from Porlock," a disruption in the "distinct recollection" of his dream in which Coleridge claims to have dashed out the first verses of the poem before the interruption forever dissolved his vision. Lamb, however, unlike Coleridge, is not disturbed by business. Indeed, in taking a porcelain teacup, an emblematic commodity of imperial trade, as his means of access to Coleridge's magnificent dome, Lamb makes business the very stuff of his imagination.

What is particularly ingenious in the porcelain emblem with which Lamb replicates the visionary genius that he associates with Coleridge is that it reveals the industrial trade upon which Coleridge's genius actually was built. The economic might and commercial supremacy that China commanded in part due to its monopoly on porcelain had long been an object of competition for British manufacturers, who hoped to gain some share of the lucrative market. While British competition with China in porcelain production was not effective until after the turn of the century (as will be discussed later in this chapter), the domestic porcelain industry had already wrought significant benefits for at least one major Romantic. In 1797 Coleridge was granted an annuity by Thomas Wedgwood, brother and business partner of Josiah Wedgwood, the visionary potter whose strategic provocation of consumer demand for porcelain had catapulted the two to the ranks of England's wealthiest men. This annuity freed Coleridge from teaching and clerical duties, affording him the financial security and leisure to read that were not available to his charity school classmate, Lamb. The latter's essays for the *London,* such as "Witches, and Other Night-Fears," acknowledge this link between genius and class privilege—a link that Lamb further exposes in "Old China" by alluding to the material conditions enabling Coleridge's poetic production. It is not so much the capacity to imagine the country of China, Lamb points out, that is the sign of Coleridge's poetic genius, than it is the manufacture of porcelain china, which provides the necessary economic conditions for poetic composition.

In this insightful analysis of the increasing centrality of business to Romantic imagination, Lamb reasserts the economic sophistication that distinguishes his orientalism from that of Keats. Lamb chooses a commodity over a priceless work of art precisely because its status as a commodity ensures its accessibility, for anyone with the ability to pay. This consumer version of imagination is fundamentally democratic and exists because of empire, the current "favourable circumstances" then responsible for British imports of oriental porcelain, as well as the disposable income that allows Elia to purchase his china cup. Yet although the china teacup is affordable—and apparently has descended so much in price that it has become, as Elia unconcernedly describes it, a "cheap luxury" (270, 271)—this affordability does not compromise its aesthetic and symbolic value. As Marx points out, one of the defining attributes of the commodity is its value-added fiction, in which mass-manufactured items can resonate with profound appeal. Porcelain is a particularly effective symbol of consumer pretensions because of its history. Once a rare object worth its weight in gold, and still an artifact prized by connoisseurs, porcelain epitomizes the conspicuous consumption that social theorists ranging from Veblen to Bourdieu note is instrumental to asserting class elevation.[41]

Of course, the affordability of porcelain china, as the debate between Bridget and Elia originally suggests, was only a recent phenomenon, but before I review how historical developments in British relations with China brought about that shift in trade, I first want to explore certain aspects of Lamb's style and how they adapt aspects of Coleridge's poetry. In the preface to "Kubla Khan," Coleridge describes his dream as one in which "all the images rise up before him as *things,* with a parallel production of the correspondent expressions, without any sensation or consciousness of effort." Coleridge thus describes a scene of spontaneous poetic composition typical of high Romantic mythology, but in doing so also betrays a fundamentally material logic underlying imagination, in which an "anodyne" activates "a profound sleep," images rise up as things, and their words come to Coleridge, similarly spontaneously, like the rocks and fountain that are flung from the earth in the poem itself. It is precisely this model of imagination as an acquired rather than organic process that would prove so convenient to Lamb. In both the literary process by which Coleridge created "Kubla Khan" out of *Purchas* and the countless other literary works that John Livingston Lowes and Elinor Shaffer have shown the poet to have referenced, as well as the more material process by which Elisabeth Schneider, Alethea Hayter, Barry Milligan, and Alan Richardson have all shown opium to instigate Coleridge's imagination, Coleridge presents imagination as a process of ingestion and regurgitation that inadvertently lays the groundwork for the stylistic appropriation and recycling that Lamb so ingeniously would employ.[42] Thus, if for Coleridge, "with the exception of some eight or ten scattered lines and images, all the rest had passed away like the images on the surface of a stream," it is precisely this model of imagination as a series of received "things" that enables Lamb to present himself as one poised to collect and recycle those same "scattered lines and images." In his prosaic rewriting of "Kubla Khan," Lamb achieves transcendence precisely because he treats words as things, in pragmatic recognition of the actual terms by which Coleridge portrays them.

Such a rhetorical process by Lamb might be described as a kind of desublimation, a materializing conceit that dredges up from Coleridge's sublime vision the physical circumstances that make that vision possible, and re-presents as its literary emblem the very industrial product enabling Coleridge's poetic production. In "Old China" in particular, this materializing desublimation is Lamb's prismatic reprocessing of words and images from "Kubla Khan," such that individual terms and images are taken from their original context, scrambled, and reinserted, often with an entirely different meaning, into a new composition with an entirely different formal and discursive shape. This scrambling, moreover, is not limited to a single essay, but can also take place in other installments of the *London* series, as "Witches, and Other Night Fears," the other essay to specifically reference "Kubla Khan," also demonstrates. It is precisely this capacity to repetitively consider a topic that makes Lamb's Elia essays an archetypal example of late Romantic capitalization upon the post-Napoleonic periodicals. Indeed, in an intriguing twist upon the "dynamic relationship" between individual contributions that Mark Parker has previously identified as a key aspect of periodical culture, the Elia essays accrue meanings not just from the connections of individual essays to the adjacent articles and publications in the issue in which it appeared, but also between different installments of the same series. This temporal continuity of the *London* essays evokes the ceaseless import and manufacture of mass-manufactured commodities like porcelain, and further illustrates the parallels between Lamb's imperial and periodical writing. Indeed, in Lamb's other references to China and commodities within the Elia essays, the series begins to simulate the whole of the contemporary British and China trade. This conceit of historical evocation hinges upon opium, the one element of Coleridge's dream-vision without obvious analogue in "Old China," and a commodity whose crucial role in Sino-British trade is precisely the historical development that Lamb references to inaugurate "Old China"'s access to the porcelain associated with Coleridgean genius.

China for Sale

In her perceptive discussion of the periodical form, Margaret Beetham points out that the periodical is a paradox that creates novelty out of repetition. "Every number of the periodical is the same in that it offers its readers a recognizable persona or identity," Beetham observes, "but every number of the periodical is [also] a new number which is different from all previous numbers," and which "must function both as part of a series and as a free-standing unit which makes sense to the reader of the single issue."[43] This tension between necessary repetition and desired originality helps account for the oft-documented resistance to the periodical format among high Romantics, but it also provided unusual opportunities for accrued meanings from installment to installment, and over the course of a series or run. With their serial production during the best years of the *London,* Lamb's Elia essays provide a particularly rich example of this distinct periodical attribute. In addition to their recurrent interest in Chinese artifacts and commodities, most Elia essays are characterized by a number of formal and thematic similarities. Thus, to apply a Proppian or Barthesian structural analysis to "Old China," "Recollections of the South Sea House," "Oxford in the Vacation," "Recollections of Christ's Hospital," "The Old Benchers at the Inner Temple," "Witches, and Other Night Fears," "Mrs. Battle's Opinion on Whist," and "Blakesmoor, in H——shire," to name just the essays cited in this chapter, most Elia essays are characterized by a consistent structure and content. The typical Elia essay (1) begins with an effusive confession of aesthetic taste, (2) incorporates some discussion of nostalgic recollections, and (3) concludes with a return to modern consciousness and common sense that causes Elia to moderate his nostalgia.

Such oscillation between memory and emotional realization as occurs in the Elia essays may recall the "out-in-out" structure that M. H. Abrams identifies as distinctive to the greater Romantic lyric, illustrating again how Lamb reprocesses Coleridgean, high Romantic poetry into prose.[44] More to the point, though, this recurrent structure of the Elia essays calls attention to the series' representativeness of the periodical format in general, and particularly foregrounds the analogy between periodical collaboration and industrial production that underpins the link between Lamb's literary and imperial employment. In their constant repetition of consistent concerns and attributes, the Elia essays themselves display the "likeness [that] is identity" in the production or import of manufactures such as porcelain teacups. Moreover, if this attribute of serial manufacture reveals the essays to be more like the commodity they feature than has previously been recognized, this is especially true of the brand those publications bore. These essays "written under the signature of Elia," as they were described in the subtitle to the *Elia* and *Last Essays of Elia* volumes, are like the chop marks on the bottom of porcelain objects that were originally the mark of the artisan, but were later imitated in the imprimaturs of porcelain manufacturers. In effect, they are a form of literary branding that Lamb developed in simulation of contemporary import or manufacture. Indeed, his success at this literary career modeled upon present-day imperial employment is particularly evident in the mutual benefits he enjoyed at both jobs. As Elia became the acknowledged star of the *London,* Lamb was paid at twice the rate of other contributors and became the magazine's most highly paid author. This fame also induced reciprocal improvements for Lamb as an India House clerk, as evidence suggests that as his literary fame grew, the author also was increasingly indulged by his supervisors at the East India Company.[45]

At times Lamb also profited on his professional knowledge of the contemporary porcelain industry by conducting private sales of porcelain, such as he did for his friend, the poet and Quaker businessman Bernard Barton.[46] Such direct profiting from his imperial employment is another instance of the professional connections between Lamb's literary and imperial interest, but it is less interesting than how Lamb used the time and space portrayed in his essays to revisit economic and consumer history. It is significant that in the series' opening essay, "Recollections of the South Sea House," Lamb already identified himself with economic controversy. The House is inextricable from the South Sea Bubble, the massive financial speculation for stock in the South Sea Company, an early venture into offshore investment that suddenly collapsed in September 1720, sending a generation of English investors into financial ruin. Such widespread economic misfortune, one would think, would be dangerous waters for the *London,* yet remarkably, however, Lamb's essay does not shy away from this history, and indeed draws attention to that episode. The essay explicitly names "the breaking of that famous BUBBLE" and acknowledges its pernicious nature ("that tremendous HOAX"), even capitalizing the nouns—a common typographic practice in the eighteenth century, but by 1820 increasingly archaic (142). Yet, intriguingly, the essay raises that historical specter only to emphasize its epochal remove. The archaic capitalization by which the "BUBBLE" is represented already alludes to its anachronism, and Elia builds upon this idea in his evocative description of the building itself. Describing the South Sea House as a *"poor neighbour out of business"* (143; emphasis in the original), Elia recalls this early disaster in British foreign economy only to neutralize its relevance to the present day. In August 1820, exactly a century after the eve of the breaking of the Bubble, when Elia sees the South Sea House, he is not reminded of its past, but instead sees the building as the antithesis of the "stirring and living commerce" in the adjacent buildings (143).

As an early publication in the *London,* and the first installment of what would become the Elia series, "Recollections of the South Sea House" thus establishes the tone and outlook of the *London Magazine.* "Situated . . . in the very heart of stirring and living commerce,—amid the fret and fever of speculation—with the Bank, and the 'Change, and the India-house about [it], in the hey-day of present prosperity" (143), the South Sea House should embody, like Waterloo Bridge, the metropolitan reminders of contemporary imperialism, or what the *London*'s prospectus described as the "'image, form, and pressure' [at the] *heart* [of] this great Empire." Yet because Elia has already described it as defunct and irrelevant, the essay voices an openness to cultural encounter and territorial expansion that typified the progressive Whig perspective of the *London.* Importantly, such a description of the empty, "almost cloistral" (143) monument at the core of empire is both evidence of the nation's distance from the destructive propensities of eighteenth-century investment in foreign goods and economies, and a metaphor for the role of Lamb's essays within the *London.* In their shared use of the same metonymy of global empire within urban topography with which the *London* debuted, Lamb's essays for the *London* distill aspects of the massive experience of contemporary empire into the quaint, comfortable, and small-scale world of his "familiar" essays.

One of the decisive events marking the imperial expansion that the *London* celebrated was the opening of China to British trade, which initiated in the year before the magazine's launch, and to which at least one of the essays alludes. In 1819 the English adventurer Stamford Raffles seized the southeast Asian island of Singa Pura (Singapore) in the name of the East India Company.[47] With this territorial foothold into the once closed Chinese empire, this annexation precipitated rapid increase in British knowledge about China. Lamb parodies this fact in the September 1822 essay, "A Dissertation upon Roast Pig," one of the other essays to allude to Chinese commodities, and in fact Lamb's most sustained and specific depiction of China. In this essay, nominally about the culinary delights of roast pork, Lamb exhibits the expanding factual awareness of the foreign that would typify later-nineteenth-century culture, and which certainly was visible to Lamb from his vantage at the India Office. The essay, written in a parody of a scholarly dissertation, begins with an apocryphal Chinese fable supposedly told to Elia by Thomas Manning ("my friend M." [245]), Lamb's Sinologist friend who became one of the earliest British explorers to enter China after Singapore's annexation, and also includes pseudo-scholarly references such as "Cho-fang," supposedly an ancient Chinese dynasty (245).[48] The premise of the anecdote is the accidental discovery of the taste of roast pork when a bumbling Chinese pig farmer, Bo-bo, inadvertently sets fire to his house with a litter of baby pigs inside. In this facetious depiction of the birth of civilization—what Levi-Strauss would later call the difference between the raw and the cooked—Lamb offers a comically superior perspective upon China that differs dramatically from the awe of Coleridge's eighteenth-century vision in "Kubla Khan." Bo-bo, the proverbial village idiot, is a buffoonish foil to the Khan's magisterial acts of superiority, and in further suggestion of the Chinese race as a primitive and ignorant civilization in dire need of English guidance, Lamb portrays the Chinese villagers bringing society to near collapse. In their insatiable demand for the exquisite flavor of roast pork, the Chinese burn their houses until "the insurance offices one and all shut up shop," and "it was feared that the very science of architecture would be . . . lost" (246).

Significantly, the only thing that saves China, according to the anecdote, is a "sage . . . like our Locke" (246), and it is in this allusion to a key figure of English intellectual history that the "Dissertation" signals its variation upon all the desirable attributes once associated with China, but which were increasingly under revision with the nineteenth century's changes in Sino-British trade. By portraying the Chinese as an ignorant and primitive society whose consumer desire precipitates social regression, and by allying the proper or correct practice of that consumer behavior with England, Lamb effects a remarkable rewriting of history, essentially denying the long history of Chinese economic might over Britain, as well as Britain's own history of self-destructive financial speculation, such as that which occurred in the South Sea Bubble crisis and during chinamania. Of course, such gestures of historical erasure are not unique to Lamb, nor are they the only instance in his essays where Lamb accords a supposedly foreign commodity or history distinctly Western characteristics. In *Robinson Crusoe,* Defoe portrays his English castaway instructing Friday in the use of the barbecue and the canoe—despite the fact that both technologies were in fact devices that European colonists adopted from Polynesian natives.[49] Somewhat similarly, "Old China" includes descriptions of Elia's teacup that hint at a Western rather than oriental origin. Horses, trees, and pagodas are involved in an English country dance ("dancing the hays"

[270]); other animals ("a cow and rabbit couchant" [270]) are described in the language of English heraldry; and the ostensibly Chinese lady is crypto-Catholic, "half-Madona-ish" (272). In these suspiciously indigenous terms, Elia seems to acknowledge the fact that the willowware pattern favored by Western consumers and collectors was in fact an "export" design, meaning that it was created by Chinese manufacturers solely for the Western market.[50]

The "Dissertation upon Roast Pig" is thus an essay about British imperial destiny that enacts the very conditions it describes. Through its portrait of Chinese consumers rendered abject by their relentless desire for consumer fulfillment, the essay both displaces the kind of debilitating consumer desire that Bridget seems to fear in "Old China" and also alludes to the new commodity within British and Chinese trade that was so instrumental in the facilitating of the confident sense of English economic superiority that pervades, however facetiously, the "Roast Pig" anecdote. This commodity was opium, an addictive stimulant, like coffee and tea, which Britain cultivated in their other colonial outpost of India and which the new trading settlements in the South China Sea enabled Britain to begin exporting to China. Although the paralysis of Chinese society that would cause Commissioner Lin to wage his vendetta against British opium trafficking did not occur until the following decade, "Roast Pig" already seems to anticipate these conditions through its depiction of addled Chinese consumers and the social degradation their consumption depicts. Lamb's prescience is inspired, in part, by his close reading of Coleridge, whose allegory of succession both enables Lamb's literary accession as well as forecasts an English curtailment to oriental fantasy. In effect, Lamb resolves the problematic history of chinamania—in typically desublimating manner—by literalizing it as a mania in China itself.

It is important to clarify here that Lamb's essays for the *London* are not simply reflecting the cultural and historical symptoms of imperial expansion that the magazine would also have reported more directly. More interestingly, the essay series also simulates and reinforces the very historical processes those essays describe, particularly profiting upon the protracted and infinite temporality of the series to accrue resonances that yield benefits in later essays. As an essay preceding "Old China," for example, "Roast Pig" lays the conditions for Elia's guilt-free pleasure in his teacup, both in the general sense by which the essay's parodic depiction of China references the growing British confidence arising from empire, and in the more specific way that depiction alludes to opium, the key transitional commodity within Sino-British trade. And although opium was a crucial component in the changing balance of power between China and Britain that metaphorizes Lamb's accession to Coleridgean imagination, Lamb does not rest with this oblique reference but instead also includes in "Roast Pig" a more specific allegory of the porcelain trade. Throughout the eighteenth century, Western preference for Chinese porcelain was based on a perceived superiority of their product, typically attributed to their clay. Although domestic porcelain distributors such as Wedgwood, Minton, and Spode were soon aided by the local discovery of similar resources toward the end of this century, Chinese porcelain still maintained a translucence and refinement attained by superior firing technique. "Roast Pig" alludes to this modern industrial quest for fire through the anecdote's comic fable about combustibility, as well as—once again—a typically desublimating pun. The word "porcelain" was thought to derive from *porcellana,* a term applied to ceramics because of its resemblance to the luminous hardness of cowrie shells used by the Portuguese traders who first introduced porcelain to the West. Those shells themselves had gained the name from "a fanciful resemblance between their backs and the backs of little pigs, [also] commonly called *porcellana.*"[51]

As an instance of early imperial culture within the contemporary periodical press, the "Dissertation upon Roast Pig" thus illustrates the acute and timely consideration by which literary contributions evoked some of the more subtle aspects of contemporary imperial development. Through its literal interpretation of the etymology of porcelain, Lamb's essay plays upon the homophony of "porcelain" and "porcine" to speciously dramatize the history of porcelain manufacture. Moreover, because "Roast Pig" co-opts that manufacturing secret as an English rather than Chinese achievement—essentially repeating the same conceit in *Robinson Crusoe,* whose fable of economic progress hinges upon the hero's quest to fire pots[52]—the essay executes a radical gesture of historical revisionism that is less interested in the facts of contemporary industrial competition than in foreshadowing the imminent triumph of British domestic porcelain manufacturers. By the time of the British opening of China, domestic porcelain manufacturers perfected their firing techniques and—as the suggestive Western attributes within Elia's teacup imply—had been producing successful imitations of oriental porcelain patterns for some time. (Indeed, in a further point of comparison between Elia's teacup and Keats's urn, some scholars have suggested that the object of Keats's attention was not an actual antiquity but rather one of the faux "Etruscan" vases by which the Wedgwood company first shot to fame.[53]) These domestic manufacturers benefited tremendously from the havoc in the Chinese economy wrought by British opium trafficking. As Chinese consumers soon found themselves paralyzed with desire in the same manner in which English consumers had once yearned for Chinese porcelain, British manufacturers and traders began a reciprocal export to China of their own domestic porcelain product. In 1823—the very same year as "Old China"'s publication—Spode supplied the Canton branch of the East India Company with its own version of "old blue." The balance of trade between England and China definitively shifted with this development. By 1826, only a few years later, the flow of silver between England and China had reversed, in England's favor.[54]

The "Dissertation upon Roast Pig" secures this modern era of guilt-free consumption in a nostalgic anecdote with which the essay closes, and which enables the restatement of modern sensibility by which so many Elia essays conclude. In the anecdote, Elia recalls a childhood moment of charity, when he had given a beggar a cake made for him by his aunt. Although his impulse was selfless, the humor of the episode lies in the fact that Elia now regrets his act, having convinced himself that the beggar "was a counterfeit" (248), and that to honor his aunt he ought to have consumed the cake himself. Elia uses the anecdote to justify his appetite, which revels in the epicurean taste of roast pork, but the story functions, as with the Chinese fable with which "Roast Pig" opens, as a parable legitimating consumer desire. As Denise Gigante has already noted, eating is a recurrent theme throughout Lamb's essays.[55] Although Gigante does not dwell on the more abstract significations of Lamb's depiction of taste, this recurrent emphasis on eating is also a literalization of the economic concern with consumption that drives so many of the Elia essays, and which the "Dissertation upon Roast Pig" asserts so that Elia, in the final essay, can "just look" at his china teacup.

What makes Lamb's essays for the *London* such an ingenious use of empire within contemporary periodicals, then, is his ability to embed his authorial promotion within the historical processes his periodical publications describe. Because porcelain offers Lamb a potent connection to Coleridge and the vision of exotic China by which Lamb figures Coleridgean imagination, and because porcelain was then an object of imperial trade becoming increasingly affordable to English consumers, the very representation within his essays of these relationships further realizes the link between his authorial and clerical "writing" upon which the *London* essays are built. In short, Lamb equates and even bests Coleridge as his essay series—a serial production of literary commodities that simulates the attributes of the commodity it portrays—presents a productivity and infinitude that far surpass Coleridge's sublime, but solitary and incomplete, poem.

This ability to synthesize imitation and originality that Lamb demonstrates throughout the Elia essays is best summarized in Edward Bulwer-Lytton's description of Lamb's capacity for "stamping" each essay with his individual style and personality. Lytton's comment, with the evocative echo of mechanical reproduction inherent in the onomatopoeic verb "to stamp," emphasizes the similarity and interchangeability between the various essays "under the Elia signature," and typifies the industrial production and commodity capitalism that Lamb exploits so effectively as a model for his authorial class promotion. We will see this industrial trope of stamping again in Hogg's Gothic novel, *The Private Memoirs and Confessions of a Justified Sinner,* and will also visit another version of the imitation and originality conflict within periodicals in the third chapter's discussion of Letitia Landon's work in the literary annuals. For now, though, it is sufficient to establish the imperial triumphalism with which industrial "stamping" is associated by Lamb, the exemplary collaborator with post-Napoleonic periodicals. In poignant contrast to the imperial triumphalism that Lamb enacts in his essays for the *London Magazine,* for Hogg the effects of magazine incorporation that are signified by this figure of stamping instead ring with the defeated tones of personal and authorial tragedy.

Two

Deciphering *The Private Memoirs*

James Hogg's Napoleon Complex

While Lamb found magazine collaboration to have uniformly positive effects, James Hogg underwent a more malignant process. His bizarre Gothic novel, *The Private Memoirs and Confessions of a Justified Sinner,* the 1824 work for which Hogg is best known today, is commonly recognized as an autobiographical allegory about the author's wranglings with *Blackwood's Edinburgh Magazine,* the powerful monthly with which Hogg was affiliated from the magazine's inception.[1] In the novel, set in Scotland mostly during the era of religious controversy and the move toward Union in the late seventeenth and early eighteenth centuries, Hogg allegorizes *Blackwood's* power over him through the figure of Gil-Martin, a mysterious personality who befriends Robert Wringhim, a religious zealot, and who either convinces Wringhim to commit crimes or frames Wringhim by committing the crimes himself. In this symbolically suggestive narrative of impersonation and corruption, Gil-Martin's Svengali influence over Wringhim is a compelling allegory of both the initial appeal that *Blackwood's* held for Hogg and the detrimental effect the magazine later exerted over him through the "Noctes Ambrosianae," a comic series that appeared in *Blackwood's* from 1822 to 1835, and which disseminated buffoonish caricatures of Hogg that competed with his hard-won authorial reputation. Thus, in the novel, as the friendship that Wringhim first thought to be a sign of divine favor increasingly reveals itself as Satanic possession, the *Private Memoirs'* Gothic plot charts Hogg's growing disillusionment with *Blackwood's* by symbolically portraying magazines as a demonic power capable of the worst feats of impersonation and disempowerment.

The critical scholarship on the *Private Memoirs,* however, rarely connects this autobiographical allegory to the 1817 "Chaldee Manuscript," Hogg's contribution to the first issue of *Blackwood's,* and a controversial text that would greatly shape the magazine as well as Hogg's future relationship with the periodical; nor does the scholarship connect Hogg's conflicted relationship to contemporary magazines with the distinctive discursive complexity for which the *Private Memoirs* is best known. The latter includes a metafictional, highly self-reflexive narrative that depicts its own composition and publication—at one point in the novel specifically portraying *Blackwood's* itself—as well as an overall discursive and generic heterogeneity, described in a contemporary review of the novel as an "exaggerated and extravagant style of writing," and by a modern critic as "a fitful narrative, characterized by numerous false starts, false endings, and digressions."[2] This convoluted narrative form alternately takes up and discards various genres (ranging from Gothic to historical novel, supernatural tale, and comic folklore), careens through various discursive voices and aesthetic tones (such as religious fanaticism, antiquarian scholarship, and Scottish dialect), and layers and embeds narratives with lunatic abandon. For much of the critical scholarship that first rediscovered the novel in the twentieth century, the deeply heteroglossic and almost internally contradictory style of the *Private Memoirs* has been celebrated as a proto-modernist trait, as demonstrated by the novel's indeterminate ending, which leaves unresolved the question of whether Wringhim's memoir is a historical mystery or the ravings of a religious maniac.[3] But in the more contemporary context of post-Napoleonic periodical engagements, the *Private Memoirs'* distinct style could also be recognized as an extreme instance of the calculated motifs of some late Romantic writing, and hence a result of the quintessentially modern experience of commercial capitalism. Certainly as a text developed in response to *Blackwood's,* one of the most popular and influential monthly magazines of the era, the *Private Memoirs* is consistent with the tropes of exotic materialism found in other magazine collaborations such as Lamb's. In the *Private Memoirs,* this turn to an exotic artifact arises, literally, in the novel's denouement, in the form of an exhumed "Scots mummy."[4] This corpse, believed to be the mummified body of Robert Wringhim, is unearthed in the contemporary frame with which the novel concludes, and it is accompanied by a "rolled," "rotten, and yellow" document whose physical attributes, particularly when adjacent to an excavated mummy, strongly evoke Egyptian papyri (173).

This second chapter thus presents Hogg as an antithetical figure of post-Napoleonic magazine collaboration, whose periodical engagement begins with all the optimism of Lamb's collaboration with the *London*, but soon shifts, with the worsening of Hogg's relationship with *Blackwood's*, into an antagonistic relationship that ultimately finds the author realigned with the different literary form of the novel and actively seeking to combat *Blackwood's* by cannibalizing the magazine's chief literary attributes. As with Lamb, the specific exotic motif that Hogg invokes in his periodical engagement evokes an imperial context to portray the author's evolving relationship with a magazine. In the case of Hogg's use of Egypt, its significance is informed by the contemporary context of Napoleonic Egyptology, and it is particularly tied to Hogg's Scottish nationality and the "auld alliance," the long-standing political and cultural alliance between Scotland and France that existed based on their mutual opposition to England. As key icons of contemporary Egyptology, such as the Rosetta Stone, became the centerpieces of a highly politicized contest between British and French imperial power, Hogg adopted those emblems, first invoking Egyptian antiquity in a pro-imperial British triumphalism, and later as an emblem of Jacobite or Napoleonic opposition to empire, whose reversal of his earlier emblem conveys his initially enthusiastic, but later deeply regretful, position on periodical magazines and *Blackwood's* in particular.

Thus, this second case study of an archetypal periodical engagement of the post-Napoleonic era contrasts with the first both by examining a less positive relationship with magazines and by shifting the terms of the comparison. While Hogg and Lamb are both minor writers whose imperial metaphors indicate the extraordinary opportunity they saw in periodicals, Hogg would become a victim of this topical rhetoric, as the Edinburgh literati behind *Blackwood's* "Noctes Ambrosianae" series would use imperial categories—specifically, the linguistic distinction between core and periphery in Scotland—to insist upon Hogg's provincial exclusion from metropolitan intelligentsia. Moreover, if nationality occupies the preeminent role in Hogg's periodical engagement, comparable to class in the previous chapter on Lamb, this second case study also expands the range of periodical engagements by examining a work that was developed in reference to a magazine but was not published within that series itself. The *Private Memoirs* may be a novel that appeared independently, but its autobiographical allegory and the Egyptian, imperial motif used to portray that allegory demonstrate the continuing importance of periodicals, and *Blackwood's* in particular, within Hogg's literary oeuvre. Indeed, although the vexed relations with *Blackwood's* that caused Hogg's turn toward novels illustrates his antithetical relationship to Lamb's positive experience of magazine collaboration, the Scottish author also closely resembles the archetypal imperial periodical contributor in that even after his break with magazines, his literary productions still exhibit unmistakable stylistic influences from the periodical form. The famous complexity of the *Private Memoirs,* I will argue, is directly related to the magazine format that the novel expressly indicts, and further demonstrates the ineluctable importance of magazines for late Romantic, post-Napoleonic authors.

The Egypt of the North

The notorious reactionary and partisan nature that *Blackwood's* exercised in the first decades of its existence is perhaps best illustrated in the scurrilous "Cockney School of Poetry" series of articles, the first of which appeared in *Blackwood's* first issue, and which remains today a touchstone for Romantic history as well as the specific culture of nineteenth-century periodicals. The bigoted and class-based attack by which the article assaults Keats and the "indelicate" and "vulgar" Leigh Hunt exemplifies the conservative, high Tory culture in which *Blackwood's* was born, and which was further characterized by the magazine's consistent endorsement of genteel and aristocratic authors such as Wordsworth, Scott, and especially Byron (who gained the magazine's staunch support despite obvious conflicts between the magazine's conservative politics and Byron's more liberal commitments).[5] This strong identification with the old-order status quo foreshadows the ad hominem, often vindictive caricatures in the "Noctes Ambrosianae," and it would also provide the environment for De Quincey's rabidly isolationist writings against empire. Thus, if the *London* was the journal of Whig supporters of empire and other British citizens actively interested in the expanding horizon of the British world, *Blackwood's* could be seen as its de facto opposite. (And, indeed, the *London* was founded in part as an alternative to the popular Tory journal.) As Kim Wheatley has noted about the magazine,

Blackwood's specialized in a paranoid hysteria often associated with reactionary conservatism, and its staunchly nationalist ethos showed little interest in things beyond British borders.[6]

In the political continuum of post-Napoleonic periodicals, then, *Blackwood's* might then be associated with an anti-imperial position. But as with the deep respect the magazine accorded the Union apologist Walter Scott, *Blackwood's* was not always as consistent on this position as it might have liked to be. Indeed, its very identity as a Scottish publication that would become one of Britain's most popular periodicals positioned *Blackwood's* amid a national literary renaissance that seemed to compensate for the post-Union loss of political autonomy with a mounting cultural influence. In these days, when an "Edinburgh imprint was worth more than a London," an influential magazine from that capital could exercise cultural authority comparable to the political influence the nation had surrendered, and thereby undermine colonial absorption by asserting a literary influence that made Edinburgh an alternate capital competitive with London in cultural influence.[7] In the case of *Blackwood's,* it is worth noting that despite the magazine's overt commitment to old-order values, it was itself a product of unquestionably modern and progressive developments.[8] While the black letter typeface and portrait of the sixteenth-century Scottish historian George Buchanan in the magazine's masthead were both archaic gestures clearly intended to signal *Blackwood*'s reactionary ethos, the journal prefigured the *London* in making urban culture a sign of its literary newness. The new magazine debuted in April 1817 as the *Edinburgh Monthly Magazine,* and although that launch aborted a few months later due to the abrupt departure of its first editors, it retained a metropolitan emphasis in its title when it resumed in October as *Blackwood's Edinburgh Magazine.* Moreover, the magazine itself was strongly identified with influential local citizens. The authors and contributors whom William Blackwood called upon for the venture drew heavily from young members of the educated and professional classes, such as lawyers like John Gibson Lockhart and the recent appointee to the university's Faculty of Law, John Wilson. Even the offices of William Blackwood, in 17 Princes Street, were located in the "New Town," a region of Edinburgh developed in the previous century and whose neoclassical order testified to its modernity and progress.

At any rate, *Blackwood's* certainly was associated with modernity for Hogg, a former shepherd and farm laborer who was largely self-taught, and for whom the new periodical represented an unprecedented opportunity for his literary ambitions. Like Lamb, Hogg had first begun publishing in the 1790s, and by the post-Napoleonic era he was another middle-aged author of limited literary repute. His most successful publications were pastoral works such as the 1807 *Mountain Bard* and the 1813 *Queene's Wake,* and thus, despite his 1810 move from his native Borders to Edinburgh to pursue a literary career, still arguably represented only a literary variation of Hogg's previous agrarian career. But the author, like his country, was embroiled in a reinvention from the agricultural to the literary, and thus it was fitting that he seized upon periodicals as the vehicle of his modernization. Early in his time in Edinburgh, Hogg had previously ventured into periodical publication with the *Spy,* his largely self-authored weekly literary journal that he produced from September 1810 to August 1811. With the collaborative authorship and extensive distribution possible from a prominent Edinburgh publisher, *Blackwood's* promised even greater opportunity. Indeed, for a former farm laborer whose professional metamorphosis and urban relocation had in part been necessitated by the Acts of Enclosure that were then rendering agricultural employment obsolete, affiliation with a periodical magazine would have been the crowning episode in Hogg's reinvention from archaic farm worker to active participant in the new economy of post-Union Scotland. Not surprisingly, his involvement with William Blackwood's new periodical is concurrent with the journal itself, beginning with a poem that appeared in the first issue of the journal in April 1817.[9] But it is the "Translation from an Ancient Chaldee Manuscript," Hogg's contribution to the periodical when it relaunched as *Blackwood's Edinburgh Magazine,* that best demonstrates the power that the aspiring author initially accorded the magazine format.[10]

As Hogg described it in the accompanying cover letter with which he submitted the work to William Blackwood, the Chaldee Manuscript is a "beautiful allegory," written in an "eastern idiom," whose oriental setting is a rhetorical vehicle by which to glamorize the Scottish literary capital, particularly the great "Book" to be founded there.[11] Accordingly, the manuscript, which appeared in *Blackwood's* with an editorial preface describing its discovery, purports to be a found text, and it uses a parody of Holy Writ to describe the establishment of *Blackwood's Magazine.* In scriptural chapter and verse, the Manuscript mixes aspects of the Old and New Testaments, remapping the landscape of literary Edinburgh as the biblical Orient of the Levant. The Tweed becomes "the river Jordan, which is by the Border" (1.44, 3.27); Ettrick Forest, where Hogg formerly lived, is "the forest of Lebanon" (2.13); and Edinburgh itself, "the great city" (1.1), becomes, by implication, Jerusalem—an apt evocation of the literary Promised Land that it certainly represented for Hogg.

In its extravagant rhetoric and blatant self-advertising, the manuscript is clearly intended to achieve the success that it facetiously portrays. To this end, it aggrandizes the magazine's birth by recasting it as Scripture. In a blend of Annunciation and Moses on the Mount, for example, the manuscript depicts William Blackwood visited by a mysteriously veiled and enclouded figure who "gave unto the man . . . a tablet, containing the names of those upon whom he should call" (2.7). Through this borrowing of Old Testament narrative, the Chaldee Manuscript endows the new magazine venture with the majesty of commandment.

For Hogg, the purpose of such hyperbolic rhetoric is to promote *Blackwood's* while also arguing for his inclusion in it. Just as he had done in *The Queen's Wake,* where Hogg depicts himself inheriting a harp awarded by Queen Mary to an earlier bard from Ettrick Forest, the author uses a self-referential historical fiction to inflate an emblem that authorizes his own text. In the Chaldee Manuscript, this ploy of creating an exalted backstory for his authorship is doubly important, as it has the additional advantage of compensating for Hogg's possible obstacles and inadequacies. Like Lamb and Keats, Hogg lacked a classical education, and he was sometimes perceived as a pretender among the Edinburgh literati. Indeed, Hogg was far lower in social status than either Lamb or Keats, and thus perhaps even less likely to be accepted into the urbane circle he hoped to join. His distance from the social class to which he aimed to gain entry was crystallized, as it was for all Scots at the time, by the linguistic criteria that encapsulated the compromises of the Union. As is widely known, the literary and intellectual culture of post-Union, Enlightenment Edinburgh prized the ability to speak unaccented English.[12] For Hogg, whose thick rural burr was insurmountable, biblical parody was a means of circumventing the problem of accent by substituting an elevated written discourse that potential readers would have recognized and found amusing.

Adding to its ingenuity was the fact that this biblical orientalism in some way approximated the classical learning that Hogg lacked. The conceit did so in two ways. First, Hogg's facetiously antiquarian celebration of literary Edinburgh in the Chaldee Manuscript plays upon the cherished Scottish notion of Edinburgh as the "Athens of the North." This epithet, popular in the post-Union era of literary prominence, emphasizes the intellectual authority that modern Scotland supposedly shared with ancient Greece and, in the monument-building typical of imperial pride, was monumentalized in Edinburgh on Calton Hill, a knoll near the New Town that in 1822 was crowned with a partially completed replica of the Parthenon. Or, with specific regard to the oriental antiquity portrayed in the Chaldee Manuscript, Hogg likely is also playing upon the Higher Criticism, a vein of biblical philology that sought to substantiate Christian history by redacting corroborating texts excavated in the Near East. The Chaldee Manuscript simulates this contemporary culture of Higher Criticism through its archeological pretensions as a found text. As described in the preface, the manuscript is supposed to be one "of many admirable pieces of writing, which had been supposed to be lost for ever," but is now the object of "resuscitation[ ]" (89).

Both of the above antiquarian conceits delineate Hogg's tactic of strategically allying himself with the larger entity provided by periodical affiliation. His trope may be biblical, but in his willingness to assimilate into larger orders, the manuscript also highlights suggestively imperial attributes in its description of how individual contributions to the magazine are "magnified" or "increased greatly" (1.18, 2.20). Similarly, Hogg puns on the biblical word "host," using the theological term to emphasize how a magazine is greater than the sum of its parts. The result of such puns is that even the most biblical moments of the Chaldee Manuscript convey attributes of rationalized production and incorporation within magazines that for Lamb were explicitly identified with the imperial, and they suggest the same for Hogg as well. This evocatively imperial metaphor that Hogg accords *Blackwood's* in the Chaldee Manuscript is particularly apparent in the figure of the veiled editor who appears to William Blackwood with the commandment to launch a new magazine. In keeping with the manuscript's biblical parody, the enclouded figure is a flourish of biblical mystery, and it may also be Hogg's version of the pictorial frontispiece of *Waverley,* in which Scott, the would-be anonymous author and "Great Unknown," is "portrayed" as a bust whose face is entirely hidden behind a curtain. But in accordance with the imperial dimensions of the biblical metaphor, the figure is also a placeholding metaphor for the magazine's editorial office, which at the time had not yet been filled.

That Hogg invested much in this biblical and oriental conceit, and that he took pleasure in it, is apparent. In his accompanying remarks to William Blackwood, Hogg noted that he liked the "eastern idiom" so much that he was "afraid I shall not easily get quit of [it] again."[13] This optimism about magazines illustrates Hogg's initial similarities with Lamb. As with "Old China," the Chaldee Manuscript is a contribution to a contemporary periodical that is explicitly compared to a tangible artifact of contemporary imperial culture and that uses those connotations of rarity and splendor to assert the work's aesthetic value. The antiquarian conceit of a found text in which the Chaldee Manuscript is framed may suggest the general context of oriental archeology, as conducted in relation to the Higher Criticism. More important, though, and in closer parallel with the imperial consumer culture dynamizing the Elia essays, the manuscript also has a more specific, and explicitly imperial, referent in Napoleonic Egyptology and particularly in the Rosetta Stone, an iconic Egyptian antiquity and trebly inscribed stone tablet that was expected to provide the key to deciphering Egyptian hieroglyphs, and which thus was one of the preeminent trophies of Napoleon's campaigns. The stone, first discovered in 1799 by Napoleon's *corps des savants,* was requisitioned by the British in the 1801 Treaty of Alexandria as part of their defeat of France. Its import is evident in the fact that the stone—along with "Memnon's Head," the colossal bust that inspired "Ozymandias," and which was the reason, along with the Elgin Marbles, for building the new British Museum—was one of the few antiquities that the British refused to return to the defeated French. Indeed, in the same way that "Ozymandias" coincides with the Egyptian exhibits at the British Museum, the Chaldee Manuscript was likely also inspired by the current exhibition of the Rosetta Stone, whose place in the museum's Egyptian collections ensured that it was much in public consciousness in 1817, around the time of Hogg's composition of the manuscript. The Chaldee Manuscript clearly alludes to the stone in the prefatory frame, which claims that the original document currently resides in "the great Library of Paris," while the "celebrated Silvester De Sacy is at present occupied with . . . the original."[14] The French orientalist scholar Silvestre de Sacy, "a gentleman whose attainments in Oriental Learning are well known to the public," was the leading western scholar of Egyptian hieroglyphs, and one of the many philologists then devoted to trying to decipher the Rosetta Stone (89). His mention, as well as the general reference to the Parisian library, acknowledge the current prominence of France in oriental and Egyptian research.[15]

The imperial connotations of the manuscript's Egyptian associations are so pertinent, in fact, that they are not diminished by the fact that Hogg may not have originally been responsible for the Chaldee preface. In the letter to William Blackwood that accompanied the manuscript, Hogg requested "the editor of the Magazine . . . to add a short history of its preservation in the archives of Rome."[16] Although it is not Egypt that Hogg suggests here, his request that a layer of Roman antiquity be applied to the text still is consistent with the imperial dimensions evident in the manuscript, and shows him anticipating the topically imperial connotations better realized in the final, Egyptian frame.

More important, and in a device directly attributable to Hogg, the manuscript's actual text formally resembles the Rosetta Stone by ingeniously evoking Egyptian hieroglyphs. This occurs in the manuscript's elaborate roman à clef, which uses verbal ciphers to reference Edinburgh personalities by replacing their proper names with oblique descriptions of the individuals themselves. For example, Archibald Constable, publisher of the *Edinburgh Review* and the *Scots Magazine,* and William Blackwood's chief competitor, is described as "the man that is crafty in counsel" (1.16, 36) and Walter Scott—already commonly referenced as "the Wizard of the North," and then immersed in the construction of Abbotsford, the baronial home that would consume Scott's life and savings for more than two decades—is "the great magician who dwelleth in the old fastness" (1.44, 3.27). In the wittiest references, the manuscript's paratactic code literalizes an individual's surname in rebus-like ciphers that use words invoking pictures synonymous with that surname. Thus, William Blackwood is "the man whose name is as ebony" (1.22, 33; 3.5, 6; 4.2), and Hogg himself is the "boar" (2.13). Such references to surnames resemble heraldic language in the use of visual images as signifiers for other, verbal signs, and as Nigel Leask has suggested about the Egyptian imagery in other Romantic writing, the manuscript names "could be seen as the products of an imperial heraldry which incorporated the symbols of the conquered into its own coats of arms."[17] Indeed, in the antique, oriental, and specifically imperial conceits of the Chaldee Manuscript, the rebus-like code more specifically simulates the ideographic attributes of Egyptian hieroglyphs, which prevailing theories of hieroglyphic translation then held must be such a system of pictorial images functioning as verbal signs.[18] So evocative of Egyptian hieroglyphs is the Chaldee Manuscript, in fact, that these puns on proper names even resemble cartouches, the oval outline surrounding a collection of adjacent ideograms that in hieroglyphic writing signifies a proper name. Because a reader of the Chaldee Manuscript must disrupt the progressive reading of a sentence to isolate the self-contained code of the surname, the work's roman à clef accurately simulates how proper names are distinguished in a hieroglyphic text.

Like Lamb and Keats, then, Hogg in his early career exemplifies the benefits to be gained from collaboration with the post-Napoleonic periodicals. His initial enthusiasm about participating in *Blackwood's* is evident in his commitment to a specific exotic leitmotif—Egypt—which, like Greece or China for Keats and Lamb, activates a symbolic system strongly associated with contemporary imperialism. For Hogg, the specific power of Egypt as a representational "empire of signs" derives—as did China and Greece for Lamb and Keats—from its historical meaning in post-Napoleonic Britain, as well as from its place within the author's individual subjectivity. In the case of Hogg, this context is his Scottish nationality and the power that Egypt exercised in the British national imaginary. "Every thing now must be Egyptian," noted Southey in 1807, when five thousand British soldiers were sent to Egypt to defend British holdings against the Turks, sparking a wave of Egyptian fashion among the British.[19] As in chinamania, this "Egyptomania," as it was occasionally known, had its preeminent emblems. These were the mummies and pyramids that embodied the mystical and monumental achievements of the ancient civilization, and also centered upon specific items such as "Memnon's Head" and the famous Rosetta Stone. In Scotland in particular, such enthusiasm for Egypt reflected the nation's military involvement in North African campaigns against Napoleon, where Scottish troops had been important forces in key battles. These battles, including some in Egypt itself, marked the shift in North Africa toward British occupation, and hence a shift in Scottish interest in Egypt.[20] During the military victories of 1814 and 1815, in notable replacement of the white cockade their Jacobite fathers and grandfathers might have worn, many Scots pinned to their lapels ribbons emblazoned with the names of previous military triumphs, including "Egypt."[21] Hogg, notably, himself participated in these festivities. The poem of his that appeared in the first issue of *Blackwood's* was a reprint of verses that Hogg composed upon this occasion.

But as Scottish participation in British imperial triumphalism surrounding Egypt indicates, this contemporary context of Napoleonic Egyptology that Hogg references in the Chaldee Manuscript is intriguing for its identificatory relationship with Union. The reasons for this counterintuitive identification by Scotland with England will be discussed momentarily; what is pertinent here is the numerous, often contradictory ways in which Egypt signified for Scotland over time, and particularly in reference to England. Scottish national interest in Egypt began with a legend, circulated in the medieval era, that the Scots people were descended from Scota, a daughter of a pharaoh in the time of Moses.[22] But by the eighteenth century, Egypt's significance for Scotland had reversed, as the 1707 Union with England prompted Jacobite broadsides that used biblical typologies to portray Egypt as England and Scotland as the oppressed Jews. As Murray Pittock and Coleman Parson have both shown, this typology was central to a revolutionary allegory prophesying the inevitable freedom of this "Chosen People."[23] Indeed, it may explain the curious tendency toward Egyptian details in the architecture of Scottish Freemasonry, a cultural organization in Scotland with strong Jacobite associations. In those buildings, Egyptian architectural details possibly elaborate upon the biblical typology by alluding to Jewish slave labor in constructing the pyramids.[24] This more recent Semitic association with Scotland may be the more immediate context of the Chaldee Manuscript. As Hogg, who had joined the antiquarian Society of Dilettanti immediately upon his arrival in Edinburgh, well knew, "Chaldea," the purported origin of the "Chaldee" manuscript, was a region of ancient Mesopotamia that was the site of Babylonia (now Iraq) and that was known to be populated by Semitic peoples.

The Rosetta Stone references in the Chaldee Manuscript, however, partake in a much more recent and topically imperial significance of Egypt, and in their enthusiasm for the Egyptian which had previously been the sign of their national antagonist, they represent yet another change in the many tergiversations that Egypt had undergone in Scottish national history. One reason for the more recent identification with Egypt—and the English imperial power then responsible for that representational fashion—may lie in the "auld alliance," the long-standing medieval political alliance between Scotland and France that is based upon mutual opposition to England, but which underwent significant changes in the Napoleonic period.[25] Murray Pittock has previously argued that during the Napoleonic era, Scottish involvement in British campaigns against Napoleon was rationalized as restoring the Bourbon monarchy, therefore constituting a form of the auld alliance simply gone underground.[26] In terms of Scottish interest in Egypt, then, the shift in Scottish identification from Jews to Egypt is not contradictory, but consistent with the current dimensions of the auld alliance, where Scots who once figured England as their Egyptian oppressor soon identified with Egypt due to their role in British resistance to Napoleonic power.

It is precisely this imperial version of Egypt that Hogg uses in the Chaldee Manuscript to illustrate his early enthusiasm for magazine collaboration. Specifically, by invoking the recent Scottish identification with English imperial triumph in Egypt, Hogg uses empire as a sign of his willing cooperation with magazines. In fact, Hogg's evocation of the Rosetta Stone does not rest with the hieroglyph-like epithets in the Chaldee Manuscript. The text also stakes a position in the contemporary race to decipher the stone by presupposing the hieroglyphs' translatability—an act with significant political connotations. Napoleon's interest in Egypt had always been driven as much by its symbolism as the birthplace of civilization as by the tactical value of its geographic location. This more abstract obsession with Egypt was embodied particularly in the contemporary quest to decipher hieroglyphs, as to penetrate that lost language was to claim the majesty of that history, rather like Napoleon—or Napoleon's hero, Alexander himself. It was precisely for these reasons that the Rosetta Stone was prized for its value immediately upon discovery, and why the English insisted that the French surrender that trophy. Even as Britain assumed territorial control of Egypt by 1801, for the first two decades of the nineteenth century France and many other European countries remained engaged in a fierce race with Britain to decipher the hieroglyphs.

The Chaldee Manuscript claims victory in this race through a premature assumption of decipherability. Composed and published in 1817, the Chaldee Manuscript appeared at a time when the artifact had not yet been decoded. Yet because a roman à clef lacks any interest if it is not decipherable, the Chaldee Manuscript—unlike the real artifact that is its emblem—is eminently accessible to translation. Most of the names and figures cited in the roman à clef were readily recognized by literate readers of the contemporary periodical press, and in further guarantee of its intelligibility, later versions of the manuscript often circulated with an accompanying key. Within the politicized context of the race to decipher the stone, this attribute of decipherability was significant, as it manifests a premature faith in Britain's imminent translation of the stone. While historical analyses attuned only to imperial history might note how the text celebrates the imperial project, for Hogg it is most important to observe that this triumphalism is a professional motif for his authorial ambition. For Hogg, this anachronistic portrait of a decipherable Rosetta Stone uses British triumphalism to exhibit his current faith in the corporate enterprise of magazines.

At this moment in the Chaldee Manuscript, Hogg looks a lot like Lamb and Keats, in the sense that the imperial icon at the center of his magazine contribution clearly functions as an emblem of successful magazine collaboration. But notably unlike Lamb or Keats, for both of whom their imperial icon was an unequivocally triumphal symbol, for Hogg the imperial metaphor proved poignantly accurate, as it also forecast authorial compromises that magazine collaboration entails but which Hogg had not adequately predicted. The same corporate and collaborative nature of magazine collaboration that Hogg exalted in the biblical imagery of magazines as "host" also meant that Hogg's contribution to *Blackwood's* was available for the emendations of other contributors also affiliated with the magazine. Thus, although the original Chaldee Manuscript does not appear to have had more than the 46 verses found in one surviving manuscript version of Hogg's, other figures associated with *Blackwood's,* such as John Gibson Lockhart and John Wilson (soon to be identified with the editorial role previously depicted as the veiled figure in the Chaldee Manuscript[27]), quickly composed many more stanzas, such that the allegory metastasized to 180 verses. Of course, such additions by different authors are common in the collective and collaborative authorship in magazines, but Hogg had no opportunity to correct these changes. Lockhart—aptly metaphorized in the manuscript as "the scorpion, which delighteth to sting the faces of men" (2.12)—had added to the manuscript numerous lampoons aimed primarily at Whigs not associated with the *Blackwood's* circle. In one of the most notorious descriptions, for example, Lockhart referred to the naturalist John Graham Dalyell as a "beast of burden . . . [accustomed] to do all manner of unclean things," a man "[with] the face of an ape" and whose "nether parts were uncomely" (3.36). But in an exclusion that might have been an omen of the limits of Hogg's inclusion in *Blackwood's,* William Blackwood forwarded the proofs of the expanded Chaldee Manuscript too late for Hogg to have any effect. Still, Hogg corrected those proofs, and in the comments with which he returned the proof corrections to William Blackwood, he warned that the manuscript's easy translation would now be a liability. Noting that "the third chapter . . . is very faulty—the characters are made too plain and the language of scripture completely departed from," Hogg cautioned that he was "certain of its popularity as well as of its being blamed."[28]

The venomous strain of ad hominem caricature that Lockhart and others added to the Chaldee Manuscript casts a substantially different light on the text's imperial conceits. In retrospect, it reveals the violence implicit in Hogg's originally naïve—but actually profoundly prophetic—imperial metaphors. As Hogg perceptibly foresaw, the subsequent publication of the manuscript brought scandal. Outrage over the scabrous characterizations in the Chaldee Manuscript immediately sparked numerous libel and slander suits, as injured parties took to the courts to gain redress. To add force to the lawsuits, some plaintiffs also cited the manuscript's pseudo-biblical discourse to level charges of blasphemy. The effect of litigation, and the more general scandal that greeted the manuscript, was considerable. Although William Blackwood soon stopped the presses, removed the manuscript, and reissued a new edition of *Blackwood's* that included a statement of regret regarding the offending article, the controversy surrounding the Chaldee Manuscript ensured that the magazine was a sensation from the start. According to John Wilson, the October 1817 issue sold over ten thousand copies. More important, with such a sensational debut, the magazine's publisher could not help but recognize the value of controversy as a strategy for market differentiation and maintaining reader interest. In the future, and despite Walter Scott's warnings against "satire so markedly personal," William Blackwood tacitly encouraged his contributors to continue Lockhart's ad hominem style by establishing a regular fund for payments in future libel and slander suits.[29]

The importance of this decision by William Blackwood to provide for future suits should not be underestimated. By institutionalizing these settlements into a regular cost of doing business, such payments seem, in retrospect, like fees for use, comparable to the commissions paid to magazine contributors writing under personae that are the property of the periodical, not the author. Today, Romantic scholarship usually associates *Blackwood's Magazine* with the "Cockney School" essays, whose first installment also appeared in this first issue of *Blackwood's* and which is also known to be of Lockhart's authorship, but it is the Chaldee Manuscript, rather, that defined *Blackwood's* for its first readers and that exercised such a formative influence in the immediate history of the magazine. (At its worst, some detractors accused the magazine of being "the vilest production that ever disfigured and soiled the annals of Scottish literature."[30]) For the periodical industry at large, this commitment by *Blackwood's* to vitriolic personal satire would galvanize existing and future journals, particularly encouraging the *London Magazine,* with its genial, inclusive style, to be founded partly as a cultural and tonal alternative to *Blackwood's.*[31]

For Hogg, the Chaldee Manuscript had both immediate and lasting effects. Although Hogg escaped accountability for the libel suits because of the same anonymization enforced by the corporate practices of the magazine that dismayed him, the overall effect of the Chaldee Manuscript was to precipitate a decisive change in Hogg's literary ambitions. First, in 1818, less than a year after the Chaldee fiasco, Hogg quitted Edinburgh, apparently in wholesale reassessment of the literary capital. Although his destination was the Altrive farm that he had acquired through his literary fame, and which thus represented a promotion from his former life as a shepherd to that of a gentleman farmer, this end to Hogg's Edinburgh residence also suggests its causal origins in the disastrous turn of the Chaldee Manuscript. It certainly signaled an end to his pursuit of inclusion among the Edinburgh literati represented by *Blackwood's.* Relations between Hogg and *Blackwood's* only grew more rancorous in subsequent years. In the August 1821 issue of the magazine, a vicious review excoriating a new edition of *The Mountain Bard* caused further antipathy between the two parties. Correspondence between Hogg and Lockhart or Wilson notably subsided during this period, as Hogg redirected his authorial aspirations toward another city and circle—that of the London-based press Longman and Company. More to the point, this shift in his literary professional focus was sited in a generic change, as Hogg seemed to abandon periodicals for avowedly single-author genres, such as the novel, which he would publish with Longman and which included *The Private Memoirs and Confessions of a Justified Sinner.*

In the longer range of *Blackwood's* influence over Hogg, the author himself became subject to the personal satire for which his *Blackwood's* contribution was responsible. In 1822, several years after Hogg's break with *Blackwood's* and at the height of the magazine's popularity, *Blackwood's* began the "Noctes Ambrosianae," the comic series that would prove such a nuisance for Hogg. In the manner of the Chaldee Manuscript, the "Noctes" are metafictional and self-promotional texts about the making of the magazine itself. The series is named after Ambrose's Tavern, an Edinburgh watering hole so popular among *Blackwood's* contributors that the place appears in the Chaldee Manuscript.[32] Each installment of the series, which all take the form of a dramatic script, is a fictional dialogue, supposed to transcribe conversations between various figures associated with the magazine. Its regular characters include "Christopher North" (John Wilson), "Thomas O'Doherty" (William Maginn, later editor of *Fraser's*), "Timothy Tickler" (Robert Sym, John Wilson's uncle), and the "Ettrick Shepherd," a character based on a signature Hogg first employed in *The Mountain Bard.* But while Wilson, Maginn, and Lockhart were all active contributors to the series, Hogg by then had little to do with *Blackwood's,* a fact that freed the other figures to make the erstwhile contributor a frequent butt of jokes. This occurred in the "Noctes" in the portrait of the shepherd as a blustering, rustic character whose ignorance and rough manners were gross exaggerations of Hogg's provinciality. Perhaps most damagingly, the dialogue-style transcriptions of the "Noctes" portrayed the shepherd in dialect, with truncated words, phonetic spellings, and antiquated vocabulary sufficiently different from Hogg's written works as to suggest an unlettered figure, incapable of writing anything of literary merit.

Previous considerations of the "Noctes" history emphasize only the authorial consequences of this fictional representation, without recognizing the imperial dimensions with which it was embodied.[33] Because the magazine possessed a far wider realm of circulation than Hogg's individual publications, the "Noctes" caricature of him was devastating, capable of countering—and even eclipsing—the small, hard-won recognition that Hogg had earned through his own publications. For Peter T. Murphy, for example, the "Noctes" persecution of Hogg exemplifies the capacity of fictional representations in magazines to "poach" reality from their real referents.[34] The alienation Hogg suffered demonstrates the dark underside of periodical print capitalism, which can gain such momentum that it continues without stopping or guidance. But while this characterization of Hogg's periodical engagement is sensitive to the consequential power of post-Napoleonic periodicals, one must also recognize how the "Noctes" reworked the motifs of imperial absorption by which Hogg first conceptualized *Blackwood's* in the Chaldee Manuscript. One reason why Hogg's metaphors of British imperial triumph had been so apt for the magazine was that those political tropes metonymized the linguistic emphasis upon standard English that distinguished the Edinburgh literati. By contrast, the use of dialect to portray Hogg in the "Noctes" Chaldee-style personal satire reiterated the differences between the self-taught former shepherd and the urbane, English-speaking Edinburgh literati. In short, it reinforced the regional and class separation that Hogg, through his affiliation with *Blackwood's,* had sought to overcome. The imperial metaphor that Hogg had first used to celebrate *Blackwood's* thus proved both ironic and poignant. Not only did the linguistic caricature by which the "Noctes" lampooned Hogg rely upon the same criteria of metropolitan assimilation that the author had hoped to overcome through his topical allusions to imperial Egyptology; but that imperial metaphor also proved prescient, as it projected the assault that the magazine would actually conduct upon Hogg.

It is precisely this conflict between the literary and the oral, evident in the "Noctes," that is widely thought to be the autobiography allegorized in *The Private Memoirs and Confessions of a Justified Sinner.* In its portrait of Gil-Martin's demonic power of "setting his features to the mould of other people's," such that Wringhim "generally conceived [himself] to be two people" (82, 106), the novel is a graphically Gothic portrait of "Caledonian anti-syzygy," the internal splitting of personality suffered by all upwardly mobile Scots who recognize that assimilation into the ruling culture is dependent upon surrender of their national linguistic heritage.[35] By all accounts, Caledonian anti-syzygy is a depressing experience. As David Daiches describes it, "If you talk and, as it were, feel in Scots and think and write in standard English, then your English is likely to be highly formal and in some degree de-natured."[36] This aspect of linguistic difference raises another point of deviation in Hogg's periodical engagement. Whereas Lamb's collaboration with magazines was so triumphally imperial that, in essays such as the "Dissertation upon Roast

Pig," he manifests early forms of the racial prejudice associated with imperial culture, Hogg's disempowerment amid magazines is evident in the ethnic prejudice to which he himself was subject, in the form of the linguistic differentiation that *Blackwood's* constantly emphasized. In the *Private Memoirs,* these hardships are portrayed in form as well as narrative. Part of the famous complexity of the novel is the discursive cacophony that arises from the vast array of characters and scenarios it unfolds. Although Leith Davis does not feature Hogg in her astute study of heteroglossic propensities in Scottish literature, Hogg might be an archetype of her analysis, as it is the antagonism between author and assimilationist periodical magazine (*Blackwood's*) that shapes both the plot and the complex form of Hogg's novel.

Decipherment

The famously complex form of the *Private Memoirs* results from several factors. First, the novel has a labyrinthine narrative structure, which takes place in two historical settings more than a century apart, and which is told through several sources, with one narrative often embedded within another. The novel opens with the "Editor's Narrative," an objective, third-person narration about the birth and life of Robert Wringhim, an antinomian zealot, whose life is reconstructed, as the editor puts it, from "history, judiciary records, and tradition" (64). This biography is succeeded in the novel by the first-person narrative of Wringhim himself—the titular "private memoirs and confessions" that supposedly have survived to become the actual, physical novel, and which retell from Wringhim's perspective the sad trajectory of his friendship with the mysterious Gil-Martin. This quintessential twice-told tale concludes by returning to the "Editor's Narrative," which recounts the circumstances of Wringhim's death and also describes the discovery and modern-day printing of Wringhim's memoir, which is recovered as the manuscript exhumed with the mummy thought to be Wringhim's corpse. Importantly, this second "Editor's Narrative" differs from the first by registering a more subjective, confused response. "What can this work be? . . . an allegory; or . . . a religious PARABLE? I cannot tell" (165). Such uncertainty as the editor expresses regarding generic form reiterates the variegated and heterogeneous shape of *The Private Memoirs and Confessions of a Justified Sinner: Written by Himself: With a*

Detail of Curious Traditionary Facts and Other Evidence, By the Editor, whose full title exemplifies its complex narrative and discursive form. Throughout these various discursive and narrative forms, moreover, the shape-shifting novel is further varied by a motley diversity of discursive voices, ranging from the editor's pomposity to Wringhim's religious fanaticism, and a vast set of characters and texts in between.

A number of critics have already noted a connection between empire and the novel's formal complexity. Nicola Watson, for example, calls attention to a Jacobite quality to Hogg's novel, which for Watson stems from the irresolute narrative created by the many competing letters and documents cited in the narrative, and which dismantle any potential for narrative discipline. "In presenting these two narratives as crucially incompatible and mutually chafing," Watson argues, where the "solipsistic, unverifiable, autobiographical and archaic" undermines the "social, official, historiographical and above all modern," Watson interprets the *Private Memoirs* as using its narrative complexity to undermine the hegemony of the post-Union Scottish state.[37] Perhaps more obviously, the *Private Memoirs* also provokes comparisons between itself and the historical novels of Walter Scott, albeit only to underscore the difference of Hogg's novel from Scott's formulaically consistent pro-Union narratives. Like Scott's many novels, the *Private Memoirs* is set in a key moment of national history. Wringhim is born around 1687 and dies in 1712, such that the main action of the narrative takes place against the background of Union, and indeed Wringhim and his brother George Colwan are involved in partisan conflicts between the Whigs and Royalist Cavaliers (their political representativeness is further underscored by the alliteration of their names with their political affiliations). Historical figures such as the Duke of Queensberry, the chief architect of Union, and Thomas Drummond, a gentleman whose service in the Austrian army and death in the 1715 uprising are incorporated into the fiction, also appear. Indeed, as was widely noted at the time of the novel's first publication, the *Private Memoirs* is so reminiscent of Scott's work that Hogg's novel was widely accused of imitating the more prominent author's recent novel, *Redgauntlet,* which appeared in June 1824, only a few months before the *Private Memoirs,* and which is also about Covenanters. (In fact, Scott began his novel after Hogg.) But whereas Scott's novels are characterized by a straightforward narrative that neatly resolves all tensions, often using the device of a marriage plot, Hogg's novel follows a reverse trajectory, which begins with a wedding whose unhappy consummation results in a division of the family house, and which concludes in Wringhim's mysterious and inexplicable death.

Such obvious thematic and structural differences between the *Private Memoirs* and Scott's novels reflect Hogg's political differences with Scott. Hogg had always been more ambivalent on Union than his literary benefactor, and he voiced more reservations regarding the process as his professional distance from Scott and Edinburgh increased. Not surprisingly, then, when Hogg uses the device of a found text, his development of that antiquarian conceit unfolds in a manner notably at odds with its typical function in Scott. The novels of Scott that employ this conceit—such as *Waverley, Rob Roy,* and *The Antiquarian*—all use the found text as a device that authorizes the historical pretensions of the fictional narrative, and thereby enhances the ultimate resolution of the narrative. The *Private Memoirs,* by contrast, does not offer resolution, and indeed looks past the immediate comparison with those of Hogg's contemporary, Scott, to instead recall the historical and narrative indeterminacy surrounding *Ossian,* the famous poetic fragments that in the eighteenth century became a germinal text of Scottish national pride. The pompous metropolitan editor in the *Private Memoirs* whose investigations recover Wringhim's manuscript resembles Samuel Johnson, whose 1775 travel memoir, *Journey to the Western Isles of Scotland,* famously doubted the authenticity of the Ossian fragments. And like Johnson, whose doubts about Ossian were ignored by the Scots who chose instead to celebrate inauthenticatability as a sign of national pride, the *Private Memoirs* shows the editor defeated in his efforts to make sense of the mysterious history.

These aspects of the novel's narrative indeterminacy place the *Private Memoirs* within the national literary history outlined by Katie Trumpener, who sees antiquarianism as an ongoing conceit throughout the literature of the Celtic periphery. By Trumpener's classification, which distinguishes between historical novels and national tales in the respective attention they accord to individual or collective historical experience, the professed commitment to "private" narrative in Hogg's novel is indicative of the author's regional and subjective allegiances.[38] Yet although all of the above approaches to the *Private Memoirs* have persuasively demonstrated the political resonances underlying the novel's narrative indeterminacy, none of these approaches have connected that formal attribute to the professional allegory that is also supposed to explicate the novel, and which was itself defined by the colonial contours of the Caledonian anti-syzygy that was the paradigm of Hogg's sufferings by *Blackwood's*. Indeed, it should be significant that the autobiographical novel is a metafictional text that reprises both the "Noctes" and the Chaldee Manuscript in portraying the conditions of its own production and circulation. The editor, notably, blames "the printers, with their families and gossips" for circulating so many different versions of Wringhim's history that the narrative is irretrievably distorted (175). This allegation about the distorting power of print representation, which might also characterize the history of *Blackwood's* and its influence over Hogg, suggests a more direct relevance of the novel's Jacobite connotations to the Caledonian anti-syzygy that Hogg suffered in the "Noctes," and which began with the Chaldee Manuscript.

Indeed, the *Private Memoirs* is more specific in its evocation of *Blackwood's* than has previously been recognized, as a key scene in the novel suggestively evokes the Chaldee history. This takes place at a printing house, where Wringhim stops during his flight from Gil-Martin in order to publish his autobiography, presumably in hopes of posthumously correcting his reputation. Like Hogg with his "eastern idiom," Wringhim publishes his narrative as a religious pamphlet, with "a shade of allegory [then] the very rage of the day" (153). And as with Hogg's initial hopes for the manuscript, Wringhim's optimism in publication is conceptualized by Hogg as an archetypal Romantic scene of literary immortality: "I put my work to the press, and wrote early and late; and encouraging my companion to work at odd hours, and on Sundays, before the press-work of the second sheet was begun, we had the work all in types, corrected, and a clean copy thrown off for farther revisal. The first sheet was wrought off; and I never shall forget how my heart exulted when at the printing house this day, I saw what numbers of my works were to go abroad among mankind" (153). But if this scene recalls the optimism with which Hogg initially submitted the Chaldee Manuscript to *Blackwood's*, the progress of that episode also portrays the consequences of the distorted, collaborative version of the manuscript that the magazine actually published. Even more evocative of the Chaldee history, the novel alludes to Lockhart's intervention into Hogg's manuscript, as Wringhim hears news of "the devil having appeared . . . in the printing house, assisting the workmen at the printing of my book." This textual arrogation then further rehearses the Chaldee controversy as the printer, like William Blackwood, arrests Wringhim's press run and accuses him—in language again recalling the outcry over the Chaldee Manuscript—of "a medley of lies and blasphemy" (153). In the end Wringhim is lucky to escape with one printed copy. To this sad, sole reminder of his original optimistic hopes about publishing, Wringhim adds final, handwritten comments, in a gesture reminiscent of the futile proof corrections that Hogg added to the expanded Chaldee Manuscript, as well as the handwritten manuscript of "The Boar," a second biblical allegory that Hogg wrote about the Chaldee controversy.[39]

The *Private Memoirs* is thus more directly connected to *Blackwood's Magazine* than has previously been recognized. In addition to the general, allegorical evocation of Hogg's persecution within the "Noctes," the novel also portrays the origins of the magazine's tendencies within the Chaldee Manuscript. Allusions to the Chaldee history pervade the novel. Gil-Martin, whom Wringhim imagines to be "the Czar Peter of Russia" (89), recalls Archibald Constable, the prominent publisher and a man who liked to go by the nickname the "Czar of Muscovy";[40] and Wringhim first meets Gil-Martin while reading a strange Bible, "having columns, chapters, and verse, but in a language of which I was wholly ignorant" (85) and which might recall the Chaldee Manuscript. Indeed, the *Private Memoirs* is so exact in the evocation of Hogg's history with *Blackwood's* that the novel even develops the Scottish national history against which Hogg's relationship with the magazine was framed. Like the historical figures who mingle with fictional characters in Scott's novels, the printer who interrupts Wringhim's press run is "Mr. James Watson," a "compositor, in the Queen's printing house," and a real Scottish patriot once jailed for his Jacobite publications (151).

All these details add to the Jacobite sympathies long recognized within the narrative, but the novel's overall anti-imperial thematic does not end there. In further extension of the novel's formal and thematic likeness to the Chaldee Manuscript, the *Private Memoirs* also builds upon the manuscript's Egyptological motif. In addition to the mummy and papyrus-like manuscript unearthed in the novel's denouement, the *Private Memoirs* also more suggestively resembles the manuscript's pretensions toward the Rosetta Stone. The novel recalls the contemporary culture of decryption when Wringhim promises to provide a "key to the process, management, and winding up of the whole matter" (153). And although it might go too far to suggest that the multigeneric and heteroglossic novel deliberately simulates the triple inscriptions on the stone, the *Private Memoirs* certainly includes puzzle-like moments such as those in which the manuscript evokes the stone. The scene in the printing house turns, like the manuscript, upon a rebus-like pun. Gil-Martin is a "printing devil," the conventional industrial term for a printer's assistant, but also a literal definition of what the demonic Gil-Martin is when he intervenes in Wringhim's print run.[41] As in the hieroglyphic plays on proper names in the Chaldee Manuscript, the moment is a verbal transcription of the visual image produced by the plot.

To be sure, these moments of reference to contemporary Egyptology are small, and surrounded as they are by the abundance of information provided in the novel's multiple narratives, they never exercise the thematic coherence that they do in the Chaldee Manuscript. Still, however, it is precisely the vestigial remnants in the novel of the Egyptological motif that Hogg first associated, so optimistically, with *Blackwood's* that exercise the most profound symbolic resonance in the novel, and that link the novel's Jacobite setting and narrative indeterminacy with its autobiographical content and complex discursive form. One of the most important paradoxes of the *Private Memoirs* is that despite its genre and its publication by Longman, the novel inherits Hogg's aborted ambitions with *Blackwood's*. This conceptual relationship is implicit in the novel's recycling of the antiquarian device within the Chaldee Manuscript, and explicit in the physical and temporal evolution from disrupted "Manuscript" to published "Memoir" that the latter work implies. The novel is full of moments that suggest the novel's compensatory relationship to the Chaldee history. When Gil-Martin first begins to misappropriate Wringhim's name, Wringhim's solution—as it was after the usurping of the Chaldee Manuscript—is merely to "sit down and write" again (67). Later, as he nears the end of his life, Wringhim concludes his memoir by threatening a curse on anyone who "trieth to alter or amend" it (165). These moments of metafiction portraying authorship and literary dissemination foreground the novel's continuity with the Chaldee Manuscript. Yet another of the "many admirable pieces of writing which had been supposed to be lost forever," as the manuscript was introduced in its fictional preface, the *Private Memoirs* compensates for the altered and withdrawn Chaldee Manuscript by finally making it to print. This occurs in the novel's contemporary setting in the second and final "Editor's Narrative," when Wringhim's manuscript is unearthed to become the actual, commercial novel that the reader holds in her hand.

In this leap from metafiction to material reality, the *Private Memoirs* achieves an extraordinary accomplishment of late Romantic literary materialism. Through a prevailing antiquarian conceit, the *Private Memoirs* extends the Egyptological motif that drove the Chaldee Manuscript, and thus demonstrates the deep connections between the two works from before and after the souring of Hogg's relationship with *Blackwood's*. But whereas the Rosetta Stone had previously been invoked by Hogg as an imperial emblem that used British triumphalism as a metaphor for Hogg's optimism about magazine collaboration, this later invocation of imperial culture, as might be predicted by the more specific invocations of Jacobite history within the novel, must also be anti-imperial, in order to convey Hogg's newly jaded perspective on the magazines he had once represented so enthusiastically as empire. That the *Private Memoirs* returns to the same Rosetta Stone emblem that had been instrumental to the Chaldee Manuscript is not contradictory, as the icon had undergone important changes in connotation that dramatically reversed their topical significance in imperial Britain. In 1822, little more than a year before the *Private Memoir*'s composition and publication, the French prodigy and protégé of Sylvestre de Sacy, Jean-François Champollion, announced his solution to the Rosetta Stone. Champollion's breakthrough, which corrected previous attempts at hieroglyphic decipherment by suggesting that some groups of hieroglyphs function as letters with discrete sounds, was announced in an article, the *Lettre à M. Dacier*, that was reproduced throughout Europe and Britain, often in periodical magazines, and that would have been well known in Edinburgh, particularly to intellectual and antiquarian clubs such as the Edinburgh Society of Dilettanti to which Hogg belonged. (In an earlier instance of the role of periodicals in disseminating imperial culture, the nine-year-old Champollion first learned of the Rosetta Stone through the French newspaper the *Courier d'Egypte*.)

The effect of Champollion's triumph retrieved the Egyptian symbol for Hogg. Because Champollion, then just thirty-two years of age, made his breakthrough working with only rubbings of the stone while the stone itself remained in England, his achievement epitomized high Romantic notions of solitary genius. In other words, the stone could be reclaimed by Hogg as a sign of his independent authorship, despite—or indeed because of—the dispossession he shared with Champollion. Indeed, in the politicized race to decipher the stone in which Britain and France had been embroiled since the stone's discovery, Champollion's achievement effectively reversed England's previously triumphal connotations of Egyptology. With Champollion's decipherment, the Rosetta Stone's significance shifted from British military victory and back to France, particularly the singular genius that many Romantic authors first celebrated in Napoleon.[42]

As decipherment thus re-presented the Rosetta Stone as an emblem of French triumph and English defeat, the artifact was once again the perfect emblem of Hogg's authorship. Now an emblem of his antimagazine novel, Hogg's allusions to the Rosetta Stone in the *Private Memoirs* demonstrate the ubiquity of empire as a model for conceptualizing periodicals, even among those authors opposed to the magazine format. Like Lamb, Hogg also relies on empire as a paradigm for periodical engagement. Where Hogg deviates from Lamb is in the formal evocation of the imperial object that he takes as his emblem. For where Lamb's many essays serially suggest the mercantile trade of commodity culture, and therefore partake in the optimism of contemporary imperial expansion, Hogg's singular novel takes as its icon a singular artifact, asserting the unique and priceless qualities that inhere in the Rosetta Stone. (Not insignificantly, then, Hogg's novel is more akin to Keats's "Ode on a Grecian Urn.") Equally significantly, the *Private Memoirs* also breaks with certain aspects of Egyptology that Hogg otherwise carefully details, and intriguingly it does not evoke the transparency that decipherment would seem to offer. Despite his promise to include a "key," Wringhim never does provide one, and as all the previous criticism shows, the *Private Memoirs* is dedicated to literary and narrative indeterminacy.

Indeed, the novel is something of a monument to indecipherability, including numerous specific details—such as Gil-Martin's tendency to walk on only one side of Wringhim (the left); the number of different burials Wringhim undergoes (three);[43] or the day on which Wringhim first meets Gil-Martin ("the 25th day of March 1704" [82])—that initially look like clues but ultimately serve as red herrings that illustrate the impossibility of resolving the narrative. Like the four trial scenes that occur in the novel, but which fail to come to resolution or even result in false conviction, the *Private Memoirs* constantly presents the appearance of closure only to defer it.[44] Although this deliberate indeterminacy may seem inconsistent with the novel's identification with the French triumph at decipherment, the model for the novel's aesthetic form is the post-decipherment split that occurred in the Egyptological craze after Champollion. During the height of Egyptomania, one branch of faddists believed that hieroglyphs were not a common script but rather a secret code limited to an elite few. After decipherment these "pyramidiots" clung to this belief, in an Ossian-like faith that only they understood the true mystery of ancient hieroglyphs.[45]

The deliberate mysticism of the *Private Memoirs* has much in common with pyramidiotism. If the Chaldee Manuscript had offered a premature accessibility in exchange for Hogg's inclusion in the urbane circle it portrays, the novel, by contrast, withholds translation, in an equally anachronistic evocation of a still opaque Rosetta Stone that figures the author's independence from the literati that had once co-opted his text. In short, the novel's indecipherability implies that Hogg, like Champollion, holds the key to the artifact, but keeps it all to himself. More generally, though, in the emphasis on epistemological power implied by the novel's revival of the Rosetta Stone's motif, the *Private Memoirs* invokes the distinctly textual vein of Egyptology that after decipherment increasingly distinguished the difference between France and Britain. French Egyptology, Edward Said has noted, was always more attuned to the epistemological symbolism of hieroglyphs and Egypt's history of ancient mysticism.[46] This predisposition only intensified with the triumph of decipherment, and it continues today in a national enthusiasm for Egyptology, as well as in Anglo-American associations of French intellectualism with obscurantism.[47] Magdelene Redekop's deconstructionist reading of the *Private Memoirs* is a particularly apposite example of the continuing importance of Egypt in French intellectual tradition. Praising the novel as a "book of the dead"—referring to the iconic texts of the ancient Egyptian occult—Redekop inadvertently continues the long association of French intellectualism with Egyptian hieroglyphs that is also apparent in her theoretical model, Derrida's *On Grammatology*.[48]

Hogg's conceit in the *Private Memoirs* thus might be summarized as his "Napoleon complex." A phrase that most literally means a set of attributes or elements relating to Napoleon, the term has come to mean in colloquial usage the aggressive or exaggeratedly belligerent style adopted by an individual to compensate for perceived physical deficiencies. The *Private Memoirs* certainly fulfills both definitions, and indeed is a synthesis of both. The novel incorporates a number of obscure, but nevertheless profoundly significant, allusions to the quintessentially Napoleonic trophy, the Rosetta Stone, and does so in retributive compensation for the belittling manner in which Hogg was portrayed in *Blackwood's* "Noctes Ambrosianae" series. More subtly, but equally powerfully, Hogg's method in this triumph of Egyptological mysticism is inspired by Champollion's example of seizing triumph from defeat. This latter aspect of Hogg's Napoleon complex, and the specific form of belligerence that it takes in his writing, underlies the formal complexity that characterizes the novel and that has previously been misunderstood as simply a reflection of the novel's Jacobite indeterminacy. As I will show, by turning to the one "key" to the novelistic revisiting of the Chaldee-esque Rosetta Stone that Hogg actually does provide, the famous heteroglossia of the *Private Memoirs* is, more specifically, Hogg's cannibalization of the miscellaneous attributes of the magazine format that by the time of the novel he had forsworn.

Magazines, That Bold and Manly Style

The heteroglossic indeterminacy that characterizes the *Private Memoirs* is exemplified in a passage often cited by scholarship as the "episode at Auchtermuchty." In this episode, Wringhim's manservant recounts to his employer a conversation that he had heard from a local woman, herself recalling a conversation she had heard between two raven birds, or "corbies" (137). With its variety of embedded speakers differentiated by gender, class, and even species, the episode illustrates the *Private Memoirs'* tendency to employ heteroglossia only to make it irrelevant, as midway through the conversation one of the birds, which previously had been speaking in dialect, suddenly switches to standard English.[49] This sudden, spontaneous, and apparently unmotivated linguistic shift is characteristic of the *Private Memoirs* in the way that it marks linguistic difference to no apparent purpose. A compelling detail, yet no more than part of an "aulde wive"'s tale (135), the linguistic shift within the bird's speech becomes part of the novel's characteristic indeterminacy.

This collapse between English and dialect that occurs in the Auchtermuchty episode has obvious relevance to the novel's allegory of Hogg's experience with *Blackwood's* magazine. In view of Hogg's history as an object of the magazine's linguistic caricature, the novel's simultaneous depiction of both dialect and English within a single character emphasizes their compatibility and coexistence, in notable correction of the "Noctes" representation of Hogg, as well as past studies of the author. Penny Fielding and Ian Duncan have both called attention to the importance dialect bears in Hogg's fiction. For Fielding and Duncan, this narrative emphasis on dialect, which is often associated with privileged or otherwise admired characters, symbolizes Hogg's rehabilitation of the means of his previous abjection, and thus must be emblematic of his postmagazine shift in genre to the novel.[50] The *Private Memoirs* certainly is consistent with this characterization of Hogg's emphasis on dialect after the "Noctes." The novel associates dialect with privileged characters such as Bell Calvert and Hogg's good friend William Laidlaw, who "speaks excellent strong broad Scots" (174), and further privileges dialect by juxtaposing it with the rhetorical bombast of Wringhim, Reverend Wringhim, and Rabina Orde, whose conflation of biblical rhetoric with monomaniacal delusion comments suggestively upon the Chaldee Manuscript. Yet this very emphasis on dialect within the metafictional novel also asserts the ability of dialect to coexist with literary achievement. Notably, Wringhim's genial brother and father both speak alternately in Scots and in English. Their discursive fluidity, as in the Auchtermuchty episode, suggests, in departure from Duncan and Fielding, a more complex discursive and generic variation favored by Hogg. As already noted by Ian Campbell, "Hogg is out to pervert any easy equation between language level and social class or degree of inherent goodness."[51] Rather than suggesting orality as a discursive form privileged above English, the *Private Memoirs* suggests that for Hogg, orality is simply another discursive form, equally as important as publication, and merely one element of the discursive multiplicity that is the true formal objective of contemporary publication.

In fact, a similar synthesis of English and dialect occurs in the voice of Hogg himself, through a letter attributed to Hogg that was published in *Blackwood's* in August 1823.[52] The letter, which begins in the mode of the "Noctes," opens by recalling a recent conversation between the Ettrick Shepherd and "Christopher North"—the fictional persona in the "Noctes" associated with John Wilson, and a character, despite the magazine's collaborative nature, frequently presented as the *Blackwood's* editor.[53] These references to "Noctes" characters, along with the detail that their conversation took place at "Ambrose's[,] . . . that celebrated tavern," clearly present the letter as inspired by the "Noctes." And, indeed, in the letter as in the "Noctes," the Ettrick Shepherd is portrayed as an aspiring but dialect-speaking author who looks to the Edinburgh literati for literary instruction. According to the anecdote, North had urged the eager shepherd, presumably in consideration of the shepherd's rustic background, to "write something of the boundless phenomena of nature." The uneducated shepherd, in keeping with the disparaging portrait in the "Noctes," responds by incorrectly pluralizing "phenomenons" and mistakenly references it as "a French word" (188).

Presented within the metafictional conceits of the "Noctes," the *Blackwood's* letter exerts the same verisimilitude as the Chaldee Manuscript, and it is obviously a strategy by Hogg to stimulate interest in and enhance the effect of the forthcoming novel. But in its prefiguring of the novel's characteristic heteroglossia, the 1823 letter also gains retribution for the damages inflicted on Hogg since his 1817 collaboration with *Blackwood's.* In assertive fulfillment of North's invitation, Hogg provides the story of the Scots Mummy—an undoubted phenomenon of great interest, which for four and a half full-length magazine columns clearly shows that he does know the meaning of "phenomenon." Moreover, in keeping with the scientific nature of the report, the letter combats the "Noctes" by showing that the shepherd speaks plain English. Precisely at the moment in the letter where Hogg describes the discovery of the Scots mummy, the shepherd's diction switches to standard English.[54] This seamless switch from dialect to English decisively rejects the "Noctes" lampoon of the shepherd, and further secures this assertion by using Hogg's real name ("JAMES HOGG") in the letter's concluding signature. In that byline, the author preempts the impersonation and possession that the novel details, and he insists upon the indivisibility of his two selves—the Ettrick Shepherd and James Hogg, a dialect speaker who is also capable of writing flawless standard English.

After all, it is hardly insignificant that it is not a "Scot*tish*" mummy that is disinterred, to use the adjectival indicator of nationality that might be expected to label this Caledonian antique. Rather, by calling the mummy "Scots," Hogg uses a noun referring to language—and, more specifically, dialect—to clue the reader into the novel's autobiographical concern with linguistic representation. A similar clue also occurs in the shepherd's misinterpretation of "phenomenon." "Phenomenon" was a contemporary nickname for Thomas Young, the English polymath who had been Britain's chief hope to decipher the Rosetta Stone. Young authored an article on hieroglyphs in the 1819 *Encyclopedia Britannica* and was responsible for the early insights into translating cartouches that facilitated Champollion's breakthrough. In conjunction with the mummy, the word hints at the Rosetta Stone motif that binds the *Private Memoirs* to the manuscript, and as an incongruously Francophonic assertion also alludes to Hogg's specifically Napoleonic motif. (Indeed, the shepherd's misclassification of "phenomenon" as a French word is more fitting than it initially appears, as the misstatement highlights the fact that it was the French, in the end, who earned the crown of translation that Young sought.)

Thus, although I have previously suggested that Wringhim never provides the key to his memoirs that he promises, the actual letter published in *Blackwood's* a few months in advance of the novel might well be that key. Despite its publication outside of the novel itself, Hogg's archeological letter announcing the Scots mummy works, rather like Champollion's historic *Lettre à M. Dacier,* to provide the clue to the novel's connections to the Egyptological motif of the Chaldee Manuscript. Just as Champollion's reprinting in magazines trumpeted French victory in the race for decipherment, Hogg's letter advertises his own symbolic triumph, deftly simulating the role of periodicals in disseminating imperial culture as well as using that imperial motif to figure his professional independence from that form.

The synthesis of English and dialect in both the *Blackwood's* letter and the Auchtermuchty episode thus is symbolic of Hogg's authorial position by the time of the novel. In their mutual synthesis of English and dialect, both passages suggest Hogg's insistence, against the representations of the "Noctes Ambrosianae," upon his own heteroglossic flexibility. This is a slightly different interpretation of the apparent tension between print and orality previously cited by Duncan and Fielding in their approach to Hogg, and indeed one that argues for a slightly different significance of the novel's generic form. For while the *Private Memoirs* is, undoubtedly, a novel, its multiple references to Hogg's history with *Blackwood's* also suggest, more important, its relevance to periodicals, and thus the ways the novel's formal attributes might derive from that earlier arena of Hogg's literary aspirations. In the second "Editor's Narrative" with which the novel concludes, the editor recounts how he first heard the story of the Scots mummy from "an authentic letter, published in *Blackwood's Magazine for August,* 1823," and "signed JAMES HOGG, and dated from Altrive Lake, *August 1st,* 1823" (165, 169). This detail clearly ties the fictional novel to the actual world of contemporary *Blackwood's.* The "extract" from which the fictional editor quotes the Scots mummy history matches the actual letter from Hogg that really did appear "in *Blackwood's Magazine for August,* 1823." And in further completion of the metafictional circle of verisimilitude that Hogg began with the Chaldee Manuscript and that went astray with the "Noctes Ambrosianae," but which Hogg hijacks back for himself by the time of the *Private Memoirs,* the editor, who is intrigued by the story, assembles a party of associates to join him in an expedition to investigate the mummy, "taking Blackwood's Magazine for August along with [them]" (170). His friends are closely associated with *Blackwood's* and are described in the novel in a barely obscured roman à clef that recalls the Chaldee Manuscript. The figures whom the editor contacts include "W——m B——e" (William Beattie, a prominent figure in Ettrick), "Mr. L——w" (William Laidlaw), and "Mr. L——t of C——d, advocate" (169)—clearly a reference to Lockhart, then a lawyer residing in Chiefswood.

In thus fictionally portraying *Blackwood's* and its affiliated personalities, Hogg co-opts the very practices of impersonation and fictional caricature that the "Noctes Ambrosianae" had once used so destructively against him. Indeed, as many readers have already noted, the novel is full of *Blackwood's*-style in-jokes that reverse their usual function to instead make the *Blackwood's* elite the butt of Hogg's jibes. The editor, a pompous know-it-all who claims that "no person . . . will ever peruse [the manuscript] with the same attention" as himself (174), bears intriguing similarities to Wilson; Walter Scott is diminished in the narrative to a mere reference as Lockhart's father-in-law and the loaner of the horses that the editor uses for his expedition; and Lockhart himself is forced to acknowledge that "Hogg has imposed as ingenious lies on the public ere now" (169). As to the shepherd himself, "the very man we wanted to make our party complete" (169), whom Hogg is careful to include in the second "Editor's Narrative" in order to complete its evocation of the "Noctes," Hogg portrays himself in notably rehabilitated terms. Although the Edinburgh party is able to locate the shepherd, he is not where the magazine article originally suggested, and he is too preoccupied with agricultural responsibilities to become involved with the editor's expedition. Thus turning his back on the Edinburgh literati, the shepherd symbolically declares his independence of the magazines that Hogg had once sought so assiduously to join.

The *Private Memoirs* thus is Hogg's alternative to magazine collaboration, even as it remains deeply dependent upon its fictional embedding within the contemporary world of magazine culture. This is not contradictory, and indeed is highly strategic, reflecting a pragmatic recognition of the power of print in the modern era. As both Susan Stewart and Margaret Russett have pointed out, the late eighteenth and early nineteenth centuries witnessed an extraordinary number of literary parodies and forgeries, reflecting the irony that, in an era of industrial publishing, existing texts can be authenticated or combated only by production or comparison with additional texts.[55] Under such conditions, these scholars point out, the most adaptive strategy is to accept the opportunities imposed by that structure. Thus, Peter T. Murphy has described the case of James Scott, "the Odontist," a Glasgow dentist whose name and profession were adopted by the "Noctes" circle with little familiarity with the actual person, and who—in a prescient, almost postmodern resignation to the opportunities provided by the impersonation—did not combat the false representation but instead chose to profit socially from it, by dining out on invitations extended on the popularity of the "Noctes," and then good-humoredly performing the songs and quips attributed to him but which, of course, he had never invented.[56] Similarly, for Mark Schoenfeld, *Blackwood's* sphere of influence was so extensive that Hogg had no choice but to work within the intertextual conventions of the "Noctes."[57] Like the odontist, when Hogg went to London in 1832, he found himself answering to the Ettrick Shepherd title. More to the point, and in a specific depiction of the kind of literary proliferation described by Russett and Stewart, Hogg responded to both the theft of the Chaldee and the damaging caricatures in the "Noctes" by producing more texts, particularly memoirs and autobiographies that aimed to reclaim authorship of the Chaldee and thereby counteract the representations of the "Noctes." In addition to "The Boar," the unpublished biblical allegory that Hogg wrote about the Chaldee controversy, Hogg repeatedly returned to the Chaldee history. In the revised edition of his 1806 *Memoirs of the Author's Life,* which Hogg republished in 1821 and again in 1832 and 1834, as well as the "Memoir" that Hogg prefixed to his 1832 *Altrive Tales,* Hogg always included mention of the Chaldee episode.

Lamb's essays, of course, exemplify one kind of this constant literary production, but where Lamb responded to contemporary print capitalism by mirroring the conditions of endless manufacture, Hogg's solution to the peculiar conditions of his magazine collaboration was a variety of unrelated texts that each sought to correct the Chaldee history through different rhetorical means. As an allegorical autobiography, the *Private Memoirs* is simply another version of the same corrective strategy of additional, combative publications. Indeed, it provides insight as to why Hogg, unlike the victims of the Chaldee Manuscript, never sought legal redress from *Blackwood's.* Instead of legal resolution, Hogg's novel is his literary retribution, standing as both literary testament and generic alternative to the assaults of *Blackwood's Edinburgh Magazine.*

Such a retributive interpretation of the *Private Memoirs* would suggest that the novel is intended as market competition for *Blackwood's,* testing the powerful name in contemporary publishing by competing with the novels that the publishing house also was engaged with producing. This is, for example, the suggestion of Peter Garside, who compares the *Private Memoirs* to the many novels on Scottish subjects that *Blackwood's* sponsored in the early 1820s, and who notes that although Hogg was then writing for Longman, the *Private Memoirs* features a number of attributes then commonly associated with the novels *Blackwood's* promoted. Thus, according to Garside, "Hogg in his *Confessions of a Justified Sinner* contrived to write a Blackwoodian novel of his own." For Garside, this similarity in form between novel and *Blackwood's* imprimatur is not inconsistent with the fact that the autobiographical content of the *Private Memoirs* still positions it as "an anti-Blackwoodian novel." Rather, it is precisely the simulation of attributes identified with *Blackwood's* that indicates the novel's function to compete with *Blackwood's* in its own market, in further, material expression of its unmitigated antipathies.[58]

While I think Garside is right to emphasize the numerous, even overt, similarities that the *Private Memoirs* shares with *Blackwood's,* I differ on the literary form in question. As an autobiographical record of Hogg's entanglements with *Blackwood's Magazine,* the *Private Memoirs* is, first and foremost, a novel about a magazine, as demonstrated in its heteroglossic and multigeneric contents. Moreover, both magazines and the miscellaneous, multivocal contents that distinguish the format from the self-contained narrative of novels were forms that played an important role in Hogg's authorial development, even before his involvement with *Blackwood's.* The *Spy,* the weekly newsletter that Hogg wrote entirely himself, and which was one of Hogg's earliest endeavors in Edinburgh, is a tour de force of authorial inventiveness in which Hogg simulated a periodical by alternating between various fictional personae. (Ironically, the *Spy* prefigures the very periodical customs of fictional personae that the "Noctes" would later use so destructively against him.) More generally, if the *Spy* foreshadows the heteroglossia of the *Private Memoirs*, the magazine also exemplifies Hogg's gift for generic variability and discursive multiplicity, an attribute that he displayed again in the 1817 *Poetic Mirror*, a collection of imitations of contemporary poets (such as Byron and Wordsworth), and which originated when few of these authors responded to Hogg's request for contributions for another periodical that he hoped to found. Both the *Spy* and the *Poetic Mirror*, then, stand as examples of Hogg's ability to simulate the miscellaneous variety of literary and linguistic forms associated with a periodical. Although this talent might be attributed to Hogg's economic necessity, which necessitated a prolific and highly productive creativity that ranged from ballads and long poetry to novels and even an award-winning treatise on sheep (the 1817 *Shepherd's Guide*), this style must also be understood as an artifact of the periodical industry in which Hogg was shaped.

Such mercenary variability in authorial style may seem unusual given our conventional notions of Romantic genius, but it reflects the powerful influence of periodicals in the post-Napoleonic period, and to which Hogg was particularly responsive. Hogg's genius was to convert what could be seen as a handicap into an opportunity. Byron, for example, representing what might be called a more conventionally Romantic ambivalence about magazine attributes, once confessed that he thought "the periodical style of writing hurtful to the habits of the mind, by presenting the superficies of too many things at once."[59] Hogg, by contrast, clearly admired this quality of internal variety within magazines, and credited that miscellany with extraordinary power. In an 1817 letter to William Blackwood, from just before the Chaldee Manuscript was published, Hogg remarked that

> of all things connected with the Magazine I like that best of intermixing all things through other. A general miscellany should exactly be such an *olio* that when a man has done with a very interesting article he should just pop his nose upon another quite distinct but as good of its kind. One may then if they please begin with a review or a poem

> or anything he pleases in short a reader should have no rule to go by but the table of contents. I like such bold and manly freedom how superior is that.[60]

In these remarks Hogg voices a taste for the miscellaneous contents of magazines that also exemplifies his authorial style. "Apparent freedom is part of the pleasure of the magazine," Mark Parker has already pointed out.[61] Hogg is no different. What he likes best about magazines is their function as a "general miscellany," an "olio" "intermixing all things through other," into which a reader, bored or disappointed with one contribution, can "just pop his nose upon another" text.

What I am arguing here is that the *Private Memoirs* is just such a text—a novel that actively simulates magazines, in cannibalistic appropriation of the very attributes of *Blackwood's* that had proved to be so popular with contemporary readers. The famously heteroglossic novel thus is a way for Hogg to take ownership of the heteroglossic impersonation that the "Noctes" had conducted upon him, but it is also, more simply, a subversive appropriation of the very attributes of miscellany and generic diversity that make magazines so "superior," "bold and manly." Several important studies of novels and their relationship to other literary forms have similarly suggested how market pressures caused self-contained narratives to incorporate other generic formats with which they competed, such as anthologies and other periodical forms. In *The Presence of the Present,* for example, Richard Altick suggests that magazines and other periodical publications exercised a shaping influence upon the novel.[62] More recently, Leah Price builds upon this idea to argue that in the late eighteenth and early nineteenth centuries, commercial demand for anthologies also required novels to register this internal heterogeneity to better compete in the current literary market.[63] For Hogg, this more ambitious form of his appropriation of *Blackwood's* methods goes far beyond the mere recycling of the "Noctes" elements in the second "Editor's Narrative," or even the real and fictional entanglement of novel with magazine through the 1823 *Blackwood's* letter, and extends to the novel's very narrative form. Hogg's authorial style in the novel is less the traditional Romantic solitary genius, and instead more akin to an editor, whose mastery of a vast number of discourses, narratives, and fictional texts reflects the hegemony of periodical miscellany within the post-Napoleonic period. Similarly, at times the *Private Memoirs* gets notably close to the time and date precision of periodical publication. For example, entries in Wringhim's journal are tagged with specific dates, as if they are news reports, and the editor bids his readers to "attend to the sequel" (165), as if self-consciously emulating the serial publication of the literary culture with which he is identified. At such moments, the novel actively simulates the very form and aspects of periodical magazines, and thereby represents itself less as a conventional novel than as a novelistic periodical, or a periodical novel.

Indeed, one might go so far as to argue that as a novel that uses its heteroglossia to simulate and thus to compete with periodical magazines, the *Private Memoirs* beats *Blackwood's* at its own game, by using its heteroglossia to engross readers in a way that a periodical cannot. Unlike Lamb, Hogg did not want to create a work that would serve a magazine by its possibilities for constant reproduction. Instead, his whole point in competing with *Blackwood's* is to create a singular artifact that can assimilate the attributes of magazines but also surpass it in readerly appeal. This project is aided by the convenient fact that the miscellaneous contents of magazines are inherently conflicted—or "disruptive," to use Margaret Beetham's term—and thus produce confusion.[64] In the *Private Memoirs,* this quality, combined with its numerous puns, conflicting details, and ultimately irresolvable plot, all contrive a narrative that invites constant rereading, in a vain attempt to make sense of the novel's narrative excess. This propensity of Hogg's to endlessly defer the neat narrative resolution that characterized other Gothics (such as Radcliffe's) arguably made the *Private Memoirs* a publication worth its cost. Indeed, it suggests, by correlation, why the Gothic as a commercial line was characterized by a relentless production of new publications. With its inevitably tidy conclusion, most Gothics defeated the possibility for suspenseful rereading, and thus required the genre—like a periodical—to constantly produce new versions as the only way to maintain reader (consumer) demand. That the *Private Memoirs,* by contrast, can provide so much information and still withhold an easy solution demonstrates Hogg's virtuosity. Full of the tantalizing lure of the Gothic, but resolutely withholding explanation, the *Private Memoirs* defies the expiration associated with Gothics and periodicals. Indeed, even as it cannibalized their very attributes, Hogg reverses the "essentially authorless text" that Klancher attributes to nineteenth-century periodicals.[65]

In the next half of this study, I will examine two other periodical engagements in which an author's editorial activities are more explicit. In Landon's work with the literary annuals and Byron's founding role in the *Liberal,* both poets exhibit the late Romantic, post-Napoleonic tendency to conceptualize periodical collaboration in topically imperial terms. This continuity of the imperial motif likens their periodical involvements with those of Hogg, Lamb, and Keats, but Landon's and Byron's periodical engagements also differ from the previous by being involved with periodical forms substantially different from the quintessentially post-Napoleonic format of the monthly magazine. Thus, before moving on to this different stage in the discussion, it is worth summarizing the similarities and distinctions between Lamb and Hogg, who are both utterly exemplary in their involvement with the monthly magazines, even as they respectively illustrate positive and negative examples of periodical collaboration. Like Lamb, Hogg conceptualized his periodical involvement in imperial terms, merely distinguishing between British and Napoleonic motifs in order to signify his changing position upon such periodical involvement. But whereas Hogg, like Lamb, initially used empire precisely for its capacity to telegraph a triumphal paradigm of social mobility and improved class status, the subsequent exclusion exerted by *Blackwood's* upon Hogg ultimately made his periodical involvement a case study in the use of that imperial metaphor for the linguistic or ethnic persecution of Hogg as a periodical victim. One might even argue that *Blackwood's* required Hogg's abjection in order to establish the magazine's superiority.

At any rate, his stark difference in experience with periodicals can be encapsulated for Hogg in the word "stamp," which occurs twice in the final pages of the *Private Memoirs,* and which conveniently contrasts with Bulwer-Lytton's praise of Lamb's ability to "stamp" all his *London* essays with his unique authorial sensibility. In Hogg's novel the term arises first when the editor evaluates the *Blackwood's* letter, acknowledging that it bears "the stamp of authenticity" (169); the second reference occurs in regard to Wringhim himself, whom the editor describes as "the greatest wretch, on whom was ever stamped the form of humanity" (175). Both of these uses, it is apparent, are tragic, and both obliquely acknowledge the tension between original authorship to industrial publication that occurs in magazine collaboration. But whereas in Lamb's case the term had been used as an accolade, in the *Private Memoirs* it tellingly occurs as an epithet of irony and pity.

Three

"But Another Name for Her Who Wrote"

Corinne and the Making of Landon's Giftbook Style

Letitia Landon died in Africa in 1838, a fate that may at first seem to be an extreme instance of imperial involvement, far exceeding the past three case studies in the degree and actuality of her foreign experience. But if Landon's death on foreign shores appears an extraordinary case of imperial engagement, it also exaggerates what was actually an ambiguous and often invisible relationship to empire in her literary and periodical writing. Best known for her work in the giftbooks and literary annuals, the lavishly bound and heavily illustrated yearly volumes that were a publishing phenomenon in the 1820s through the 1840s, Landon is widely associated with the highly conventional brand of sentimental poetry favored in that format, and consequently she is not known for particularly hard-hitting topical or political commentary. (As Thackeray famously disparaged the giftbooks, for example, her verse for the format is like that in all annuals, in which "Miss Landon, Miss Mitford, or my Lady Blessington, writes a song upon the opposite page, about water-lily, chilly, stilly . . . plighted, blighted, love-benighted . . . lost affection, recollection, cut connexion, tears in torrents, true love token, spoken, broken, sighing, dying, . . . and so on." His essay, which has become a touchstone of critical scholarship on the history and culture of the annuals, went on to claim that "they all bear the same character, and are exactly like [those] . . . which appeared last year."[1]) Similarly, the *Literary Gazette,* the weekly miscellany in which Landon debuted and to which she continued to contribute verse (and even became silent editor), was notorious for shameless puffing that suggested a pragmatic opportunism far less concerned with cultural and political journalism than it was in literary logrolling. Thus, throughout the numerous verse pieces that Landon contributed to the *Gazette* over her extensive involvement with the magazine, the poet maintains the same conventional, utterly predictable sentimentalism for which her giftbook verse often is dismissed. In the *Gazette* and in her work for the giftbooks and annuals, Landon shows little of the sophistication about contemporary imperial expansion that she experienced by the time of her death.[2]

The several imitations of *Corinne* that Landon composed over her career might be a further instance of her characteristic atopicality. Beginning with *The Improvisatrice,* the title poem to her breakthrough 1824 volume of the same name, and arguably as early as Landon's debut poem on Rome, which appeared in the *Literary Gazette* when the poet was only seventeen, Landon repeatedly produced imitative homages to Madame de Staël's best-selling 1807 novel about a gifted female lyricist in Napoleonic Italy. (As in *Corinne,* the heroine in Landon's adaptations is an "improvisatrice," the feminine version of an *improvisatore,* the kind of unstudied Italian troubadour whose spontaneous overflow of powerful feeling was widely believed to embody Romantic genius.) Yet although Landon's many poetic imitations maintain the Italian setting and the female heroine at the center of *Corinne; or, Italy*—as goes the novel's full title—her adaptations are notable in that they dispense with a political allegory originally central to the novel, in which the abandonment of the Italian heroine by her British lover symbolizes the English failure during the Napoleonic wars to come to Italy's aid. By ignoring this allegory, Landon may simply be following a pattern common among many nineteenth-century women writers who, like Landon, looked to Staël's novel as a model for female literary ambition. At the same time, though, Landon's unquestioned prominence within the contemporary periodical industry also reveals the oddity of this late Romantic appropriation of a Napoleonic artifact. Unlike Lamb or Hogg, Landon cannot be identified with a distinct imperial position whose politics offer insight into her professional perspective on the periodical industry. Erasing or suspending the topical and imperial leitmotifs that prove so useful for other periodical collaborators, Landon's most significant engagement with a territory identified with recent Napoleonic history is distinguished by the utter absence of that topical motif. And as if to further underscore her deviations from the typical conditions of late Romantic collaborations with the post-Napoleonic periodicals, almost all of Landon's adaptations of *Corinne* never appeared in the periodical format for which the poet is best known.

For some scholars and critics of Landon, this seemingly apolitical relationship to empire in her poetry may be explicable by her gender, as her sex and contemporary codes for social propriety limited her to literary formats targeted at female and mixed audiences, and hence required uncontroversial and often egregiously derivative literature.[3] But just as class and nationality provide the paradigm, but not the sole content, of Lamb's and Hogg's periodical collaboration, Landon's gender should be recognized only as a springboard for highly advantageous strategies of authorial self-promotion, in which Landon, like her male contemporaries, also capitalizes upon current imperial and political motifs to advance her profile within the contemporary periodical press. Her emulative interest in *Corinne* is a perfect example of this tactically gendered motif. By focusing on *Corinne,* Landon embraces a text recently consecrated by female authors, and in her repeated poetic adaptations of the novel, she uses the plot to figure her own self-promotion. Her success at the technique is evident in the persistence of such authorial self-reference throughout her other, non-*Corinne*-related periodical verse, and it is encapsulated in one of the authorial signatures by which she was known. Like Lamb and Hogg, whose mobility within the contemporary periodical marketplace was marked by the increasing currency of their literary personae (Elia, the Ettrick Shepherd), Landon too was known by a variety of signatures and sobriquets. The most famous of these rubrics may be "L.E.L.," the initialized signature famously remembered by Bulwer-Lytton as the "three magical letters" that captivated readers during the 1820s;[4] but after the *Improvisatrice,* Landon was equally well known as the "English Corinne," an epithet that acknowledges her as the living embodiment of Staël's fictional character. Indeed, as if to specially acknowledge her propensity for domesticating and diffusing Napoleonic history, Landon's sobriquet replaces the second half of Staël's title ("Italy") with a new linguistic or territorial affiliation ("English"). This change encapsulates the depoliticized bent of Landon's poetry, and her uses of *Corinne* in particular.

This chapter on Landon thus differs from the two previous case studies by turning its attention to more exceptional kinds of periodical collaboration. This approach can seem awkward in that it explores a negative, referring both to how the poet's *Corinne* adaptations suppress the political content originally crucial to the Napoleonic novel, and to how these works might have influenced her style in the giftbooks and literary annuals, despite the fact that almost none of her *Corinne* adaptations appeared in the format for which she is best known. Past approaches to Landon's oeuvre have often suggested general similarities throughout all of her verse, particularly emphasizing a propensity for self-representation and self-reference that characterizes both her giftbook and *Corinne*-based productions, but few scholars have yet demonstrated a more specific connection between these two apparently disparate veins in Landon's literary production, or explored what this characteristic poetic technique of Landon's owes to the Napoleonic text from which so many of Landon's nonperiodical texts were inspired. Accordingly, this chapter examines the *Improvisatrice,* Landon's first and most important *Corinne* adaptation, to show how the deliberate depoliticization of Napoleonic content so characteristic of Landon's poetry provided a crucial precedent for the techniques of authorial self-promotion that the poet would perfect in the giftbooks and annuals.

Although I will begin by reviewing Landon's techniques in the giftbooks, a style that follows the *Improvisatrice* in chronological order, it is only by first examining the prevailing attributes of Landon's giftbook verse that its origins in Landon's suppression of the novel's Napoleonic politics becomes significant. This unusual use of imperial motifs, where Napoleonic history is reduced to a mere figure for a stylistic technique, puts Landon at one extreme among late Romantic uses of empire, but it also asserts the comparability of Landon's case to past periodical engagements. Indeed, although Landon's collaboration with giftbooks encompasses a variety of different giftbook series, unlike the single periodical series favored in the previous case studies, and although the giftbooks are not usually considered a periodical comparable to the monthly or quarterly magazines with which those other authors are involved, Landon's borrowing from *Corinne* is as invested in a Napoleonic artifact as are the exotic and imperial artifacts adopted by Keats, Lamb, and Hogg. As such, her characteristically post-Napoleonic use of empire to figure a method of authorial self-advancement presents an intriguing instance of late Romantic uses of empire. In her use of the motif to portray her relationship to contemporary periodicals, Landon exhibits an utter ease with both empire and periodicals that far exceeds that of Lamb and Hogg. Indeed, in the same way that Lamb and Hogg present opposite cases of periodical collaboration, Landon exemplifies a purely apolitical use of empire within the periodicals that Byron, in the final chapter, works against.

Second-Order Style in the Giftbooks and Annuals

With their bound form and long delay between installments, the yearly parlor albums known as giftbooks or literary annuals are often singled out from other periodicals, despite their obvious commonalities in serial publication and miscellaneous contents. Both Richard Altick and Walter Graham, for example, distinguish between the two in their separate references to the format. For Graham, the format's commercial success cannibalized verse magazines, which abruptly ceased production during the height of the subgenre and resumed only after the annuals began to fade; and for Altick, the higher prices of giftbooks exclude them from truly representing the mass audience attained by periodicals.[5] Yet to treat annuals as wholly unconnected to their unbound cousins is to overlook the many ways in which that form retains attributes closely identified with periodicals, even to the point of reproducing key aspects of post-Napoleonic periodical culture. In her analysis of periodicals, for example, Margaret Beetham cites the middle-class tendency to bind favorite magazines as evidence that the periodical is really "a kind of book."[6] Although Beetham is interested in the paradox that magazines and reviews ultimately become bound volumes, her comment might also be applied in reverse, to interpret the luxuriously bound giftbook album as a ready-made—and more ornate—version of the periodicals' customary final form. And even more specifically addressing the defining qualities of annuals, Margaret Linley has argued that the form's vending of aristocratic personalities, highly remunerative rates of authorial payments, and wide distribution all constituted a textual embodiment of contemporary trends toward cultural democracy.[7] Her Benedict Anderson–like account of a society constituted by their consumption of these serial publications places the giftbooks at the forefront of contemporary culture, and it certainly presents the literary annual as an intriguing and important variation upon the periodical format. To rephrase Michael Wolff's oft-quoted insight about the place of periodicals in nineteenth-century literary history, one might say that the giftbooks and annuals were a basic unit of culture and society during the height of periodicals that occurred in the later Romantic, post-Napoleonic era.[8]

As one of the most prolific contributors to this distinct periodical format, Landon exemplifies many of the major stylistic techniques and stratagems particular to the form. She was a prominent contributor to many editions of the most respected and long-running giftbook series, such as the *Keepsake* and the *Literary Souvenir,* edited individual volumes and proposed ideas for new series to publishers, and in some cases single-handedly provided all of the letterpress for entire giftbook volumes (as she did for the 1832 *Easter Gift,* the 1833 *Book of Beauty,* and the 1838 *Flowers of Loveliness*). With such extensive involvement throughout all levels of the giftbook industry, Landon can be seen as an exemplar of the chief stylistic attributes and characteristics of giftbook verse in general. The scene in *Middlemarch* that is often cited by scholarship on the annuals exemplifies Landon's representativeness for the giftbook phenomenon as a whole. In the passage, Rosamund Vincy leafs through an edition of the *Keepsake* and teases Lydgate for "know[ing] nothing about Lady Blessington and L.E.L."[9] Here Eliot uses a giftbook as a sign of Rosamund's bourgeois taste, but the more general point that might be made of the vignette's equation of Landon (and Blessington, a fellow giftbook contributor) with the new form of publication that "marked modern progress at that time" is that it accurately depicts Landon's interchangeability with the periodical format that exercised such commercial and cultural impact at the time of the novel's setting.[10]

By illustrating Landon's representativeness for the periodical format, I want to show how her most distinctive poetic techniques exploit conventions within the giftbook format itself. The giftbooks and annuals traffic in a fundamentally value-added aesthetic, whereby the luxuriously bound and illustrated albums use their visual and physical attributes as material evidence of the worth of the texts' literary contents. (The term "embellishment," commonly used to reference the albums' visual illustrations, is a particularly overt example of how the format conflated physical and literal attributes. Although the term suggests a supplementary or additive quality to illustration, the fact that illustrations increasingly constituted the main cost of giftbook production indicates their centrality in conferring the volumes' prestige.) This conceit of value-added merit to the albums legitimated their high price—which often cost as much as a guinea, far in excess of the shilling or half-penny cost of many other periodicals—and greatly exaggerated the material pretensions toward value implicit within the metaphors of museums and collecting already common among the albums' periodical cousins. Just as monthly or quarterly magazines proclaimed the merit of their contents by likening themselves to cultural monuments such as museums and repositories, the giftbooks and annuals also invoked conceits of material value through titles that likened the albums to economically or sentimentally precious items such as flowers (*The Iris, The Flowers of Loveliness*), jewels (*The Pearl, The Bijou, The Amethyst, The Cameo, The Diadem*), or souvenirs (*Friendship's Offering, Pledge of Friendship, The Keepsake, The Remembrance, Easter Gift, New Year's Gift, Anniversary, The Literary Souvenir*). In some cases the format further loaded the issue by choosing for its title an object that is itself a metaphor for another kind of value—as was the case with the *Forget-Me-Not,* named for a flower that is itself named for a souvenir.

Of course, in comparing themselves to individually precious items, the giftbooks also differed from their more frequent cousins in narrowing the scope of their material emblems, but it is precisely this attenuation in the size of the emblems that intensifies the giftbooks' metonymic rhetoric. Rather like Keats evolving from diminutive sonnets to an ode whose ambition inflates the minor object it describes, by likening the whole periodical to the precious physical icon or item previously invoked in individual magazine contributions, the giftbooks accorded an extraordinary importance and value to all their literary contents. As Herbert Tucker notes, "All those Cabinets and Boxes among the gift annuals declared themselves so many decorative microcosms of the architectural spaces they graced." As they gave "fresh point or subliminal appeal to literary periodicals that bore architectural names," the albums constitute an extreme example of the material tendencies underlying much late Romantic periodical culture.[11]

It is just this value-added tendency of giftbooks that Landon cultivated in her own poetry. Past studies of Landon have all noted her propensity toward self-reference, often achieved through an intermediary image or representation that directs attention away from that image and ultimately back toward the original source—hence the author—of the text. The beautiful, often dead, women who litter Landon's poems with remarkable frequency are perhaps the most obvious instance of this transitional motif. As Judith Pascoe notes, Landon's recurring images of dead women are an idiosyncratic way by which the poet figures authorial autonomy through a graphic image of physical indifference.[12] The precedent for such authorial representations is Sappho, Corinne's classical predecessor in a genealogy already well documented by Yopie Prins, but even the more general observations of Landon's tendency toward self-reference that do not identify a single image as the source of this motif similarly note the thrust toward authorial evocation that her poetry invariably takes.[13] Richard Cronin, for example, notes that Landon's verse constantly produces "moments in which the poet disappears into the poem, but the poem is itself only a representation of the poet," and Angela Leighton, in a comment whose metaphor serendipitously parallels Landon's writing to the imperial artifacts evoked in other post-Napoleonic periodical writing, observes that Landon's repeated scenes of dead beauties show how "the woman has become her own work, her own Grecian Urn."[14] As the similarities between these comments all illustrate, what is striking in Landon's giftbook verse is how she uses reference to one thing (visual illustration; the image of a dead woman) as a kind of figural transponder by which to refract attention to her authorial self. Where the material tendencies of late Romantic writing manifest in visual emblems such as those invoked by Shelley, Keats, Lamb, and Hogg, Landon makes herself that subject.

With such fluctuations through alternately visual and verbal forms of value, Landon's poetic technique has obvious parallels to the value-added precepts of the giftbook format. With its similarly mediated transition through one form to another, the conceits of literary and material value underlying the giftbooks set the precedent for Landon's poetics within the form. Indeed, for Jerome McGann, Landon's poetry is throughout characterized by how the poet "rehearses established forms and ideas, echoes and alludes to recognized authors and styles." In a deliberate, self-conscious mode of derivative production, McGann argues, Landon converts imitation into a type of poetic creation. Although McGann may be no different from the many readers of Landon who note the derivative, highly conventional nature of her verse, his characterization assesses this attribute as an index of her imaginative creativity. For McGann, precisely "because . . . such . . . signs may be effectively deployed as second-order signs of the presence of a poetical discourse," the derivative, highly conventional propensity within Landon's poetry is not an indicator of imaginative inadequacy, but instead a deliberate, manipulative, and remarkably pragmatic approach to literary prestige.[15]

Examples of this value-added, second-order quality to Landon's verse are ubiquitous, but a particularly overt instance occurs in "Corinne at the Cape of Misena," a poem of Landon's that appeared in the 1832 installment of the giftbook series the *Amulet*, and which is the only instance of direct intersection between Landon's two chief authorial concerns. In the poem, which accompanies an engraving of a portrait by François Gérard of Madame de Staël, costumed and posed in the manner of her heroine, Corinne, Landon initially seems simply to fulfill the ekphrastic obligation of literary contributions to the visual giftbooks. "How much of mind is in this little scroll, / Whereon the artist's skill has bodied forth / The shapes which genius dreamed!" Landon begins, presumably referring to the literary "genius" embodied by Staël and praising the painter's ability to portray that mental power.[16] In such hortatory comments upon Staël's genius and the ability of the artist to visually depict that gift, these lines partake in the homage then common among women writers who admired Staël and her novel, as well as specifically demonstrate Landon's lifelong admiration for author and character. Indeed, in her fluent ability to proceed on from that start to three long verse paragraphs totaling an even hundred lines, Landon both fulfills the usual function of giftbook letterpress—to simply provide verbal "embellishment" of the visual images that were widely regarded as the format's primary attraction—and illustrates the reasons for her status as one of the era's most prolific contributors to the giftbooks and annuals.

But even as "Corinne at the Cape of Misena" exemplifies the basic functions of giftbook verse, it also provides an illuminating insight into the second-order gestures by which Landon overcame those conditions. The conventional giftbook format of recto letterpress and verso engravings, which ensured that readers saw text only as a secondary, subordinate contribution to the visual element, was not always as stable as it initially appears. In "Corinne at the Cape," for example, Landon combats that convention from the very outset of the poem. Because the "scroll" that Landon mentions appears nowhere in the engraving, her references to "mind," "genius," and "artist's skill" become unhinged from their putative reference to Staël and Gérard and instead hint at Landon herself. Thus floating free from their assumed reference, the terms of artistic and intellectual creativity exalted in the poem retract from the verso's visual image and suggestively settle, in the limited options available within the *Amulet*'s pages, on the recto text, the only possible analogue to a "scroll" within the album, and an emblem of "mind," "genius," and "artist's skill" that refers to Landon herself. This substitution of Landon for Staël that the poem performs is explicit; later in the poem, and in direct articulation of the connection of Staël's novel to her own techniques of second-order literary production, Landon proclaims that "Corinne / Is but another name for her who wrote" (lines 38–39).

In this direct assertion of her appropriation of Staël's fictional heroine, "Corinne at the Cape" might at first seem simply to acknowledge the importance of Staël's novel for Landon and so many of her female contemporaries. More generally, though, the comment also illustrates the ability to co-opt aspects of another author's legacy that McGann, Cronin, and Leighton all identify as typical of Landon's second-order style. Nominally discoursing upon the assigned visual subject, in apparent compliance with giftbook conventions, Landon also launches a metacommentary that displaces the poem's implicit focus from visual image to her textual self. This substitution subverts the usual emphasis upon visual illustration that Thackeray and many others disparaged in the giftbooks, and reinvents the annual as a periodical with as much potential for authorial promotion as others found in the more familiarly "literary" magazines. Indeed, the fact that the image that Landon uses to launch this deflection is one that incorporates multiple forms of creative genius only makes the point all the more strongly. In displacing the poem's focus from the author, character, and visual artist present in the portrait, Landon denies all of the forms of artistic contribution within the hybrid visual and literary giftbook album, therefore ensuring that she would become the page's sole subject.

Indeed, the third and final verse paragraph in "Corinne at the Cape" reiterates Landon's interchangeability with Staël's character through yet another giftbook convention. Another aspect of the giftbooks' value-added tendencies was the propensity for recycling past publications, which appealed to publishers by economizing on cost while also prolonging a work's revenue stream. Landon understood this strategy well. In one idea for a new giftbook series, for example, Landon proposed to the publisher Charles Heath that they pull from the "infinity of female portraits" previously printed by him and reassemble them in an annual by "giving them a completely new literary character."[17] Such a publication would give Heath a new entry in the profitable giftbook market while also employing Landon at little more cost. Indeed, Landon herself uses a similar tactic of strategic recycling in "Corinne at the Cape." Part of the one hundred lines of the poem is not original poetry but in fact is an extract from Staël's novel, which Landon interpolates into her poem in an authorial variation upon the industrial convention of textual recycling. Although Landon precedes the interpolation with an admission that these "words, too truly, are the singer's own" (line 60), and concludes the extract with a footnote acknowledging that it is "translated literally from Corinne's song," the second-order techniques still adopt Staël's text primarily for Landon's benefit. Both in the practical way that Landon extends her work with little effort and in the more subtle way that she heightens her identification with Corinne, the prevailing conceit within the insertion is that these words belong as much to Landon as to Staël or her fictional heroine.

Such an effort by Landon to foreground herself through an ingenious adaptation of giftbook conventions is hardly unique. In an intriguing essay entitled "Pocketbooks and Keepsakes," which appeared in the first edition of the *Keepsake,* Leigh Hunt argues for the form's authorial possibilities by playing upon the sentimental economy in which annuals were marketed and purchased as ready-made gifts. Observing that giftbook contributors "have the pleasure of writing our words, this moment, *with* a keepsake, *on* a keepsake, and of dipping our pen *into* a keepsake," Hunt puns upon that conceit to proclaim, "Thus are we a gifted writer in one sense, if in no other."[18] Notably, Hunt's conceit depends upon the same deflection of meaning from physical or material attributes within the album to the more abstract merits of the literary text that Landon employs in "Corinne at the Cape." Indeed, as might be expected of an author so inextricable from the giftbook industry, Landon also engaged in the transactional motifs that Hunt introduces. One recent critic, relying upon anthropological notions of gift theory, has argued that Landon's distinctive "poetic excess makes a show of linguistic generosity," throughout which Landon "expects—and receives—payment . . . tendered in money, as well as in worship."[19] This way of reading Landon suggests that the excessively ornamental language within her poetry is Landon's way of securing indebtedness from her readers, as Landon exploits the transactional conceits of giftbook culture to figure her own writing as a gift, and thereby foreground the process of literary dissemination. Or, in a striking inversion of the rhetoric of generosity that giftbook contributors often use to claim literary posterity, Adriana Craciun points to an intriguing strain of curses in Landon's poetry. For Craciun, this rhetorical penchant is only a variation upon the transactional motifs that giftbook authors borrowed from the form. As Craciun observes, the "'curse' in Landon's works is [a] stubborn insistence on the material, corporal, and historical specificity of literary production" and a rhetorical device for mystifying what is otherwise a straightforward acknowledgement of an author's desire to impress upon her readers.[20]

Of course, as the only instance of Landon's *Corinne* interests that directly appears within a giftbook, "Corinne at the Cape" is an example of Staël's role in inspiring Landon's second-order techniques that is particularly overdetermined. But before pursuing the more subtle ways in which Staël's novel inspired the technique so characteristic of Landon's giftbook verse, it is worth first noting how the poem illustrates how such giftbook poetry as Landon's ought to be read. Many efforts to revisit this oft-disparaged body of nineteenth-century poetry attempt to ennoble the work by elucidating the complexity and inherent coherence of individual poems. In her reading of Landon's contributions to the *Bijou*, for example, Cynthia Lawford argues that the poems deliberately clash with the genre's visual emphasis, and in similar approaches to Mary Shelley's and Elizabeth Barrett's giftbook contributions, Sonia Hofkosh and Beverly Taylor also demonstrate how those authors' texts resist the emphasis upon female beauty that giftbook images commonly espouse.[21] Significantly, such approaches to giftbook poetry depend on close reading to illustrate and demonstrate an individual poem's fulfillment of those criteria, but in so doing they also overlook the associative and more desultory forms of reading by which periodicals often were approached.[22] Landon's poetry, by contrast, requires precisely such a superficial approach, as suggested in the literary allusions and intertextual references that McGann recognizes are a crucial component of her second-order style. "Corinne at the Cape," after all, makes little sense if read with no attention to the visual image, no knowledge of Staël's novel, or no awareness of the fact that to many British readers in 1832, "Corinne" referred as much to Landon as it did to Staël. Indeed, without close familiarity with both Staël's novel and the various conventions of giftbook verse by which Landon converts the commission into the opportunity for her own self-reference, "Corinne at the Cape" appears far less interesting than it actually is.

What "Corinne at the Cape" helps us see, then, is that in her giftbook verse Landon develops a whole mode of literary production that is based upon the systemic assumption of a more desultory and indifferent mode of reading than that usually assumed in criticism and sought after by high Romantic writers. This deliberately superficial kind of reading that attends to reference rather than content might be better described as comparative rather than close, and is particularly suited to giftbooks in that it recalls the distracted ways by which periodicals and their contents often were read. As a solution to the peculiar conditions of giftbooks as a type of periodical, Landon's second-order style is far afield from the work of Hogg, Lamb, and Keats, whose works all make sense as self-contained, independent texts, and whose aspirations for this typically Romantic ambition are encapsulated in those texts' self-comparisons to the precious items that each of those works invokes as their visual emblem. Indeed, if the physical metaphors common among nineteenth-century periodicals differ among giftbooks in their shift toward likening the whole volume to a beautiful or precious object, Landon's genius is to invent a poetic style that anticipates the subordinate place of any one text within a larger work. Just as Leigh Hunt imagined an authorial practice in which contributors troped the transactional conditions under which giftbooks circulated, Landon's poetic practice in the literary annuals riffs upon the superficial reading methods commonly applied to all periodicals and converts that reading method into a blueprint for her own literary production. This aspect of her poetry may account for the long marginalized status of her giftbook verse, but it is also an ingenious method of redirecting readerly attention to her authorial self. As one recent critic has remarked, "To get at the root" of Landon's poetry, "the reader must look past" the giftbooks' visual images or other texts invoked by her verse and instead look at "its second remove, its poetic translation."[23]

The aforementioned allusion to the "second remove" in Landon's poetry resembles my description of what I have been calling her "second-order" style and reiterates the oblique and tangential attention required by her giftbook poetry. But what of Landon's many *Corinne* adaptations, which for the most part were not published in periodicals, but whose overt imitation of a best-selling novel of the previous generation must surely constitute one of the most obvious examples of Landon's second-order style? Notably, Landon's commissions for the giftbooks and her homages to *Corinne* are contemporary. She appeared in the very first English giftbook, the *Forget-Me-Not* of 1823, and only months later was composing the *Improvisatrice,* which appeared in 1824. Her subsequent *Corinne* imitations, which include "Erinna," in the 1827 volume *The Golden Violent and Other Poems,* and "A History of the Lyre"—about "Eulalia," another improvisatrice—which appeared in the 1829 volume *The Venetian Bracelet,* coincide with some of the years of Landon's greatest labor for the giftbooks. These works certainly ensured for British readers the conflation of Staël's heroine with one of the era's leading contributors to the giftbook format.

Indeed, such contemporaneity between Landon's *Corinne* adaptations and her work with the giftbooks suggests some role of the Napoleonic novel in the general development of Landon's second-order style. As Landon emerges as the contemporary, English incarnation of Staël's fictional character, the poet's first and most prominent instance of second-order style occurs by deliberate suppression of the imperial allegory with which Staël's novel originally was conceived. This peculiar application of empire to her later work in the giftbooks is a further point of contrast between Landon and her male contemporaries among the periodicals, as Landon seems to reduce *Corinne*'s political content only to a framework for her distinct poetic style. But if Landon's indifference to contemporary empire within works like the *Improvisatrice* constitutes an extreme instance of late Romantic engagement with the post-Napoleonic periodicals, it nevertheless remains an intriguing instance of late Romantic uses of a Napoleonic-era artifact that can be compared to Keats, Hogg, and Lamb. Indeed, it is precisely this utter absence of empire within the *Improvisatrice* that suggests Landon's relationship to both empire and periodicals is even more enthusiastic and uncomplicated than Lamb's. Hence, although Landon is often lumped with other writers of her gender, her canny use of empire is best understood when compared to her male contemporaries in the periodicals.

Second-Order Style in the *Improvisatrice*

In suggesting that *Corinne* adaptations such as the *Improvisatrice* omit the politics that distinguished Staël's novel, I am hardly the first scholar to observe that Landon's poetry is characterized by a systemic indifference to contemporary history. "While frequently drawing on historical, or mythological, or literary figures," Glennis Stephenson has already noted, the author "ignores the specifics of the actual story and prefers instead to produce her own text."[24] This description of Landon's indifference to history recalls the fluctuation from reference to self-representation that underlies second-order style, and might be an excellent introduction to the function of empire in the *Improvisatrice.* At the same time, though, it overlooks how that poem's suppression of imperial history mimics a device in *Corinne* itself, and hence ignores how what appears to be Landon's apoliticism in fact stems from Staël's novel itself. The plot of *Corinne,* which Staël conceived after a tour of Italy she had undertaken with Schlegel in 1805, frequently uses the architecture and history of Italy's imperial monuments to stage its plot of female genius. The narrative follows a prolonged tour of Italian landmarks, monuments, and locations; key scenes in the novel are set in specific Italian spaces, and two of the four lyric passages embedded in the novel as transcriptions of the heroine's improvisations make location so important that it is included in the improvisation's title ("Corinne at the Capitol" and "Corinne's Chant in the Vicinity of Naples," in book 2, chapter 3, and book 3, chapter 4).

Within the larger critique of empire in which the novel was conceived, the effect of this locodescription was to blame Napoleon for preventing travel to these privileged destinations in European culture; but within the more literary themes of Staël's plot, this representational emphasis within *Corinne* uses its explicitly imperial references as emblems of lyric genius. This is most apparent in an early scene at the Roman Capitol, where the heroine is first introduced. In book 2, chapter 1, Corinne is depicted atop a triumphal procession through throngs of Roman citizens who chant her name and praise her beauty, intelligence, and generosity. She then proceeds up the Capitoline steps to be crowned with laurels, signifying her recognition as a lyric genius as well as equating that artistic achievement with the military and political contributions of the soldiers and statesmen who in ancient times preceded her upon this august location. Notably, such a scene depends upon the material trappings of Rome's imperial history to portray Corinne's lyric gifts. In a very literal sense, Staël is using the material form of Roman imperial architecture not for any political or topical purpose, but simply as an emblem to stage her heroine's lyric genius.[25]

This deliberate suppression of imperial or political history that Staël exerts over Rome partakes of a long literary tradition. As Leo Braudy points out, Rome is the original setting for Western representations of fame, and the Capitol is the preeminent location within that tradition.[26] The specific importance of the Capitol scene for *Corinne* is further evident in the fact that the numerous nineteenth-century imitations of the novel, which like Landon all focused on the plot of female genius, still maintain this scene. To name just two of the many admirers of Staël who produced literary or poetic homage, both Felicia Hemans and Jane Taylor reprise the "Corinne at the Capitol" scene in their own poetry, as is apparent in Taylor's 1822 address "To Mad. de Staël" and Hemans's 1830 lyric "Corinne at the Capitol." In overt homage, Hemans's poem even uses the same title.[27] Although Hemans's and Taylor's respective treatments of the Capitoline scene are substantially different in content (Taylor reprises the scene as part of her unequivocal admiration for Corinne's dedication to the arts, while Hemans uses the scene to launch a predictably conservative commentary upon the impropriety of Corinne's public renown), the fact that both authors reproduce Staël's original conceit affirms the depoliticized importance of Rome's imperial architecture as emblems of literary genius. Described by Ellen Moers as "one of the most important scenes in the book," the early scene at the Capitol is so crucial to the novel's plot of lyric genius that many subsequent female authors invariably return to that scene, invoking the imperial setting with the same totemic importance that other post-Napoleonic authors use visual or material icons of empire in their allegories of authorial advancement.[28]

Landon, not surprisingly, was no different. "The scene of [Petrarch] being crowned at the Capitol was always present to my mind," confessed the poet in a letter to the journalist S. C. Hall: "It gave me the most picturesque notion of the glory of poetry."[29] Although the author identified with Italy whom Landon references here is male rather than female, the quote demonstrates Landon's long identification of the Roman Capitol with lyric power, and indeed illustrates her shift from a gendered to a more general motif. In fact, this penchant was apparent from the start of her career. Landon's debut poem, "Rome," may not directly invoke *Corinne,* but in its opening declamation to the "proud daughter of fame" and the "capitol worshipped as Liberty's shrine," her poem reiterates the same identification of renown with Roman landmarks that underlies the scene of Corinne at the Capitol. Indeed, because that topic was the vehicle of the prodigy's literary debut, empire arguably was a motif of Landon's even before the onset of her *Corinne* images.[30]

Interestingly, however, in the *Improvisatrice,* Landon's longest and most explicit adaptation of the Corinne story, this convention takes an unexpected turn. The poem, a 100-page, 1,500-line narrative work about "a daughter of that land, / Where poet's lip and the painter's hand / Are most divine," appears at first to be another imitator of the feminine personification of Italian genius in *Corinne,* and it bears a title that seems to differ from the novel only by substituting the profession for the proper name.[31] Where the novel tracks a tragic love affair in which the Italian heroine is abandoned for a blonde to whom the male love interest was betrothed by his father, causing the improvisatrice to waste away and die, the *Improvisatrice* similarly tells the tale of a male protagonist who betrays the heroine for a "pale and lovely" girl" (line 1291), to whom he was also betrothed by his father, and thus also causes the improvisatrice to abandon her lyre and eventually die. This Sapphic trajectory of intense love, disrupted lyric production, and eventual death is explicit in *Corinne* in numerous comparisons of the heroine to the classical poet, and the *Improvisatrice* is likewise bracketed with sustained references to Sappho (lines 113–60, 1321–42). So close is the *Improvisatrice* to *Corinne,* in fact, that the poem even maintains minor details within the plot, such as when the heroine attends a ball dressed in an Indian turban (book 6, chapter 1, in *Corinne;* lines 743–60 in the *Improvisatrice*). As with the reduction of Roman architecture into a purely physical signifier for literary genius, this oriental headdress sported by Corinne is yet another suggestively imperial emblem for artistic sensibility within the *Improvisatrice* that Landon borrows from Staël's original novel.

But if these points of direct resemblance between poem and antecedent text suggest one reason why Landon, of all the authors who admired the novel, should have won the title of Corinne's English heir, it also highlights a key point of difference between novel and imitative poem. Indeed, it does not explain how Landon's homage could achieve that prestige when it diverges from its model in eliminating the imperial motifs so instrumental in portraying the heroine's genius. After all, Landon's characters in the *Improvisatrice* are, as she announces in the preface to the poem, "entirely Italian."[32] This pronouncement foregrounds the role of Italian identity in figuring the heroine's emotional expressiveness and artistic sensibility, but it also deviates from *Corinne* by eliminating the British citizenship of the heroine's lover and her own half-English heritage, two details instrumental to the novel's political commentary. (In the original novel, Corinne's father is English and her lover a Scot, while in the *Improvisatrice* the heroine's lover, "Lorenzo," presumably is Mediterranean like the heroine herself.) Such an erasure of the once potent political elements within the *Corinne* narrative exemplifies the suppression of empire that characterizes the *Improvisatrice,* which is most evident in Landon's egregious variation upon the important "Corinne at the Capitol" scene. Although the *Improvisatrice* remains true to the detail that Corinne was born in Florence, Landon's poem displaces the early scene of the heroine's public acclaim from the Capitol to the Arno (line 191), and therefore eliminates the imperial setting that made the Roman scene at the Capitol so important in the original novel.

In one possible explanation for Landon's omission of the Capitoline setting, David Riess speculates that the *Improvisatrice* results from the author's calculated updating of the *Corinne* story for the post-Napoleonic audiences of Landon's own time. Set in the period from 1794 to 1803, at the height of Napoleon's military ascendance, *Corinne* was of great topical interest upon its debut, but it would only have lost this significance as the Napoleonic wars faded into the past. According to Riess, Landon resolves this problem by simply ignoring those outdated elements, as the poet "takes an already popular novel and makes it even more accessible to an English reader of 1824 by de-politicizing it."[33] Riess is certainly right about the aspects of the novel's post-Napoleonic reception. When Waterloo made the allegorical content of Staël's novel irrelevant and anachronistic, *Corinne* did not, significantly, fade into insignificance. Rather, the novel enjoyed a curious half-life, both in the extensive homage to the novel by female authors and in two other veins of relevance for more general audiences, which, like the elite adaptation by Staël's literary admirers, focused on the literal rather than the allegorical portion of the novel's narrative. In the first vein, *Corinne* exercised a powerful hold on young female readers who consumed the love plot as they might devour sentimental romances by Austen or Burney. The extensive descriptions of Corinne's beauty and dress throughout the novel inspired fashions among these women readers, and even when community leaders intoned against the novel's dangerous representation of female independence, such publicity only served as free advertising to pique the interest of additional fans.[34] And in the second vein of reception, an even wider general audience appropriated the novel as one of the many literary commodities whose publication served as an ancillary industry to the newly developed tourist industry that emerged after the end of the Napoleonic wars, and in which Italy was a preeminent destination for British travelers. As James Buzard and Maura O'Connor have shown, the numerous descriptions of Italian locations and monuments within *Corinne* provided readers with a novelistic supplement or substitute for actual travel itself.[35] Indeed, at the end of the nineteenth century, the novel was still cataloged as a travel guide, in a generic expansion that seemed to give more weight to the second half of *Corinne*'s title ("or, Italy").[36]

The *Improvisatrice* certainly reflects these aspects of *Corinne*'s post-Napoleonic reception. In addition to Landon's stated emphasis on Italy, her poem also differs from its novelistic source in that Landon narrates her poem in first person, a change that foregrounds the experience of the female protagonist and therefore arguably enhances those aspects of the story in which contemporary women readers were most interested. These changes are particularly felt in the many passages in the poem that describe the heroine's body and the sentimental excesses of her physical reactions. Where Staël's improvisatrice was prone to long philosophical dialogues that instruct her lover on Italian culture and history, Landon's heroine talks about herself, and particularly how love and fame make her feel. "Each wild, / High thought I nourished raised a pyre / For love to light," proclaims the improvisatrice in one characteristic comment equating genius with romantic love (lines 175–77). Elsewhere noting that "It was not song that taught me love, / But . . . love that taught me song" (lines 151–52), the heroine recasts her genius into a medium of erotic connection. Thus, when Lorenzo first spies the improvisatrice as she performs before a crowd (in a passage recalling the premise if not the setting of *Corinne*'s Capitol scene), the heroine is indifferent to the crowd's appreciation and has pleasure only in her future lover's gaze. "I heard no word that others said," confesses the improvisatrice, as she acknowledges that she "heard nothing, save one low-breathed sigh," and "felt the thrill / Of that look burning on me still" (lines 462–63, 460–61). In such modifications of the content of Staël's original novel, Landon converts a scene originally dependent upon imperial imagery into a scenario of erotic attraction.

Unique among the numerous contemporary homages to Staël's novel, then, Landon's poem follows *Corinne*'s post-Napoleonic reception by converting its portrait of Romantic genius into a sentimental narrative of romantic love. In so doing, Landon actualizes an aspect of *Corinne* that had never before been recognized. Most homages to the novel obscured a paradox—that in aspiring to the genius portrayed in the novel through improvisation, the era's many *Corinne* adaptations expressed that aspiration through imitation, a second-order response otherwise antithetical to the improvisational genius the novel lauds. Landon's poem, however, does not elide this paradox; indeed, in taking the term as its title, the *Improvisatrice* explicitly asserts that the genius signified by the term can be achieved through second-order activities such as direct imitation. It is a paradoxical claim that no previous homage dared to advance, and it is an assumption that Landon also fulfills through her careful replication of the conditions by which the *Corinne* story remained popular in the post-Napoleonic years. By thus equating imitation with improvisation, and specifically imitating the less topical aspects of the narrative then pertinent in the post-Napoleonic era, Landon achieves the era's most compelling adaptation of the novel. Attending closely to the literal rather than the allegorical aspects of *Corinne*'s plot, Landon's adaptation of the narrative into the *Improvisatrice* focuses on reception rather than content, and it preserves only that portion of the novel that still exercised relevance with post-Napoleonic readers. It is a gesture that ought to recall Lamb in his desublimated reworking of Coleridge, and shows Landon to be the best reader of Staël's historic novel.

An interesting paradigm of this self-centered and noncreative form of authorial production may lie in the masturbatory sensationalism of the *Improvisatrice*'s many scenes of female arousal. In one passage midway through the poem, the heroine describes the experience of lyric performance with an almost orgasmic quality:

My hand kept wandering on my lute,
  In music, but unconsciously

My pulses throbbed, my heart beat high,
  A flush of dizzy ecstasy
Crimsoned my cheek; . . .
. . . .
. . . my mood
Made my soul pant for solitude. (lines 464–68, 474–75)

It is easy, as with so much sentimental verse, to see the inadvertent comedy of such passages. In its overheated transposition of Romantic sensibility and the spontaneous overflow of powerful feelings to a female body, Landon's poem becomes, unintentionally, a quasi-pornographic fantasy, as the heroine's surrender to her feelings and to her instrument produces a physical response with an unmistakably sexual tinge. This distinctly sensual quality to the poem may seem ironic and contradictory, given the genre's professed function as a polite publication suitable for proper young ladies, but it reveals another point of similarity between the poem and the periodical form with which Landon was to become so involved. The illustrations of many annuals were full of women whose revealing dress and often carefully detailed bosoms and dishabille were the object of much derision among giftbook critics. More important, in the self-centered and nonprocreative stimulation that masturbation constitutes, the scene allegorically suggests the closed circuit of artistic manipulation and production on which second-order style is based.

In keeping with the comparative approaches mandated by Landon's second-order techniques, however, the *Improvisatrice* is perhaps best understood when considered according to the systematic and general motifs throughout the poem. I have employed this approach in my previous contrast of the poem with the novel, and its insights are particularly apparent in the poet's take on the imperial landscape previously constituted in the novel by Napoleonic Italy. As the title suggested, the setting was always of equal importance in *Corinne; or, Italy.* But in the *Improvisatrice,* and despite Landon's prefatory comments describing the poem as entirely "Italian," it is an ironic fact that Landon's *Corinne* adaptation incorporates an extensive global geography in which Italy, or even the Continent, is only a small component. This occurs in the four embedded stories included within the narrative as supposed transcriptions of the effusive songs that the heroine improvises in the scene, and which simulate a similar device in Staël's novel. But where "Corinne at the Capitol," "Corinne's Chant in the Vicinity of Naples," "Fragments of Corinne's Thoughts," and "Last Song of Corinne" all enhance Staël's novel by reinforcing the setting and providing glimpses into the heroine's interiority, the embedded passages within the *Improvisatrice* are new and different stories all set in locations outside of Italy, and hence seem to have little obvious relation to the overall *Corinne* plot. As their respective titles suggest, the "Moorish Romance," "The Indian Bride," "Leades and Cydippe," and the Gothic "Charmed Cup" are set, respectively, in the Levant, India, Greece, and the Continent. Thus topographically and narratively independent of the *Corinne* plot that frames these embedded stories, these variations on Staël's Italian setting reiterate the differences between Landon's poem and its Napoleonic predecessor, or what Reiss summarizes as its "depoliticized" quality.

Yet the most obvious thing that can be noted of this variety in topographical locations is that its range of eastern and western locations encompasses a geographical diversity that approximates a global variety. (Indeed, in its combination of Greek, Continental, Asian, and North African settings, the *Improvisatrice* contains a topographical variety notably similar to that encompassed in this study.) In the expanding global consciousness of post-Napoleonic Britain, such spatial diversity can suggest an imperial compass even if the spaces portrayed are not explicit sites of imperial interest in the manner of China or Egypt. After all, all of the spaces invoked in the poem are places popular in literary and cultural interest, and furthermore are bound together by a favored site of Western history and leading destination for British tourism. This insight raises an answer to the question as to why the *Improvisatrice* omits the scene that so many other female authors saw as important. In her poem, Landon does not need to repeat Staël's Capitoline scene because she has replaced Roman imperial architecture with a more expansive and topical version of empire that serves the same symbolic purpose. That is, by replacing the single imperial space of Rome with the whole global compass of geographical diversity signified by the different settings of the *Improvisatrice*'s embedded lyrics, Landon maintains Staël's original use of the imperial motif to signify lyric genius but—as Riess suggests in a different context—updates that motif for a more topically appropriate manifestation for her post-Napoleonic audience.

There may be something peculiarly feminine in this move by Landon toward a global geographic diversity. Sydney Owenson, "Lady Morgan," tracks a similar global compass in her various novels, first depicting Ireland in *The Wild Irish Girl,* and later Belgium, India, and Greece, respectively, in *The Novice of Saint Dominick, The Missionary: An Indian Tale,* and *Woman, or Ida of Athens.* This geographical scope, moreover, was not limited to fiction. Owenson also published travel books on Italy and France.[37] Perhaps more pertinently, Felicia Hemans, Landon's poetic colleague and chief competitor, also composed works based on similar arrays of global motifs. Hemans's 1829 volume, *The Forest Sanctuary,* contains a section entitled "Lays of Many Lands," which collates various poetic vignettes about representative people in exotic places. Her earlier volume, the 1828 *Records of Women,* is a collection of poetic portraits of women from various cultures and histories, and like Owenson, Hemans's whole career seems to produce a similar global coverage, as the poet moved from *Welsh Melodies, Greek Songs,* and *Songs of Spain,* to *National Lyrics, and Songs for Music.* While the global motifs of these authors may seem to replicate the diversity employed by male counterparts, such as Byron, Southey, or Moore, the socially proscribed nature of female literary careers arguably accords their geographical motifs a greater significance. For while the variety was for the male writers merely a sort of costuming, like the ethnic dress that Byron sometimes affected, for the women writers the expansive and public nature of invoking a whole global geography was a vividly dramatic way to invoke a platform for their authorial presence. In the same way that the Capitol puts Corinne on display, some women writers portrayed their ambitions through a more typically imperial scale. A larger, more ambitious version of the Corinne at the Capitol scene, this imperial variety is a hyperbolic way to assert public visibility when the gendered conventions of propriety did not always provide for it. Thus, it is not surprising that authors as politically diverse as the jingoistic Hemans, nationalist Owenson, and seemingly apolitical Landon all use the same trope of global geography. As with Landon's adaptation of Corinne's reliance upon Roman imperial architecture, these three female authors all turn to imperial topography because of its convenience as a stage for their authorial ambition.

Of course, Hemans's and Owenson's uses of global geography span a variety of different publications, whereas Landon's globetrotting within the *Improvisatrice* adaptation is contained within a single poem. This is exactly what makes the *Improvisatrice* so prophetic of Landon's later work in the giftbooks, as the internal miscellany of Landon's long poem simulates an anthology and is unified by Landon through similar methods of authorial display. Much as the miscellaneous contents of periodicals generated meaning from the accidental connections of their miscellaneous contents, the different, explicitly non-Italian settings of the four embedded stories within the *Improvisatrice* appear to be united only in the arbitrary fact of their selection and arrangement. Moreover, in the *Improvisatrice,* Landon further showcases its internal diversity by expanding its geographic variety with the more explicitly literary diversity of rhyme scheme and stanzaic form. As with the geographical diversity, what is significant about this stanzaic variation and diversity of rhyme scheme extends beyond the fact that it distinguishes the embedded stories from each other and from the *Corinne* frame. Rather, like Hogg's early periodical, the *Spy,* whose imitations of various contemporary poets prefigure his heteroglossic diversity in *The Private Memoirs,* this stylistic variety within the *Improvisatrice* recalls various other contemporary authors and therefore simulates a miscellany of works or poems by other successful contemporary poets. The "Indian Bride" story, the third of the embedded tales, recalls poems on *sati* by Hemans and Wordsworth, and "Leades and Cydippe" and "The Charmed Cup," two of the other embedded stories, might be compared with Greek and Continental tales by Keats and Shelley.[38] Similarly, with its richly sensual description of "pomegranate groves," "Indian rubies," "giant palms," and the "mosque's gilded minaret" (lines 219, 222, 226, 227), the "Moorish Romance" both resembles the oriental romances then identified with Byron, Southey, and Moore and also typifies the highly pictorial capacities that made Landon's poetry so eminently suited to the annual form. *The Improvisatrice,* in other words, formally simulates the miscellany of different authors and works that might be found in a giftbook or album, and therefore further suggests the possible relationship between Landon's *Corinne* adaptations and her contemporary work in the periodical giftbooks and annuals.

Such similarities between contemporary publications and the *Improvisatrice* did not go unnoticed by the periodical press. "Very elegant, flowing verses they are—but all made of Moore and Byron," noted the "Noctes Ambrosianae" of the *Improvisatrice.*[39] In this snide allusion to the derivative attributes of Landon's poetry, this contemporary review from one periodical series implicitly acknowledges the poem's likeness to other miscellanies, such as the periodical giftbooks. It also illuminates the observation, often implied in previous studies of the poem, but never before explicitly illustrated, that the album-like form of the *Improvisatrice* prefigures Landon's success in the giftbook format.[40] (Similarly, another contemporary review of the volume containing the poem praised it as "a most delightful *bijou*," using a term that would later title a giftbook series to which Landon would contribute.[41]) Indeed, with its ekphrastic descriptions of portraits, by which the *Improvisatrice* is bracketed at the beginning and end of the poem (lines 33–80, 1550–78), the work arguably even anticipates the hybrid visual and literary form of the illustrated giftbook.

In fact, this connection between *Corinne* and Landon's giftbook collaborations would come full circle in "Corinne at the Cape of Misena," the poem previously referenced as the only direct intersection of Landon's two chief literary interests. The excerpt from *Corinne* that Landon incorporates into the final stanza in her poem is a translation of Staël that Landon was then conducting for Richard Bentley, a successful printer and giftbook publisher with whom Landon had previously worked, who was then planning a new English edition of *Corinne.* Based on her acknowledged celebrity as the "English Corinne," Bentley had commissioned Landon to provide metrical English translations of the prose lyrics within Staël's original novel. These translations, which converted to English and also set into meter the prose passages that Staël had provided as transcriptions of Corinne's effusions, provided Landon with the material to flesh out "Corinne at the Cape," and further consolidated Landon's inheritance of Staël's character and fame. Indeed, because Landon's translations were the first time that Staël's heroine actually exhibited the versification for which she supposedly was renowned, and because it was in this giftbook poem that her translation work first appeared, it was through a giftbook that Landon realized the claims that the novel promised but which Staël herself had never effectively provided.[42]

What previous scholars and readers of Landon have never adequately recognized about the *Improvisatrice,* however, is how the poem's anthology-like internal diversity shows the paradoxical ability of second-order methods to foreground the borrower as creative author. "My name / Is linked with beauty and with fame," claims the improvisatrice in some of the final lines of the poem (lines 1519–20). As in my previous observations about Landon's continuation of Staël's imperial motifs, the improvisatrice's ability to make this claim depends upon the same superficial or comparative modes of reading encouraged by Landon's giftbook poetry, and it is modeled for the reader in one important passage early in the poem. This occurs in "A Moorish Romance," the first and longest embedded story within the *Improvisatrice* and a work, like the poem's overall *Corinne* frame, that is an overt example of Landon's second-order propensity for derivative adaptation and imitation. As many readers have noted, the "Moorish Romance" obviously imitates Byron's *Giaour,* the earliest of the best-selling romances later referenced as his "Oriental" or "Turkish Tales." Like the overall imitation of *Corinne,* the "Moorish Romance" is a remarkably detailed adaptation. Landon's romance borrows from Byron's in narrating the fate and attempted escape from a harem of a female slave with the aid of her Christian lover, and in a remarkably explicit instance of a "name / . . . linked with . . . fame," the poem acknowledges its debts to Byron by the fact that it even keeps the same name—Leila—of the female love interest. Yet as with the *Corinne* imitation, these points of overlap should not be mistaken simply as evidence of Landon's impoverished imagination. Rather, such overt imitation is no different from that in the *Corinne* frame—that is, a deliberate claim for literary prestige by the self-conscious imitation of some other author's previously successful work. In the case of the *Improvisatrice*'s timely publication in 1824, which came immediately after news of Byron's death, this obvious likeness between Landon's poem and its predecessor had the additional advantage of insinuating Landon as Byron's heir.

This cultivated comparison of Landon to Byron was not entirely self-generated. Poems from the two authors were often published adjacent to each other, and when not referenced as "the English Corinne," Landon was also known as "the female Byron," a cognomen that acknowledged her similar tendency for erotic romances set in exotic locations. But a closer examination of the *Improvisatrice* also reveals a more sophisticated strategy that breaks down any overt imitation to instead reconstruct internal likenesses that redirect attention away from her source and instead toward Landon's own authorial self. This practice is evident in the "Moorish Romance" in the poem's depiction of brunette hair, a detail originally crucial to *Corinne* and which runs throughout the *Improvisa-*

trice's frame and other stories. From the first passages to one of the last lines of the poem, the *Improvisatrice* is rife with references to "dark hair" (line 391), "tresses dark" (line 498), "my long black hair" (line 515), "long black tresses" (line 533), "the raven tress of silken hair" (line 559), "her long black hair" (line 597), "her dark hair . . . bound" (line 854), "her black hair loose" (lines 1326–27), and "[a] cloud of raven hair" (line 1560). These details are typical of the post-Napoleonic heightening of the erotic and sensual portions of *Corinne* and also encourage the comparisons of poem to giftbook by its pictorial emphasis upon the female body. Indeed, studies that compare the *Improvisatrice* only to the giftbooks it resembles might at first see this attention to hair as part of the form's material conventions, particularly the Victorian affectations for hair jewelry that the sentimental affectations of giftbooks anticipated.

But a more topical attention to the imperial motifs common in post-Napoleonic periodicals would also note that this brunette detail—a marker of the heroine's Mediterranean origins and symbolic of her nontraditional artistic sensibility—is an element of the original novel that is cited in homage as much as the Capitol scene. (For example, in Eliot's *Adam Bede,* the heroine identifies with Corinne because of their shared hair color.) Similarly, in the *Improvisatrice,* Landon builds upon this physical embodiment of Corinne's difference from her blonde English half-sister and uses her multiethnic array of brunettes to figure a more general racial otherness, whose corporeal signification of contemporary imperial culture becomes, paradoxically, a means of signposting her own authorial self. As the repeated references to brunette hair connect the embedded stories with each other and with the overall frame, they fracture the stories' ability to recall their source text, and instead redirect attention to the one female body that unifies these otherwise discrete, self-contained stories. The hair, a detail that runs throughout both embedded and frame stories, becomes a visual embodiment of the superficial and comparative connections by which Landon's poetry is best understood. That is, as all but one of the stories end in the image of a dead female with dark hair (only the Grecian romance "Leades and Cydippe" does not), the *Improvisatrice* gradually constructs a network of figural references that point to Landon, the only female body that is consistently implicated throughout the poem's different embedded and frame stories.

Landon herself was a brunette, but this biographical fact may be redundant in the face of her poem's explicit depiction of the visual network that unites its various narrative stories. The climactic scene in the "Moorish Romance" occurs when fishermen inadvertently net the two drowned lovers, retrieving their bodies from the water, with the escaped concubine's dark hair wound round her and her lover (lines 390–411). In the self-contained context of the "Moorish Romance," the woman's dark hair is a graphic example of both the lovers' embrace and the fishing net that retrieves them from the sea, but in the larger context of the story's likeness to the other embedded stories and to the *Corinne* frame itself, that net of brunette hair also is evocative of the network of intertextual reference that binds together the various, otherwise unrelated stories. Like the imperial structure loosely suggested by the stories' geographical diversity, the network of brunette hair within the *Improvisatrice* retains an element originally strongly associated with *Corinne* and reinvents it as a figure for Staël's second-order imitator. As the dark hair of the "Moorish Romance" and all the other stories of the *Improvisatrice* combine to collectively allude not to Corinne or Staël but to Landon herself, the poem exhibits the same second-order techniques of using derivative adaptation to foreground the borrowing author's own contribution that Landon would develop to such a degree in her subsequent work in the giftbooks and annuals. Indeed, the repeated references to brunette hair work—like the poem's overall use of the *Corinne* narrative to frame other, unrelated poems—as a kind of purely literary binding that prefigures the physical binding by which such miscellaneous contents are collated in anthologies such as giftbooks and annuals.

It is worth pausing here to review how this account of Landon's literary techniques differs from other critical accounts. Most studies of Landon emphasize the gendered context of the literary form in which she published and the other literary influences, such as *Corinne,* that exercised such an important role in her artistic development. In one provocative reading of the *Improvisatrice,* for example, Katherine Montwieler claims that the poem parodies the conventions of erotic love in order to present literature, and Landon's poetry in particular, as the only site in which women readers can safely encounter such sensations.[43] Such studies promulgate a profoundly gendered account of Landon's poetic style, which manifests in the excess of her sentimental phrases and images, the improvisational effusiveness thematized by her borrowing of the *Corinne* story, and the willingness to objectify her authorial self. In stark revision of this account, however, I suggest a view in which gender provides the vehicle of Landon's authorial devices, but in which that element is less significant than the topically imperial dimensions of that vehicle. By using *Corinne*'s imperial and Napoleonic geography to enact a singularly advantageous scheme of authorial self-promotion, the *Improvisatrice* may feature all of the elements commonly associated with the poetess tradition, but in Landon's hands those elements rely upon empire to contrive their powerfully ambitious framework for authorial self-promotion.

Indeed, it is equally intriguing that the other poems in the same volume as the *Improvistrice* mirror the title poem in content and style. Many of these other poems also focus on lyric heroines who suffer or die at the vagaries of romantic love. The eponymous heroine of "Rosalie," for example, is a mandolin player who is abandoned by her lover Manfredi (notably, another Byronesque character); Isabelle of "Roland's Tower" is a lutist and singer who dies in a convent after being separated from her lover; and in "The Basque Girl and Henri Quatre," the heroine dies only after carving a record of her love onto a tree. Dark hair is also a recurrent attribute of the heroines. These similarities between the volume's title poem and its additional contents only reinforce the objective of the title poem and its embedded "episodes" and "tales." Like the long poem alongside which these works appear, these supplementary poems reiterate Landon's propensity for authorial self-reference, and they rely upon the simplest kinds of geographical diversity to loosely differentiate what are otherwise nearly identical poems.

Thus, the *Improvisatrice* is an important early document in understanding Landon's more prominent later work in the periodical giftbooks and annuals. Although the long poem was not published in a periodical, its form prefigures the embedded and miscellaneous contents of giftbook anthologies, and it also shows Landon's early development of the second-order techniques that she would use to such advantage within that particular periodical format. In her reliance upon imperial motifs within the *Corinne* narrative—or in her use, more generally, of a novel once supremely identified with Napoleonic history—Landon resembles her male counterparts among the post-Napoleonic periodicals by relying upon a geographic and highly topical imperial motif to figure her literary gifts. Indeed, her remarkably reductive and ahistorical use of empire purely as a figure for literary style may seem to suggest a wholly uncomplicated ease with the imperial and periodical project that perhaps exceeds even that of Lamb. But while Landon's drastic reduction of empire into a paradigm for the second-order style may suggest an ease with empire notably different from that of Keats or Hogg, it would be a mistake to assume that Landon was unaware of the consequences of contemporary capitalism, and hence not a sophisticated critic of both the imperial and periodical industries. Indeed, in one of the most explicit intersections of empire with the periodical giftbooks within Landon's career, we see her, like other periodical collaborators, adopting empire as a paradigm by which to portray the adverse consequences of periodical collaboration.

Empire and the Giftbook Industry

Born in 1802, Landon only knew a literary and political world transformed by the linked enterprises of empire and periodical publication. During her childhood, Landon's father, a former naval officer, enjoyed significant financial success as an army agent, and the future poet's next-door neighbor was William Jerdan, the *Literary Gazette* editor who managed Landon's literary debut (and likely became her lover). These aspects of Landon's youth and exposure to contemporary literary and political trends no doubt account for the familiarity and ease with which she adapted to those conditions, and further contextualize the conflation of imperial and periodical that occurs in her giftbook work. The "English Annuals are becoming a new branch of exportable manufacture," noted Christian Isobel Johnstone, the editor of *Tait's Edinburgh Magazine* in 1837. The trend had come to "monopolize the picture-book market . . . as, in another line of business, do Yorkshire broad-cloth and Sheffield cutlery."[44] Johnstone's comment recognizes the parallels between giftbooks and imperial exports and, as an observation from one periodical editor, also acknowledges the annual as another type of periodical. Like Lamb, whose periodical essays also simulate a mass-manufactured commodity, Landon found herself surrounded by literary and imperial industries that increasingly resembled each other.

It is, after all, precisely this familiarity with empire that distinguishes Landon from other later Romantic contributors to periodicals. Unlike Lamb and Hogg, who remembered an era before the precipitous acceleration in British expansion, Landon assumed empire to be a regular aspect of the contemporary world; and unlike Keats, whose influences included the less historically explicit elements of Wordsworth, Landon's favorite literary precursor, Staël, was an author deeply invested in the historical events of the time. Given these circumstances, it may come as a surprise that so much of Landon's writing is as evacuated of topical pertinence as it appears, but as Edward Said has pointed out in a different context, such "aesthetic silence" is precisely what betrays the existence and implicit acceptance within literary works of contemporary imperialism.[45]

A more specific glimpse into Landon's perspective on empire and periodicals, however, can be seen in her work for the admired giftbook series *Fisher's Drawing Room Scrap-Book.* Typical of the giftbooks' second-order style in consisting largely of recycled engravings already owned by the publisher, the *Fisher's* series also was distinct within the dense giftbook market for being a "landscape annual," a particular subgenre of the giftbook format whose illustrations specialized in picturesque landscape views. The "Scrap-Book" label was a common term in the industry, an acknowledgment of the recycled contents typical of many giftbooks and literary annuals (another example was the *Juvenile Scrap-book*). As such, the variant was included in Thackeray's critique of the form, as he warned "the unwary public, who purchase Mr. Fisher's publications" that they "will be astonished, if they knew but the secret, with the number of repetitions, and the ingenuity with which one plate is made to figure, now in the *Scrap-Book,* now in the *Views of Syria,* and now in the *Christian Keepsake.* Heaven knows how many more periodicals are issued from the same establishment, and how many different titles are given to each individual print!"[46] While other popular landscape annuals included *Finden's Tableaux, Heath's Picturesque Annual,* and—from the same publishers—Fisher's *Views in Syria and the Holy Land,* it was the *Drawing Room Scrapbook* that offered the most comprehensive and widely admired example of the subgenre. The *Fisher's* volumes included plates of locations throughout Britain and the Continent but was particularly known for its images of exotic locations in the east and across the globe. (In this the *Fisher's* series foreshadowed later periodicals such as the daily *Illustrated London News.*) A quintessential imperial commodity, the *Fisher's* volumes thus literally brought empire into British homes, and as such demonstrate the giftbooks' position as an exaggerated, extreme version of contemporary trends in periodicals.

During her prolific prominence in the giftbook industry, Landon edited and single-handedly wrote all of the letterpress for the *Fisher's* volumes from 1832 to 1839. In this remarkable feat of poetic productivity, Landon no doubt drew upon a personal interest in distant and exotic locations that had been fueled in childhood by her father's stories, and which may have influenced her ill-fated decision to move to Africa. In the implicitly dismissive gestures of the gendered accounts of Landon's poetry, Landon's prolific contributions to the *Fisher's* series often are explained as inevitable aspects of her financial need, but in light of the important role of imperial geography in her other poetic work, the geographical subjects of Landon's *Fisher's* poems deserve further consideration. The mandate of the *Fisher's* series meant that Landon's contributions addressed a vast variety of spaces, and thus that those volumes that Landon single-handedly completed implicitly identified empire with her imagination. If the *Fisher's* series was a textual monument to contemporary imperial culture, their imperial connotations also served Landon as an emblem of her own poetic power, far exceeding Lamb's specific interest in China by the way her volumes' broad geographical scope portrayed her genius as a limitless march of destiny that ended only where the sun never set.

But just as Hogg's motifs of Napoleonic Egyptology use empire to portray his critique of magazine print capitalism, Landon's involvement with this most imperial of literary periodicals must not be taken as unqualified consent to the more extreme and appropriative conditions of periodical collaboration. Her adaptation of empire from *Corinne* to the *Improvisatrice* has already demonstrated Landon's sophisticated adaptation of topical themes. In the *Fisher's Drawing Room Scrap-Book,* her most sustained and explicit intersection of empire with the periodical giftbooks, Landon uses the rhetoric of empire to register her objections to certain aspects of the giftbook industry. Perhaps not surprisingly, in light of Hogg's own self-referential allusions to *Blackwood's* in his professional allegory of periodical collaboration, for Landon this metaphorical identification of empire with periodicals occurs in two metacritical poems where the poet alludes to the giftbook industry itself. These works are "Macao" and "The Chinese Pagoda," a pair of poems that appeared in the 1832 edition of *Fisher's Drawing Room Scrap-Book* and that both use the specifically geographical contents of the landscape annual to portray the conditions of giftbook collaboration in oppressively imperial terms.

As giftbook poems, "Macao" and "The Chinese Pagoda" each appear adjacent to the visual image noted in poems' titles. The image inspiring the former poem is the Chinese port city then under Portuguese administration that is located in the South China Sea; the image accompanying the latter poem depicts the architectural construction uniquely associated with Chinese culture and civilization. Intriguingly, however, neither of the poems goes on to verbally elaborate upon the provided image, which might be expected within the ekphrastic conventions of giftbooks and annuals. Rather, like the turn to self-allusion that Landon conducts in "Corinne at the Cape of Misena," both *Fisher's* poems comment upon the conditions of giftbook collaboration and use the exotic oriental subject of both images as examples of challenges for the imagination. In "Macao," Landon laments that "Of all the places in the world," the image presented to her is of China, a place that for whatever reason stalls her otherwise fluent capacities for versification. The opening lines of the poem announce her predicament as she exclaims, "Good Heaven! Whatever shall I do? / I must write something for my readers: / What has become of my ideas? / Now, out upon them for seceders!"[47] Similarly, in "The Chinese Pagoda," Landon describes how receipt of the "second Chinese view" causes her to confess "to Messrs. Fisher, saying / The simple fact—I could not write."[48] Her writer's block thus provides a unique glimpse into the challenging conditions of giftbook collaboration that is intriguing because of both its explicitness and its singularity. As Glennis Stephenson notes, the sentimental affectations of giftbooks ensured that the one aspect of female experience that the form ignored was household work.[49] The *Fisher's* poems, however, chip away at this convention, not by showing household chores, but by depicting another kind of female labor—the difficulties of writing for this distinctly gendered periodical, the giftbook or literary annual. As is often the case with Landon, the poet overcomes this challenge by foregrounding it. As one critic has noted of the two *Fisher's* poems, the works illustrate Landon's "pleasure in stripping bare the framework" of the genre.[50]

In comparison to other late Romantic invocations of China in post-Napoleonic periodicals, what is interesting about Landon's depiction of Macao as an obstacle for her imagination is that she assumes a position directly opposite of Lamb's. Instead of seeing China as an index of her imaginative capacities, Landon depicts it as the obverse—she even denies any inspiration in the "'old association' / . . . [of] the willow-pattern plates," the very topic that Lamb uses in his essayistic treatment of China. But in the more specific context of poetic strategies among contributors to the particular periodical format of the giftbook or literary annual, Landon's poem recalls her second-order technique of deflecting attention from the image to the letterpress, and ultimately to the author herself. Just as we previously saw Landon do in the *Improvisatrice* and "Corinne at the Cape of Misena," in "Macao" and "The Chinese Pagoda" Landon uses the ostensible visual subject only to launch an oblique and tangential discussion that pertains to Landon herself. In the *Fisher's* poems, this ingenious substitution of authorial achievement for the poem's assigned visual subject is particularly obvious in the first poem, "Macao," where Landon compares the challenge posed by China to the variety of other foreign and exotic places she is accustomed to verbally describing in the *Fisher's* series. Noting that "Had it but been a town in Greece; / I might have raved about its altars," "Or had it only been in Spain; / . . . / . . . I might have scribbled / The rest," Landon circumnavigates the subject that confounds her with a variety of other world places that she is ably equipped to evoke. In the same way that Italy had always been evoked in her *Corinne* imitations through a handful of broadly drawn conventions, Landon uses a few judiciously selected symbols to evoke a variety of different locations and thereby resolve the writer's block she initially encountered. China is only a false obstacle within the two poems. In her uncharacteristic depiction of how "invention falters," Landon invokes that imperial location only as an excuse to exhibit the imperial variety long associated with Landon's poetic fluency, and which the *Fisher's* series in particular displayed.

A "horse in a mill has an easier life than an author," observed Landon in 1831, as she was assembling her first volume for the *Fisher's* series. Complaining that she was "fairly fagged out of . . . life," Landon noted that "this is my very busiest time, writing for the annuals."[51] Her protestations demonstrate the grueling challenges of the annual industry, which stemmed both from the relentless pace of production required of an ongoing series, and the particular challenges of composing texts to accompany existing illustrations. Interestingly, in "Macao" and "The Chinese Pagoda," Landon also portrays these obligations in notably industrial and imperial terms. In "Macao," Landon describes herself as an exploited and underserved member of the merchant marine: "I'm like a sailor set to sea, / Sent with 'no, nothing' for his sea-hoard." She notes that the real crisis of imagination is the industrial conditions under which poetry is produced: "Well the muse may turn refractory; / When all her inspiration is— / A Chinese town, and an English Factory." Similarly, in "The Chinese Pagoda," Landon likens the highly conventionalized language of sentimental poetry common in the giftbook format to a literary "joint-stock" and laments the oppressive conditions of giftbook collaboration, where with "one's publisher there is no braving." Notably, in this latter poem Landon abandons altogether any ekphrastic consideration of the commissioned image, and instead uses the poem to foreground her authorial achievements. Noting that "if in this world there is an object, / For pity which may stand alone," Landon places herself as the subject of the poem. The "object" that "stand[s] alone" that she describes is herself, a "poet with no subject, / Or with a picture worse than none."

Intriguingly, these descriptions of giftbook collaboration as a type of industrial or imperial employment show Landon simultaneously occupying an imperial and anti-imperial position. While complaining of the relentless burdens of giftbook ekphrasis and the particular difficulty of the *Fisher's* subjects, Landon also uses the imperial content of the *Fisher's* volumes to foreground her own ability. "How my ingenuity has been taxed to introduce the different places!" wrote Landon in 1833: "Forgive this . . . effusion of vanity, [but] I do pique myself on contriving to get from Dowlutabad to Shusher, and Penawa, and the Triad Figure in the Caves of Elephante, and from thence to Ibrahim Padshah's tomb."[52] This paradoxical duality of Landon's uses of empire typifies her unique perspective on periodicals. Deeply aware of the omnipotence of giftbooks—a fact of the contemporary periodical marketplace that Landon, like her other contemporaries among the periodicals, acknowledges by portraying it in imperial terms—Landon uses those imperial comparisons both to figure her own facility within the format and to critique certain conditions of the industry. This is a perfect "miracle," even Thackeray, Landon's erstwhile critic, had to acknowledge. "It may be a 'miracle instead of wit;' but it is a perfect wonder, how [she] could have penned such a number of verses upon all sorts of subjects, and upon subjects, perhaps, on which, in former volumes of this *Scrap-Book,* she has poetized half-a-dozen times before."[53]

As giftbook contributions that explicitly portray the conditions of giftbook collaboration, "Macao" and "The Chinese Pagoda" are intriguing both for their dramatic depiction of the practice of second-order style and for their identification of that practice with contemporary imperialism—both in the specific structural similarities of the capitalist practices and in the more general sense by which Landon employs geography as an emblem for her poetic faculties. Landon's turn in the two poems to a broad diversity of geographical spaces may depart from her "entirely Italian" focus in the proto-giftbook poem, *The Improvisatrice,* and also differs from the specific geographical locales favored by other periodical contributors, but it nevertheless illustrates Landon's proficiency with the format, and indeed may reflect the giftbooks' status as an overdetermined exaggeration of many of the periodicals' most characteristic attributes. What is valuable about this observation is that it demonstrates, once again, the continuity of the giftbooks and annuals with their more regular, unbound periodical cousins, and it situates Landon's prolific contributions throughout the giftbook industry as comparable to the periodical collaborations of her older, male peers working in more conventionally recognized formats and usually with one particular series. Indeed, although I have previously compared Landon to Lamb in their familiarity with both empire and the literary periodical industry that both authors figure through empire, this last insight into Landon's recognition of the oppressively capitalist pressures of the giftbook industry also suggests the so-called poetess as having much in common with Hogg. Both authors were deeply aware of the compromises of imperial and periodical collaboration, and in "Macao" and "The Chinese Pagoda," at least, we see Landon expressing her professional discontent in imperial rhetoric notably comparable to Hogg's. It shows the awareness and critique of the contemporary periodical industry that exists in an author even as apparently unconcerned as Landon herself.

Of course, I do not mean to suggest that "Macao" and "The Chinese Pagoda" are entirely representative of Landon's extensive giftbook contributions. Most of her verse for the annuals, as much of the contemporary and modern disregard for Landon would seem to imply, is utterly conventional, and when it does effect a second-order promotion of authorial identity, as Landon does in "Corinne at the Cape of Misena," it does so without any of the metacritical "laying bare of the device" that Landon undertakes in the *Fisher's* poems. Yet even if "Macao" and "The Chinese Pagoda" are but incidental works amid the massive corpus of Landon's annual verse, they remain a powerful glimpse into the place of empire in Landon's literary and periodical production. Moreover, they do so despite the fact that Landon's literary production is one in which empire is often invisible, and her emblematic periodical form is often characterized as exceptional rather than exemplary. The poems dramatize a stylistic tendency in Landon's poetry since the *Improvisatrice*, in which the second-order tendencies of giftbook poems such as "Macao" are portrayed by an evacuation of imperial history that Landon first developed through her many *Corinne* adaptations.

In one of the most thoughtful recent approaches to Landon, Tricia Lootens has argued for a wholesale reconception of the author by suggesting a turn away from her poetry—written quickly and with little revision—to consider instead Landon's novels, which the poet undertook in the early 1830s, and which Lootens claims reexamine the sentimentalism that Landon previously circulated so unselfconsciously.[54] For Lootens, one of the most provocative possibilities offered by this approach is the significance of Landon's nationality—as Lootens puts it, "by reading Landon as English first, rather than as feminine."[55] But while Lootens's urge to reexamine Landon valuably reminds readers of the importance of place and nation throughout her work, one must still always qualify how those elements shaped the literary works for which Landon is best known. In her reductive adaptations of Staël's novel, Landon may have excised *Corinne*'s Roman setting, but she kept the sentimental romance, effectively converting the topical into the stuff of popular appeal. Such uses of empire by the "English Corinne" are hardly imperial in the commercial and political manner practiced by Lamb and Hogg. Rather, they are simply structural devices that exhibit the author's genius, in the same symbolic manner as Landon retains Staël's use of the Roman Capitol in the original novel. Thackeray missed this point in his rant on the annuals, as he bemoaned Landon as a poet who "degrades" her genius.[56] It is precisely her strategic use of sentimental conventions associated with her gender—as evident in her depoliticizing take upon a prominent Napoleonic novel—that enable her claims for lyric power.

In the next and final chapter of this study, I will consider a similarly exceptional periodical collaboration by Landon's other prevailing literary model beyond Staël—that is, Byron. Although Landon, as the *Improvisatrice*'s "Moorish Romance" has already shown, frequently based her literary production upon explicit emulation of Byron, Byron's fierce harnessing of poetry to political change is obviously starkly opposed to the reduction of empire to a mere literary trope that we see in the work of his female namesake and imitator. Byron's involvement with periodicals during his exile from Britain follows a pattern antithetical to Landon's, and indeed asserts an aggressively political agenda that has far more in common with Staël. Thus, in the next and final case study of this survey of late Romantic periodical engagements with the post-Napoleonic periodicals, I will examine a unique late Romantic periodical collaboration that recruits the format toward an explicitly political and specifically anti-imperial agenda.

Four

Only "a Little above the Usual Run of Periodical Poesy"

Byron's *Island* and the *Liberal*

Byron's epigraph to *Childe Harold* famously describes the world as a type of book, in which familiarity with only one country is comparable to having read only one page.

> The universe is a kind of book of which you have read but one page when you have seen only your own country. I have leafed through a sufficient number to have found them equally bad. This study has not been unprofitable for me. I hated my country. All the peculiarities of the different people among whom I have lived have reconciled me to it. Even if I should have gained no other benefit from my voyages than that one, I should never regret the pains, nor the fatigues.[1]

In this metaphorical comparison of world to text, Byron's epigraph anticipates the premise implicit in much late Romantic writing. Like Lamb, Hogg, and Landon, Byron conflates geography and textuality, and indeed seems to foreshadow the connection of global geography to textual form that Byron's female emulator, Landon, would perfect. But closer reading of the epigraph also reveals a different significance to the metaphor, and one which assumes a political position upon that text. Byron, like de Monbron, the source of the epigraph, "hated [his] own country," and in claiming that travel "reconciled" him to his home, uses the literary metaphor as a paradigm by which to conceptualize his national subjectivity. This application of the geographical to the literary in Byron's epigraph reiterates his distinction from his would-be female imitator, whose depoliticized use of Napoleonic history is antithetical to his own, and also distinguishes him from other late Romantic associations of the literary with global geography. Where Landon uses geography as a figure for a literary device in her periodical and nonperiodical writing, and like other periodical collaborators uses empire as a parallel for the periodical industry, Byron links geography with textuality precisely because the literary promises an effective model of political response to the changing conditions of the imperial world. His explicitly political response to literature is utterly characteristic of Byron's conflation of poetry and politics, and by extension raises the question as to how the epigraph, which wonderfully foreshadows so much of Byron's work, might also prefigure his late involvement with periodicals. Although the *Liberal,* the journal that Byron cofounded with Shelley and Leigh Hunt, lasted for only four issues, its origins amid the intensifying radicalism of Byron's late poetry make the publication an intriguing episode in his oeuvre. Both it and the individual works that Byron composed with the *Liberal* in mind provide a strident assertion of the contemporary power of periodicals and an unusual and important case study with which to conclude this study of late Romantic collaborations with post-Napoleonic periodicals.

Few studies of the *Liberal* sufficiently consider the curious fact of the journal's history as an English periodical largely composed and edited outside of British shores. The short-lived journal, which was formulated while Byron and Shelley were living in self-imposed exile in Italy, was a product of the circle of authors surrounding and corresponding with them while the two were in Pisa, and it was only printed in London upon the authors' forwarding of manuscripts to John Hunt. Such unusual circumstances of publication are a notable exception among most periodicals in that they reversed the usual trajectory of the form to a nation's readers. Instead of originating from the metropole and emanating outward in the conventionally centripetal role of periodicals in consolidating national culture, the *Liberal* began in the periphery and sought entrance in the home country, in a provocative reversal of the territorial coverage by which periodicals are supposed to buttress national culture. Indeed, this spatial alterity embodied in the *Liberal* as a whole is particularly apparent in *The Island,* Byron's last complete narrative poem, and a work that he composed with the *Liberal* in mind. A fictional revisiting of the notorious 1789 mutiny on the *Bounty,* in which British sailors on commission for the East India Company revolted in an attempt to return to paradisal Tahiti, *The Island* is consistent with the *Liberal*'s progressive ideology in both subject and setting, and not surprisingly was intended by Byron for one of the magazine's early issues. Yet because the poem was abruptly removed by Byron from its original destination within the *Liberal,* neither poem nor periodical has been accorded the significance they deserve. Few studies consider the *Liberal* a significant aspect of Byron's career, and the *Island* is similarly overlooked.[2] Rarely does the criticism consider how the specific geographic space portrayed in the *Island* might have fit into the oppositional space of the periodical for which it was originally intended, or notice how Tahiti might slip into the global compass originally invoked by Byron in the epigraph to *Childe Harold.* Indeed, as the few studies to specifically explore the *Island* tend to dwell on a tonal unevenness to the poem that is particularly evident because the work is interpreted alone, those analyses overlook how Tahiti's exotic remoteness represents a last page in Byron's cosmopolitan survey of countries of the world, and thereby symbolizes a foil to the imperial island from which Byron both sought escape and hoped to use the *Liberal* to reform.

Accordingly, this final chapter, on Byron's collaboration with the *Liberal,* aims to restore both poem and periodical to their rightful place amid the other achievements of Byron's late career. As with his masterwork *Don Juan,* from which Byron was on hiatus when he wrote the *Island,* the *Liberal* and the *Island* are both politically ambitious works, whose geographical identifications exert tremendous symbolic potential and whose curiosities of style are instrumental to their political content. Byron himself was acutely aware of the challenges posed in this undertaking. In a letter to Leigh Hunt written while Byron was composing the poem, Byron remarked:

> I have two things to avoid—the first that of running foul of my own "Corsair" and style—so as to produce repetition and monotony—and the other *not* to run counter to the reigning stupidity altogether—otherwise they will say that I am eulogizing *Mutiny.*—This must produce tameness in some degree—but recollect that I am merely trying to write a poem a little above the usual run of periodical poesy—and I hope that it will at least be that;—You think higher of readers than I do—but I will bet you a flask of Falernum that the most *stilted* parts of the political "Age of Bronze"—and the most *pamby* portions of the Toobonai Islanders—will be the most agreeable to the enlightened

Public;—though I shall sprinkle some *uncommon* place here and there nevertheless.[3]

In this explicit description of the *Island* as a product of its intended destination within periodicals, Byron hints at the important role of periodicals in his late career. His comment requires consideration of the poem within its original content in the periodical, and it also invites speculation into Byron's reasons for his last-minute separation, whose consequences for the *Island* have clearly been so adverse.

First, though, it is worth noting the fact that Byron even appears in this study of Romantic collaborations with periodicals, revealing an engagement with periodicals that discloses the importance of this form for even the era's most prominent figures. As the era's reigning literary celebrity, Byron was independent of any professional need of periodicals, and among all of the authors considered here, only Byron had any significant personal experience with the exotic locations that his works portray. These singularities render Byron an exception among the four other case studies I examine, but it also makes him an especially apt case with which to conclude this book. Unlike so many other contributors to periodicals, Byron had no major precursor whose overwhelming supremacy necessitated periodical collaboration as a means by which to equal that achievement. His late turn to periodicals suggests, instead, a curious reversal in his final years, as the era's erstwhile "grand Napoleon of the realms of rhyme" was forced to battle with the continuing popularity of his earlier, more commercial, less controversial self.[4] Byron's turn to periodicals thus was predicated upon its function in and association with empire itself. His periodical involvement is anti-imperial in two senses: it is opposed both to the political empire of British territorial expansion and to the literary commercial empire constituted by Byron's past market success.

Living in self-imposed exile in Italy, and shortly to depart for Greece, Byron exhibits in the *Liberal* and the *Island* the same revolutionary fervor that fueled his anti-imperial involvement with the Carbonari and Greek patriots. Together the two works represent a singularly politicized application of empire and periodicals in late Romantic writing in the post-Napoleonic periodicals, and a telling, poignant exception to the professional metaphors in which empire was used by Byron's contemporaries.

The *Liberal* Conspiracy

"My talent (if I have any) does not lie in the kinds of composition which is most acceptable to periodical readers," wrote Byron to John Hunt, less than two months after his letter to Leigh on his plans for the *Island*.[5] Like all of Byron's comments, this remark is both deliberately deceptive and deeply illuminating. The immediate context of the statement is Byron's flagging interest in the *Liberal* and his desire to separate himself from the faltering venture, but in the more wide-reaching context of Byron's relationship to periodicals and their peculiarities of form and style, the comment obscures what was actually, for the poet, an acute and enduring awareness of the possibilities that awaited him within the format. The poet whose debut received such harsh reviews that he responded with *English Bards and Scotch Reviewers,* the satiric 1807 poem that first intimated Byron's poetic genius, was well aware of the power of periodicals to launch or sink an individual career. In that poem, Byron vowed to "make my own review," and in his brilliant demonstration of individual genius he effectively destroyed the personal attacks leveled at him by the *Edinburgh Review.*[6] More to the point, and in further recognition of the influence that the format exercised in contemporary culture, in 1811 Byron proposed to Hobhouse that they "start a periodical paper, something in the Spectator or Observer way," and again in 1820 suggested to Moore that they partner to found a newspaper.[7] Although the *Liberal* would be his only, late, and short-lived realization of this recurring ambition, the journal still attests to Byron's initial interest in periodicals through this misleading disclaimer about his lack of talent for periodical "composition." The comment, surprising enough amid Byron's typical brio, reveals a massive about-face in what was otherwise an active and long-standing interest in periodicals. Vociferously denying any interest in periodicals, Byron only betrays his disappointment by protesting too much.

Such intensity of feeling as Byron exhibits at the time of the *Liberal* can only hint at hopes he might have invested in the journal that Walter Graham exalts as the "periodical of the highest literary quality in the first quarter of the nineteenth century."[8] Occasionally cited as the first nominative English usage of the word "liberal," the journal's title referenced the Spanish democrats (*liberales*) who rebelled against the Bourbon King Ferdinand in 1820, and clearly signified a politically active, deliberately provocative publication.[9] Although the journal coyly claimed to be "not political," except insofar as "all writing now-a-days must involve something to that effect," this disclaimer was an obligatory gesture that was soon negated by any close scrutiny of its contents and history.[10] At the time of the journal's founding, Byron had left England under the cloud of his divorce and Shelley had already been living abroad for several years. Hunt was impoverished, in part due to his stints in prison for treason. These facts of the journal's origins as the collaboration of a disgraced aristocrat, a socially condemned atheist, and an editor convicted of treason inevitably sparked controversy, as reports of the forthcoming new series were bruited about in hysterical rhetoric that clearly demonstrated the combined fear and fascination that the public held for the journal. Even before the first issue appeared, one early report on the *Liberal* announced that the authors had formed "'Tria juncta in uno,' . . . to write some sort of periodical work, and send it to console their native land for their own absence."[11] Of all contemporary comments on the *Liberal,* this is remarkably restrained in its characterization. The remark describes the periodical as a sort of literary surrogate for its absent human progenitors, and only hints at the collaborative production of the journal as a governing body ("tria juncta in uno").

Other contemporary comments on the magazine were far more intemperate. Wordsworth, betraying increasingly conservative sympathies, accused the *Liberal* of being "directed against everything in religion, in morals and probably in government and literature," while the middlebrow *Imperial Magazine,* clearly ignited by the ideological challenge posed by the forthcoming publication, warned of Byron's involvement in "a school of sceptics, who . . . club their wits in a journal, for the dissemination of . . . liberal opinions."[12] While some precedent for this journalistic animosity lay in the Satanism often attributed to Byron and Shelley, what is intriguing about these references to the *Liberal* is the political and territorial cast these terms take on. In typically inflammatory rhetoric, the "Noctes Ambrosianae" played upon anti-Catholic sentiment and the *Liberal*'s Italian origins to warn in March 1822 against the forthcoming "holy alliance of Pisa."[13] Like the *Imperial Magazine,* whose ideological difference from the *Liberal* is encapsulated in their respective titles, this typically paranoid response from *Blackwood's* likens the *Liberal* to a cabal of dark conspirators. It characterizes the journal from outside British borders as a subversive publication and transgressive *agent pro-*

vocateur clearly formed to incite radical sympathies. Indeed, the conservative *New European Magazine* echoed these accusations in its allusion to the "newly arrived Manifesto of the Pisan Conspirators," and *Blackwood's* would later return to this idea when it accused the journal of attempting to reestablish "the balance of . . . power . . . which has preponderated lately too much on the Tory side."[14]

Such allegations leveled in the conservative hysteria with which the *Liberal* was greeted may not have been far from the truth. As is apparent in the above comments, early reportage on the *Liberal* often alluded to the journal's geographic origins, and it used that geographical attribute as an emblem of the political subversiveness with which the periodical was imbued. When the journal finally appeared in October 1822, this metonymic association of ideology with geography was further encouraged by the publication itself, whose full title is *The Liberal: Verse and Prose from the South.* In its expansive description of the magazine's contents, the subtitle both underscores the *Liberal*'s geographical alterity and, in the grammatically equilateral presentation of the sur- and subtitles, implies (like *Corinne; or, Italy*) the interdependent relationship of those attributes. (In the magazine's masthead, this equilateral relationship is reiterated visually by the fact that the words "Liberal" and "South" both occupy a line to themselves.) As in the preface's earlier finessing of its claim about politics (i.e., that it is "not political" except insofar as "all writing" is), the magazine thus presents itself both as a cultural review of literature from southern Europe and as a politically liberal publication for whom its literary and cultural contents are merely a displaced reflection of these more topical and political concerns.

This fuller characterization was further upheld by the magazine's actual contents, which were frequently explicitly, aggressively political. The first issue of the magazine contained Byron's fierce "Epigrams on Castlereagh," with their grim triumph in the minister's recent suicide, and was especially noted for the *Vision of Judgment,* in which Byron aligned Southey's poetic pandering with the more autocratic actions of the current monarch. Indeed, the *Vision of Judgment* encapsulated much of what the *Liberal* seemed to stand for. The poem had been the subject of dispute between Byron and John Murray, the poet's king-making publisher, who had been reluctant to publish the work. When Byron redirected the *Vision* to the *Liberal,* he finalized the break with his former publisher, which began when Murray objected to the first cantos of *Don*

Juan, and signaled his new literary and political affiliations with a more radical publisher and a far more marginal place in British literary culture. Tellingly, anticipation for the *Vision* was as nervous as it had been for the *Liberal* itself, and when the issue containing that poem finally appeared, most reviews focused on this work from the magazine's best-known contributor as indicative of the journal as a whole.

This blend of literary and political apparent in the *Vision* characterized the *Liberal* throughout its short run. "We wish to do our work quietly," claimed the magazine, and "contribute other liberalities in the shape of Poetry, Essays, Tales, [and] Translations."[15] Accordingly, the second issue of the magazine included Hazlitt's democratic manifesto, the essay "On the Spirit of Monarchy," whose ideas would have been echoed in Shelley's "Defence of Poetry," had that work appeared in the magazine as originally intended. Moreover, even when it was not explicitly political, the *Liberal* still maintained that focus through a persistent interest in Italian culture and history. "Italian literature, in particular, will be a favorite subject with us," promised the magazine, in a topographical focus that scholars have noted is a barely disguised intimation of the magazine's political agenda.[16] This promise was fulfilled in works such as the *Vision of Judgment,* which specifically references the king's refusal to grant Catholic emancipation, as well as *Heaven and Earth,* Byron's contribution to the second number of the magazine, and a dramatic monologue that included a visionary depiction of Dante. Such attention to Italy and other geographic locations within the magazine tapped into an existing trend for progressive works set in the southern continent and, as Caroline Franklin shows, employed Italian subjects to figure broader liberal causes.[17] Its content affirmed the accusations leveled at the *Liberal* upon the first news of its founding. As William Marshall observes in his important history of the magazine, both "in quality and kind," publications such as the *Vision* "seemed to justify the spirit which they had anticipated in the *Liberal.*"[18]

For many readers, the precedent to the *Liberal*'s provocative contents may have been the *Examiner,* the progressive weekly originating from the same printer and editor, and which had resulted in the pair's sentences for treason. Long a strong supporter of Shelley (it was in the *Examiner* that "Ozymandias" first appeared), and a journal to which Byron frequently directed correspondence, the *Examiner* would be the first periodical to announce the *Liberal*'s new name. Yet in both its progressive politics and its identification of that politics with geographic space, the *Liberal* also presented itself as a return to older, Habermasian concepts of periodicals as a republic of letters. As David Higgins has pointed out, the *Liberal* was developed under the founding belief "that the spirit of the 1790s can be recovered," and that in itself and its individual contributions, "the republic of letters . . . [,] clearly a representation of the Utopian ideal of the magazine," was restored.[19] Such temporal identification by the *Liberal* with an earlier era in British literary and cultural history may seem at odds with the geographical emphasis evident in the *Liberal*'s subtitle and contents, but in fact the *Liberal*'s variation upon the "empire of signs" evoked in most post-Napoleonic magazines made the magazine one of the era's most overtly spatially concerned periodical publications. Tilar Mazzeo has already pointed out how the circle of writers surrounding Byron and Shelley in Pisa generated a variety of oriental and often specifically Indian texts, whose foreign characters and exotic settings serve as symbolic reminders of the philosophical and ideological otherness of the authors.[20] Although Mazzeo does not include the *Liberal* among the texts she discusses, the same might be said of its contents. Indeed, the magazine could well be their mascot, as its identification with the "South" encompassed a global south extending from Pisa to India that dramatically asserted the extent of its cultural difference.

Like so many of its contemporaries and competitors, then, the *Liberal* is a periodical profoundly characterized by the post-Napoleonic emphasis on geographic space. Where other magazines, such as the *London*, *Edinburgh*, or *Blackwood's Edinburgh Magazine*, fashioned their institutional character through an explicitly metropolitan identification, the *Liberal* also emphasized a territorial location—albeit one with a contrary association deriving from and symbolized by its extranational ontology. For Kevin Gilmartin, such oppositional commitment on the part of the magazine might make the *Liberal* another, foreign instance of the "counterpublic spheres" that characterized so much of the British periodical press, but Gilmartin overlooks how that oppositional identity was figured in the *Liberal*'s origins outside of British borders.[21] Like Byron's self-imposed exile, and recalling the rhetoric of global coverage in the epigraph to *Childe Harold*, the *Liberal* promulgated an explicitly exilic identity whose cultural affiliation was opposed to the modern imperial society for which it was destined. The magazine was using its geographic and topographic allusions to map a symbolic cartography in which geographic motifs conveyed ideological messages. In a similar, albeit politically polarized case of topographical allusion in a contemporary periodical, Nanora Sweet has shown how recurrent coverage of South America in the *New Monthly Magazine* exhibited that journal's developing politics. The *Liberal* can be understood to be doing the same thing, such that this product of the "Pisan circle" uses geography to triangulate itself with the Lake poets and the Cockney School, two other literary circles also known for their geographic location and distinguished by different political and ideological associations.[22] In its titular identification with the "South," the *Liberal* used its contrast with two other sites in British Romantic geography to encapsulate the ideological difference in which the *Liberal* was steeped.

Indeed, so compelling was this symbolically radical geography in characterizing the *Liberal* that it was also used to describe the magazine's failure, and in fact was likely implicated in that fate. One major challenge facing the new journal was the physical distance between London and Pisa. For the always disorganized Hunt, the months it took him to journey to Italy caused Byron to rapidly lose interest—a dangerous development, given that Byron's name and wealth were instrumental in securing commercial support for the venture. These delays and logistical problems were further exacerbated by local governments in the path between Pisa and the magazine's destination in England, who extended the *Liberal*'s reputation for subversion by intercepting communications and accusing authors affiliated with the magazine of spying. As William Marshall notes, the Hapsburg authorities who had monitored Byron's associations with the Carbonari also disrupted correspondence related to the *Liberal*, and in France customs agents seized published copies of the magazine as potentially subversive material.[23] These actions hampered the magazine's launch and subsequent success, but they also reiterate the extraordinary importance of periodicals in the post-Napoleonic era. Precisely because of their efforts to limits that power, these measures by reactionary governments accord the *Liberal* tremendous social and political influence, reacting to the magazine exactly as the liberal conspiracy the journal proclaimed itself to be.

Moreover, if its geographic exceptionalism was instrumental in the magazine's failure, the journal's physical layout, which continued that theme, did not help. Format and style decisions by John Hunt ensured that the *Liberal* announced its alternativeness in its very form and visual appearance. The journal's neoclassical aesthetic was actualized in the roman typeface of the journal's title and text, whose visual asceticism stood in stark contrast to the Gothic black letter of *Blackwood's* masthead or the multiple typefaces used in many other contemporary magazines (such as Landon's frequent venue, the *Literary Gazette*). Indeed, in self-conscious differentiation from many other mass-market periodicals, the *Liberal* eschewed illustration and other forms of visual or typographic ornamentation, favoring an austere and textually dense environment that prefigured the *Athenaeum* (whose institutional commitment to textual density was so severe that at one point it would employ an almost unreadable 8-point font). In this deliberate reform of existing attributes of contemporary literary culture, the *Liberal* may recall the revolutionary manifesto of the "Preface to the *Lyrical Ballads*," whose momentous return to "plain speech" offers an intriguing aesthetic and discursive analogue for the journal. But it is also important to note that it had a contemporary analogue in Byron's own work, as after his 1819 break with Murray, Byron worked to keep *Don Juan* affordable by issuing it without illustration and in cheap paper boards. Not surprisingly for a contemporary project, the *Liberal* continues Byron's efforts in *Don Juan*. Indeed, it belongs to a time-honored British revolutionary tradition that began with Thomas Paine, and which identifies radical discourse with cheap production standards and widespread affordability of the very attributes by which periodicals, before their aggrandizement into value-added commodities like giftbooks, for which periodicals were known.

The *Liberal* had to ensure accessibility because its political radicalism and abstruse interest in classical history and literature might otherwise be off-putting. The efforts to promote the magazine, however, proved futile, as production of the magazine was hampered from the outset, and public interest in the *Liberal* dropped off rapidly after the first issue. (Shelley's death in July 1822, only five days after Hunt arrived in Italy, and a few months before the first issue appeared, dealt the final blow.) By the second number of the journal, public commentary was already anticipating the *Liberal*'s imminent demise. In December of the first year, the *Imperial Magazine* stood poised to "rejoice" that the *Liberal*'s "circulation has been less extensive than others" and that "irreligion, and a contempt of what has been revered as sacred or venerable among the virtuous and loyal, [and all] that constitute the more prominent articles of the cargo which the *Liberal* has imported from a foreign shore, [had proved] too heavy for any thing on board to render buoyant." Thus, in one last allusion to the journal's unusual coverage of global space, and perhaps a distasteful allusion to Shelley's recent death by drowning, the *Imperial Magazine* remarked balefully that the *Liberal* indeed "escaped the dangers of the sea, but . . . only to be wrecked on the coast of oblivion."[24]

With its rhetorical allusion to the *Liberal*'s mission to "import" ideological "cargo," the aforementioned remark illustrates the ambition that the contemporary press accorded the *Liberal*. Even as the *Imperial Magazine* gloated over the *Liberal*'s sinking, the very interest it showed in the esoteric journal acknowledges the agency that the *Liberal* set out to achieve. These insights support the importance of the magazine in Byron's oeuvre. Scholarship has long debated the extent of Byron's involvement in the magazine, arguing that Shelley was the glue holding together the odd trio and emphasizing how Byron's friends dissuaded him from association with Hunt.[25] Such debates flesh out an otherwise neglected history, but they also are somewhat irrelevant. Byron may have participated in the project largely to provide Leigh Hunt with work, and his interest in the project may have already been waning, but in its earliest phases Byron was a crucial element of its formation. The poet bankrolled the project, selected the title, provided many of its most prominent selections, and in general made the venture possible. As William Marshall notes of the magazine, "It must be acknowledged that Byron was responsible for it in large part."[26]

More important, and regardless of the extent of Byron's involvement, the *Liberal* still stands as one of the most interesting and overt instances of the prominent role of space among post-Napoleonic periodicals. Where the various periodicals examined in previous case studies invoke space only in the latent sense of their titular pretensions toward museums or the precious objects sited in those locations, the *Liberal*, by contrast, makes geographic space a defining element of its identity and institutional culture. (This was even more obvious because the magazine appeared at irregular intervals and at varying times of the month, and therefore failed to exploit the temporal rhythms instrumental to developing readerly habits for which periodicals are known.) Such intense and developed importance given to space within the *Liberal* is further apparent in the purpose to which the publication puts that motif. In the hands of most late Romantic contributors to the post-Napoleonic periodicals, the specific geographical motifs by which individual authors elaborated ideas latent within the periodical format existed primarily as an industrial and professional metaphor for the experience of periodical collaboration. The *Liberal,* by contrast, was conceived as a literary representative of oppositional politics as emblematized in its geographical affiliations. It did not use empire as a mere industrial metaphor, but subversively appropriated the periodical attributes of rationalization and massification that periodicals shared with empires in an ingenious attempt to use those attributes to undermine empire itself. The magazine explicitly presents itself as a liberal, alternative center that hopes to recruit sympathy, using Pisa, Italy, or—most generally—the "South" cited in the *Liberal*'s telling subtitle, as an emblem of the alternate cultural capital that it presented to imperial Britain. In fact, before settling on the title of the "Liberal," Byron first had wanted to name it "Hesperides" after the fabled "islands of the blest" of antiquity, at which the Garden of Eden was supposed to be found.[27] In both its utopian idealism and its insular yearning, this early title for the *Liberal* reiterates the revolutionary concepts in which it was conceived. It is in this context of the magazine's deeply loaded emphasis upon southern geography that the *Island*—Byron's erstwhile poetic contribution to the magazine, and a poem set in the deeply symbolic South Seas—that the poem ought to be understood.

The *Island* in the *Liberal*

As with the other geographical locations invoked by late Romantic periodical collaborators, the South Seas are a significant aspect of the *Island,* and an intriguing variation upon the *Liberal*'s southern themes. For most of European history, the remote chain of tiny islands went unvisited by the comparatively advanced societies of the northern hemisphere, and the distant location—significantly, often described in Britain as the single most remote region of the globe—occupied a privileged position in romantic geography for the paradisal images of abundance, perfect clime, handsome natives, and unaffected society that had long circulated about these distant isles.[28] These notions of a prelapsarian Eden before the Fall where love was unprohibited and labor unknown was only reinforced by the ocean that caressed the islands. Due to its immense size, the Pacific was literally a space without conflict, which sometimes seemed to have escaped the conquest that long ago had already reshaped the Mediterranean and the Caribbean. This perception of the South Sea islands as sites beyond the reach of modern civilization remained in place as late as 1730, when the collapse of the South Sea Bubble reiterated the islands' continued status as a place still impervious to capitalist exploitation.

It is for these reasons that the South Seas are an appropriate, even perfect space to be invoked by Byron within the specific geographical associations of the *Liberal.* As Diderot intimated in his 1796 *Supplément au voyage du Bougainville,* a fictional philosophical discourse on the moralities of Tahitian culture, the native inhabitants of these "Friendly Isles" were thought (like Native Americans) to be the modern embodiment of the Rousseauvian idea of the noble savage, and thus a culture sympathetically related to that of the *Liberal.* Although the "South" that the islands represented was hemispheric rather than continental, and thus more distant and extreme than any of the southern European spaces that the *Liberal* previously invoked, the South Sea islands that Byron depicts in the poem intended for the magazine clearly belong to the *Liberal*'s symbolic map. In the *Liberal,* Byron's *Island* would have been the most extreme instance of the magazine's consistent thematic interest in the south as a nonimperial, explicitly non-British place. And in more specific elaboration of Byron's political geography, Angus Calder points out that after Scotland and Greece, the *Island*'s South Sea setting is only the latest and most remote component in an island chain long associated in Byron's oeuvre with freedom.[29]

Yet if Byron's use of the South Seas relies upon a timeless romantic notion of the region similar to Lamb's use of China and Hogg's references to Egypt, his treatment of the subject is also informed, as with those of Hogg and Lamb, by contemporary transformations that extended to even that remote part of the globe. (Indeed, Lamb's apologia for the South Sea Bubble in "Old China" was published only months before Byron's *Island,* and thus, in the virtual landscape of the contemporary periodical press, foretells the modernized South Seas with which Byron contends.) By Byron's time the South Seas were no longer as secluded as before, and the forces of historical development that opened China and Egypt had also reached the South Seas, beginning with the expedition of French explorer August-Louis Bougainville in 1766–69 and climaxing with the two historic voyages of the *Endeavor* and *Resolution* led by Captain James Cook in 1768–71 and 1772–75. These meetings of northern and western hemispheres, like encounters between east and west, inaugurated a new era of knowledge with the once unfamiliar South Seas. Cook's two voyages were the "first British opening of the Pacific to exploration, discovery, and exploitation," and marked an irrevocable break from the islands' past isolation and sanctuary.[30]

The *Bounty* history is a case in point in this dramatic transformation of the South Seas by the end of the eighteenth century. The voyage was the initiative of wealthy dilettante and scientist Sir Joseph Banks, the first smuggler of tea plants from China to India, who hoped to sustain his Caribbean sugar plantations by transporting breadfruit, a plant indigenous to the South Seas, and an easily cultivated crop that slaveholders had found to be a cheap food source for their human labor. A ubiquitous figure behind various imperial projects, Banks had served as naturalist aboard Cook's first voyage, and he knew William Bligh from when Bligh was Cook's ship's master on Cook's third voyage to the South Pacific. As Tim Fulford, Debbie Lee, and Peter Kitson point out, Banks and especially Bligh thus embodied a newly professionalized phase in British familiarity with the South Pacific, and the subsequent history of the *Bounty* mutiny typified contemporary pretensions to mastery of this formerly unknown corner of the globe.[31] Selected for Banks's venture because of his previous South Sea experience, when Bligh was forced by the *Bounty* mutineers into an open boat with eighteen others and little food or water, he was able to navigate the 48-day, 3,600-mile journey toward European colonies in Dutch Java only by relying upon his previous experiences and his sailor's memory of the stars and seas.

After the heroic voyage (in which he lost only one man), Bligh returned to England to testify against the mutineers. British desire to demonstrate its authority over the region was so great that that the Admiralty launched the HMS *Pandora,* a 24-gun military frigate with a crew more than triple that of the *Bounty,* whose only commission was to return to Tahiti to arrest and capture the mutineers. This extraordinary display of imperial power was realized in 1791 when the *Pandora* landed in Tahiti and incarcerated all but the nine mutineers who had long ago left for another island. That the British government willingly incurred the expense of the twelve-month journey to the South Seas and back, for the sole purpose of arresting the mutinied sailors, and at a time when naval services might have been needed for disturbances much closer to home, demonstrates the British empire's calculated performance of symbolic power. As Greg Dening puts it in his thoughtful study of the dynamics at work in the *Bounty* mutiny, for the emerging world power of the British navy, "To win in such display of unambivalent power, material costs were unimportant."[32]

By Byron's time, then, the *Bounty* history, and the South Sea islands in general, occupied an ambiguous status, simultaneously suggesting their long-standing role as the modern emblem of undisturbed nature and also portraying the inescapable power of contemporary imperialism.[33] The mutiny by the *Bounty* sailors may have been motivated by the former—those utopian ideals that made the Pacific island a space contiguous with the democratic South idealized within the pages of the *Liberal*—but the subsequent fate of those mutineers, most of whom were executed upon trial or who died en route, decisively marked the end of South Sea isolation, as the island chain was forever incorporated into the imperial ambit. In the decades between the *Bounty* and Byron's fictional revisiting of the episode, northern expeditions to the now established trade routes rapidly increased, occasionally providing additional codas to the *Bounty* history. In 1808 and 1814 American and British expeditions separately stumbled upon Pitcairn Island, the forbiddingly rocky islet where Fletcher Christian, the ringleader of the mutiny, and a handful of other sailors and natives had fled soon after arriving in Tahiti, and whose still-uncharted status had enabled Christian to escape the *Pandora* expedition. Although only one mutineer still lived by the time of the British and American discoveries, news of this final chapter in the *Bounty* history sparked a brief revival of interest back home. Robert Southey and Mary Russell Mitford both published poems on the subject, and in 1816 a play about the *Bounty* opened on Drury Lane, where Byron had been involved shortly before his departure from England. The play, *Pitcairn's Island, a "New Melo Dramatic Ballet of Action,"* is primarily interested in the spectacular and romantic elements of the *Bounty* history, but the poems by Southey and Mitford are interesting for the conservative and moral turn that the *Bounty* history had come to occupy by that time. Southey (who, along with Wordsworth and Coleridge, knew the Christian family in the Lake District) initially had been a strident supporter of the mutineers, but in his later years his feelings on the *Bounty* characteristically reflected his mounting conservatism. In the 1820 *Vision of Judgment,* Southey celebrates Captain Cook, along with

Burke and Hastings, as one of the "Worthies of the Georgian Age."[34] Exhibiting the jingoism that Byron would later satirize in his *Vision,* Southey's poem includes the British conquest of the Pacific in his parade of British military triumph. Similarly, Mitford's poem is consistent with reports from the first, American voyage that the mixed-race descendants of the natives and mutineers on Pitcairn lived a strict and pious life. Accordingly portraying the Christian piety of the Pitcairn islanders as the embodiment of imperial manifest destiny, Mitford's 1811 poem *Christina, Maid of the South Seas* depicts the half-caste daughter of Fletcher Christian falling in love with a British sailor and returning with him to England.

In view of this ambiguous, conflicted, and even conservatively imperial status that the South Seas had achieved by the time of Byron's poem, the *Island*'s identification with that territorial space and how that location worked in the ideological space of the *Liberal* must be more complex than previously recognized. From the first news of its occurrence the *Bounty* mutiny was associated with revolutionary ideals. The crew was unusually educated, and well read about contemporary developments in France—two facts that may have influenced their decision to mutiny. For many British citizens, such connections between the mutiny and contemporary events in Europe made the mutiny's temporal proximity to the storming of the Bastille resonate with current fights for liberty. Such associations certainly would have been powerful in the *Liberal,* where the *Island* would have crystallized many of the utopian fantasies that the magazine identified with southern geography. Rather than an "empire of signs," the poem's glance back to an earlier episode in Napoleonic history would have augmented the magazine's nostalgic and idealistic notion of periodicals as a republic of letters. As a fictionalized retelling of an episode that once struck at the heart of contemporary liberals, the poem reiterated in romance what the more scholarly contents of the *Liberal* espoused in theory.

Yet even as the *Island* invites this connection between its subject and periodical setting, the poem also undercuts itself, such as is most evident in a curiously Burkean description of Captain Bligh. Canto 1 opens with a scene of the deposed captain that recalls Burke's famous passages on Marie Antoinette. Like the French queen, who from "sleep . . . was . . . startled by the voice of the centinel at her door"—as Burke describes her confrontation with "bayonets and poniards" in the *Reflections*—in the

Island, Bligh too is accosted from bed, where his "limbs are bound, the bayonet at [his] breast" (1.53–55).[35] Such surprising similarities in Byron to Burke's Ur-text of conservative ideology are surprising, and cannot entirely be explained by the aristocratic loyalties that always coexisted with the lord's liberal politics. Rather, in the context of the poem's historical subject, Byron is only acknowledging the increasingly ambiguous status that the South Seas had come to occupy at the time of the mutiny. Byron had read extensively in his preparations for the poem, having consulted Bligh's 1790 memoir, *A Narrative of the Mutiny, on Board His Majesty's Ship Bounty* (composed and published by the captain soon after his return to England), as well as William Mariner's 1816 *An Account of the Natives of the Tonga Islands,* a memoir by a British sailor who had grown up amid native islanders after his entire crew was killed (and still a major source on pre-Christian Polynesia). The poet thus would have been well aware of the changing status of the South Sea islands, and in his treatment of the historical subject he bore some responsibility for accuracy. That the *Island* includes the momentarily jingoist celebration of Bligh in canto 1 is not an incongruity but rather a pragmatic depiction of the facts of the *Bounty* history and the South Seas' newly accessible status. Cursorily remaining true to the history of the mutiny frees Byron to move on, in the *Island*'s subsequent cantos, to his real object of interest, which is life on the eponymous isle.

The poem is quite clear on this rhetorical transition. At the end of canto 1, as Bligh's boat is lowered into the sea by an impassive Fletcher Christian, a dispassionate narrative voice intones, "We leave them to their fate, but not known / Nor unredress'd" (1.201–2). In such a comment Byron briskly acknowledges the known history of Bligh's survival and the naval triumph over the mutineers, so as to move on from the facts of that imperial history to his more important concern—depicting anti-imperial fantasy, the favorite subject of the *Liberal,* and a task the poem fulfills through its fictional depiction of the romantic life available on Toobonai.

Indeed, it is only in canto 2, which introduces the characters of Torquil and Neuha, a mutineer and his native bride, that the place of the *Island* within the *Liberal* truly becomes apparent. Carefully following the *Bounty*'s itinerary after the mutiny, Byron sets his poem in "Toobonai" (Tubuai), an island 7 degrees south of Tahiti that Cook had charted but did not visit, and hence a place whose unfamiliarity with European visitors promised the *Bounty* sailors a chance to relive the wonder of the first visitors to Tahiti without risk of returning to the very location where the navy would likely seek them. In keeping with this atavistic fantasy, Byron portrays Toobonai as Eden, where

> The bread-tree, which, without the ploughshare, yields
> The unreap'd harvest of unfurrow'd fields,
> And bakes its unadulterated loaves
> Without a furnace in unpurchased groves. (2.260–63)

With this utopian image of abundance without labor and consumption without commerce, Byron's description of the island revives the older, pre-Cook idylls of the South Sea islands, and effectively portrays the seductions of the land and culture that compelled the *Bounty* sailors to mutiny. (Indeed, it is a sign of Byron's remarkable ability to re-idealize Tahiti that Byron can use breadfruit as an emblem of its idyllic perfection, in complete disregard for the plant's more recent connotations as a resource of slaveholding and the very crop motivating the *Bounty* mission.[36]) The poem's idyllic description of Toobonai thus is utterly continuous with the utopian South imagined within the *Liberal,* and the progressive, alternative society that the *Liberal* hoped to recruit also is symbolized through the poem's central romantic pair, and particularly the unusually progressive manner by which Byron portrays their sexual relationship. As a union of white male and native woman, Torquil and Neuha conventionally ought to figure imperial power, where the sexual politics signified by their respected gender roles allegorize European conquest of the femininely receptive new world.[37] Yet, as many critics note, the *Island* is curiously feminist in its depiction of Torquil's and Neuha's relationship, and repeatedly emphasizes Neuha's emotional maturity and social superiority over her mate.[38] In the scene in canto 2 where the pair is introduced, for example, Neuha, already described as a "Highborn" princess who personifies contemporary Rousseauvian notions of the South Sea noble savage, is portrayed as occupying the dominant status in their relationship (2.214). Torquil, the "husband of the bride of Toobonai" (2.211), is described in a rhetorical inversion of Western customs ("by Neuha's side he sate" [2.212]). The *Island* thus inverts colonial romance to suggest equality rather than dominion: "Each was to each a marvel," Byron asserts; "more than Europe's discipline had done, / [their love] civilised Civilisation's son!" (2.240, 270–71).

Such protofeminist descriptions are intriguing and might recall the effeminizing that occurs when the hero is cast into a harem in *Don Juan*. But as with that passage, the primary significance of Torquil's description is less about gender than in how it uses gender to invert colonial romance. In the *Island,* this radical application of colonial allegory will culminate in canto 4, when Neuha rescues her husband from the naval pursuers, but I first want to explore the tone by which the pair's romantic idyll is portrayed and the method by which Byron portrays a South Sea utopia so seductive that the *Bounty* mutineers, who burned their ship after arriving at Pitcairn, could imagine remaining there for the rest of their lives. Such dramatic rupture with home as the *Bounty* sailors undertook has poignant parallels with Byron's own exile at the time of his poem's composition. Like Byron, who a few months later would describe himself as "of no country," the *Bounty* sailors are "men without country" (1.29), and the poem presents the mutineers (like the Carbonari or later Greek revolutionaries) as rebels consistent with *Liberal* ideals, both in their rebellion against British naval autocracy as well as for their revolutionary turn toward the free love and open land promised in Tahiti.[39] Yet even as the poem strives to convey the immense seductions of the South Sea islands, the *Island* also destroys them, by way of the discursive and tonal incongruities that are such a striking aspect of the poem. In Torquil and Neuha's introductory scene, for example, their bliss is punctured by Ben Bunting, another sailor and fictional character, but a character who is as comically bathetic as Torquil and Neuha are romantic. A quixotic and Crusoe-like figure who maintains modern attributes despite his defection to Toobonai, Ben brings news of the navy's arrival, and appropriately still bears vestiges of European culture ("instead of trousers," "A curious sort of somewhat scanty mat / Now served for inexpressibles and hat" [2.480, 482–83]). With his physical embodiment of British culture, Ben is a disruptive presence in the island, whose appearance in the narrative is preceded by the noisome smoke of his pipe, which floats into air "Not like a 'bed of violets' . . . / But such as wafts its cloud o'er grog or ale" (2.436–37). This smoke, an olfactory version of the "sordor of civilisation" (1.69), is both a manifest sign of the environmental consequences of cultural contact and another instance of how his presence wrecks the poem's idyll. The topic of Ben's pipe launches a *Juan*-esque digression in the *Island,* in which the speaker apotheosizes "sublime tobacco!" (2.448) and concludes with another digressive exclamation ("Give me a cigar!" [2.459]) that only further deflates the poem's precious sentimentality. Ben, in short, has the remarkable ability to plunge the poem's romance into bathos, destroying everything that the poem sought to achieve.

Don Juan provides a useful counterpoint to the tonal upheavals in this passage from the *Island,* as the latter is often compared to the epic that defines Byron's late poetry, and from which the poet was on hiatus while drafting the *Island.* Many readers of the *Island* have noted the resemblance of the Torquil and Neuha passages to the idyll between Juan and Haidée that takes place in cantos 2 and 3 of *Don Juan.* Both couples meet through a shipwreck and achieve a sympathy that transcends their racial difference and their lack of a common language (both pairs communicate with their eyes [*Don Juan* 2.1281–1304; *Island* 2.131]). In their erotic idylls in remote islands, both couples embody innocence and sexual freedom that the poems depict with utopian perfection, even as the larger poems in which those passages nestle acknowledge the material or historical processes then undermining or supporting that existence. (Thus, in *Don Juan,* the abundance that Haidée shares with Juan and that she takes for granted is provided by her father's piracy, just as Torquil and Neuha exist in a naïve romanticism that isolates them from the other sailors and encourages them to mistake time as their only "tyrant" [2.353].) This tonal layering that the *Island* shares with the Haidée passages in *Don Juan* is particularly evident in the longer poem when Haidée hires a bard to entertain in a festive celebration. Although the lyric that the bard sings—embedded into the poem as the song on "The Isles of Greece"—might be considered a stirring account of Byron's revolutionary fervor, and indeed was often excerpted and reprinted under that auspice, the sincerity of the lyric collapses due to the narrative details surrounding the bard. The character, the poem's narrator says prior to the song, is a mercenary poet, and appears to have been introduced by Byron as a commentary upon the faithless opportunism of modern society. Thus, just as the *Island* evokes utopian idylls only to destroy them, as occurs with the arrival of Ben Bunting, *Don Juan* also makes impossible any consistent sentiment or feeling.

In *Don Juan,* this refusal of coherent position or perspective is widely regarded as typical of Byron's radical skepticism, in which the poet refuses to assume any moral or ethical perspective.[40] (Indeed, in his cynically pragmatic resistance to any consistent perspective, Byron himself is the living precedent to *Don Juan*'s mercenary poet for hire.) Such an account of the larger poem would then suggest of the *Island* that the smaller poem belongs to the same cynical vacuum and endorses no single aesthetic or ideological position. Yet instead of this complex reaction to the poem's discursive complexity, the *Island* more often than not is simply dismissed for this apparent unevenness in tone. Immediately upon the poem's publication, for example, contemporary reviews deplored Bunting's dialogue with Torquil as an example of the "doggerel, and incongruity, and bathos, and carelessness, which are crowded into almost every page" of the poem, and in an early-twentieth-century edition of Byron's works, Ernest Hartley Coleridge expressed his regret "that no one suggested the excision [of those] sections . . . from the Island's second canto."[41] Such comments present the *Island* not as a complex or conflicted work but rather as simply a poorly executed one, and they hint at another way in which *Don Juan* constitutes an important precedent to the *Island.* The excerpting and anthologizing that the "Isles of Greece" often underwent was based upon contemporary sensibilities that saw the lyrics as beautiful and compelling, despite widespread rejection of *Don Juan*'s more offensive passages. The *Island,* in a sense, seems to have undergone a reverse process, in which the Bunting passages are widely seen to be ruining what might otherwise have been a sensuous and appealing piece.

Such critical emphasis upon the poem's aesthetic inconsistencies, however, assumes that the *Island* is a self-contained text, rather than a work explicitly conceived for a periodical, and it is the context of that periodical which illuminates the philosophical and ideological commitments that distinguish the poem from *Don Juan.* After all, although Byron bet that "the most *pamby* portions of the Toobonai Islanders will be the most agreeable to the enlightened Public," he also intended to "sprinkle some *uncommon* place here and there nevertheless." Such a deliberate mixture of uncommon and familiar—what Byron called being "a little above the usual run of periodical poesy"—suggests a calculated strategy in the poem. The aim of the *Island* is "*not* to run counter to the reigning stupidity altogether," such that the poem destined for a politically provocative magazine disguises or moderates its radical politics through commercially appealing content that is so well developed that it runs the risk of "running foul of my own 'Corsair' and style." In this charged context it is profoundly significant that the bathetic Bunting coincides in the *Island* with the arrival of the British navy. Disturbing Torquil and Neuha's idyll with news of the anchored ships, Bunting precipitates an aesthetic effect shift in the poem that enacts his role in the plot. As Bunting warns Torquil of imminent battle, and the younger sailor responds with a suitably—and characteristically effeminate—chivalric vow ("Unman me not!" [2.529]), Bunting's deflationary remark ("Right, that will do for the marines" [2.531]) is typical of his bathetic effect upon the poem. Bunting may have been a mutineer, but his real role in the *Island* is to signify the South Sea islands' inability, by the time of the *Bounty* mutiny, to truly escape imperial absorption and British power. His language, dress, and even the disruptive cigar smoke that portends the assault on the islands' romantic remove are all part of a sophisticated representational strategy that uses competing discourses to portray the precarious state of the South Sea islands in the transformative decades between the mutiny and the discovery of Pitcairn.

"From the sublime to the ridiculous there is but one step," Hazlitt noted of *Don Juan*. "You laugh and are surprised that any one should turn round and *travestie* himself: the drollery is in the utter discontinuity of ideas and feelings."[42] Hazlitt's comments on *Don Juan* might serve the *Island* as well. As he suggests, the drollery produced by the "utter discontinuity of ideas and feelings" must have some philosophical or ideological purpose. In the *Island,* this objective is to portray, through Ben Bunting and other similar moments of discursive or aesthetic incongruity within the poem, the consequences of historical progress upon the romantic utopia that the South Sea islands had once represented. That parts of the *Island* recall the *Corsair* and other elements of Byron's earlier, massively commercially successful oriental romances is crucial to this strategy. Byron is using the format to attract readers who might not otherwise be drawn to such a controversial and esoteric publication as the *Liberal,* and thereby uses the poem to convert readers to the attractions of Tahiti and the reasons for the sailors' mutiny. In the midst of this tactic, the aesthetic breakdown wrought in the poem by figures such as Bunting initiates readers into the traumatic loss of that idyllic experience. As Bunting's noisome pipe smoke spoils the soft air of the island, the eponymous poem uses that aesthetic disruption to foreground the despoilment that occurs with the arrival of British imperial culture. This strategy works surreptitiously, through the subtle but inevitable regret a reader must feel over the *Island*'s perceived aesthetic unevenness. Like Coleridge disturbed from his dream, the dissolution of romance that is caused by the intrusion of Ben Bunting leaves the dreamer bereft, and increasingly condemnatory of the violent historical processes causing this aesthetic catastrophe.

The *Island* can thus be understood as a kind of literary Trojan Horse, included in the *Liberal* because its romantic contents were more likely to be accepted by contemporary readers than the rest of the magazine's esoteric and controversial agenda. Unlike the actual Trojan Horse, however, Byron's literary version of the martial strategy was not successful. The rapidly faltering public interest in the *Liberal* boded well for neither poem nor periodical, so days before manuscripts were due to John Hunt for the magazine's third issue, Byron abruptly decided to publish the *Island* independently, with the (typically glib) explanation that he wanted "to see how much the public still likes [me] out of the *Liberal*."[43] The consequences of this retraction from his original intentions were significant. The poem, Byron had once remarked, was "not good enough perhaps to publish alone," and as a consequence of his abrupt separation of poem from magazine, the context in which the newly independent poem figured was different from that originally intended.[44] Although Byron had forwarded the manuscript to John Hunt, the printer of the *Liberal* and the later cantos of *Don Juan*, with whom Byron had partnered since his break with Murray, immediately after the poem's first printing in England, Murray invoked his copyright to publish his own versions of the *Island*. This intrusion effectively resumed for readers the lucrative partnership between poet and publisher that *Don Juan* had inconveniently disrupted. At the same time, European publishers also seized upon the poem, and as they had always done of Byron's works, pirated the *Island* in special Continental editions. For Murray and the European pirates alike, their exploitation of Byron's most recent work benefited from the *Island*'s apparent return to the accessible romances of the Oriental Tales, and only consolidated with Byron's death. As news of his death reached readers around the same time as the *Island*'s first editions, the poem was consecrated as the great celebrity's last complete work. Indeed, many of the editions of the *Island* published by Murray and the European pirates were expensively illustrated and ornamentally bound volumes that stood in sharp contrast to the cheap paper boards and austerely unillustrated conditions that Byron had sought to maintain for *Don Juan* and the *Liberal.* Swiftly surpassing the magazine for which it had been intended, the accessible content of the *Island* ensured that even Hunt's cheap version was already in its third edition when the fourth—and what would be final version—of the *Liberal* was being advertised.

Thus, in ironic antithesis to the subversive original intent of both the *Island* and the *Liberal,* the poem's ultimate publication outside of the magazine laid the groundwork for conditions of reception entirely unlike those that characterized Byron's late career. And if those publications signaled a trend toward a spectacular, consumerist, and depoliticized adaptation of the *Island,* that fate was confirmed with a theatrical production based on Byron's poem. In July 1823 Sadler's Wells produced a spectacular "Aqua Drama," which used a dramatic adaptation of the *Island* as the premise for a theatrical extravaganza. This production included "REAL WATER," a "CHRYSTALLIZED BASALTIC CAVERN," and "BRILLIANTLY ILLUMINATED" "ALLEGORICAL FIREWORKS," as advertised in the program, and clearly presented a version of the *Island* drastically different from that which Byron originally intended for the magazine.[45]

"An author's works are public property," Byron acknowledged in the preface to *English Bards and Scotch Reviewers.*[46] This was the lesson about publication that Byron learned from periodical criticism at the start of his career and that informed him throughout his subsequent work. Byron was hardly unique in experiencing such authorial alienation, and he resembles other post-Napoleonic periodical contributors in portraying those conditions in notably imperial terms. When the first cantos of *Don Juan* initially met opposition from Murray and the reading public, the poet complained of the "empire" of sentiment embodied by women readers who condemned his opus for deviating from polite taste.[47] In rueful allusion to the "Women all over the world" who "[do] not admire Rousseau and hate *Gil Blas,*" Byron laments the hegemony held by reading audiences that is tantamount to a kind of territorial control. Although the poet names this connection a type of "freemasonry," and hence uses the term for democratic conspiracies perhaps more in line with the *Liberal,* his suspicion of a global network of readers is important for its conflation of literary commerce with imperial politics. Rather like the government authorities who intercepted the *Liberal* and its related correspondence, Byron accuses readers of conspiring against his literary efforts. The irony, of course, is that in this case the readers themselves are the source of strictures against transmission, as if the audience comprised of Byron's fans constitute a government or imperial power themselves.

The *Island* suffers from a similar tension. As a poem composed only a few months after the conflicts with *Don Juan,* it is not surprising that the *Island* reflects aspects of the epic poem's history. At times appealing to the sentiment favored by women readers, and at other times deflating it, the *Island,* like the *Liberal,* fell victim to the commercial omnipotence of the "empire of sentiment." If the poem originally had been conceived as a spiritual counterpart to the magazine's liberal ideals, the *Island* also was subject to the limitations of that ideal within contemporary history, where the South Sea islands were now a charted destination on numerous military and trade routes, and the liberal magazine that once hoped to harbor that symbolic space had itself been rejected by the hegemonic omnipotence of popular taste. Byron's *Island,* in short, was being remade as an imperial rather than liberal artifact, whose ability to recruit defectors to the idealized space it portrayed was undermined by the commercial interests to which it was put to use. In the context of the revolutionary ambition in which both the *Island* and the *Liberal* are imbued, the fate of both texts was also a political defeat, enacted by the superior power of contemporary taste.

How then are we to understand the fact that it was Byron who removed the poem from the journal, precipitating the misreading of the "most *pamby* portions of the Toobonai islanders" that the poet predicted? An answer to this question may lie in the changing notion of periodical power that Byron harbored after the *Liberal*'s failure. Byron's colleague in the *Liberal,* Mary Shelley, has characterized the poet's late career as one in which the commercial failures of his late works caused Byron to grow increasingly disillusioned about literary agency, such that he abandoned it for the active political dissent of military rebellion that Byron commenced when he departed Italy for Greece. According to Shelley,

> The opposition he met concerning the Liberal made him defy the world in D. Juan—Then it made him despise the Liberal itself, so that when he wrote expressly for it, he wrote tamely—as is the case

> with the Island—But, in the end, this war gave him a disgust to Authorship—and he hurried to Greece to get a new name as a man of action—having arrived at the highest praise as a poet.[48]

While Mary Shelley's account usefully places the *Liberal* and the *Island* amid the other works of Byron's late career, and her allusion to "war" acknowledges the confrontational agenda in which the magazine was conceived, her misleading suggestion of the poem's triviality overlooks the poem's original relation to the *Liberal* and the ambition for ideological opposition in which the magazine was steeped. That the *Liberal* failed, and caused Byron to remove the poem from the periodical, may have been a snag in his efforts to use periodicals to subversively undermine contemporary imperialism, but it did not entail a total and complete loss of faith in the revolutionary hopes embodied by Byron's own text. Significantly, the *Island* itself encloses lines depicting the power of verse in contesting imperial authority. Canto 2 opens with a song sung by the Toobonai islanders in ritual celebration. As Byron's footnote to the poem explains, the stanzas are an adaptation of a transcription "from an actual song of the Tonga Islanders," and it is incorporated into the poem with the same proto-anthropological attention by which Byron had also annotated Arnaout songs in *Childe Harold*.[49] In this post-Said era, such anthropological pretense to document native life must be suspect, but it also still attempts to give the natives their own voice. In the poem's revisionary reworking of colonial romance, the quotations thus are not signs of conquest but instead are converted into an anti-imperial gesture.

More to the point, Byron follows the song by explicitly asserting the capacity of verse to contest the traditional signs of imperial might. In the stanzas that follow the song of the Toobonai islanders, Byron notes that "one long cherished ballad's simple stave, / . . . / Hath greater power o'er each true heart and ear, / Than all the columns of Conquest's minions rear" (2.87, 91–92). Recalling "Ozymandias" in this claim that poetry surpasses military might in its ability to recruit human audiences, Byron asserts the transcendent agency of verse above the traditionally material forms of military and political power. However conventional, the lyric expresses hope in the potential agency of his poem, and it is an expression of faith that demonstrates the continuity of the *Island* with the culture of opposition in which the *Liberal* was founded. The difference is that by the time of the poem's publication, Byron had also begun to experience the adverse consequences of periodical power. As the *Liberal*'s commercial failure prompted the poet's abrupt removal of the *Island* from the periodical, Byron had to acknowledge that periodicals can hamper as well as help. After the failure of the magazine and the ideological defeat that failure signified, the extraordinary power of periodicals in the post-Napoleonic era was so great that the only possible remaining option for opposition was not contest but escape, the solution originally pursued by the *Bounty* mutineers.

The *Island* Alone

Many readers of the *Island* have noted that the poem presents a variety of heroes, consistent with the poem's general discursive heterogeneity.[50] Canto 1 offers a traditionally official hero in the form of Captain Bligh; canto 2 introduces Torquil as a hero reminiscent of conventional romance, complete with a name possibly derived from *Ossian;* and canto 3 presents a charismatically anti-establishment hero in the Byronic Christian. This kaleidoscopic quality of the poem enables profoundly different ideological interpretations. Depending on which hero (and canto) the reader focuses upon, audiences could find a jingoistic celebration of naval authority (canto 1), a sentimental exotic romance reminiscent of Byron's Oriental Tales (canto 2), or a heroic battle between liberty and military authority (canto 3). In the diversity and potential contradictions of these alternate heroes, the separate cantos of the *Island* might recall the miscellany of the periodical form in which the poem was supposed to appear—what Hogg extolled as that "intermixing [of] all things through other," into which a reader could begin with "anything he pleases."[51] Outside of the magazine, however, these various heroes within the *Island,* and particularly the sequence in which they appear, more specifically suggest a gradual shift from history to fiction that occurs over the course of the poem. As the poem alternates between real (Bligh and Christian) and fictional characters, transforming the actual fate of Christian and returning, in the final canto, to the purely imaginary Torquil, the *Island* metamorphosizes from a fictional depiction of what happened on the *Bounty* to a fantasy of what readers of the *Liberal* might have liked, and which the poem, through the power of fiction, can still depict.[52]

Byron begins the shift toward fictionalization in the *Island*'s depiction of Christian by dramatically revising the actual circumstances of the sailor's fate. The real Fletcher Christian had escaped recapture by the *Pandora* through his residence in Pitcairn, which the naval mission had passed by unvisited. Although Christian was murdered by his fellow residents within a few years of his arrival on the island, the British and American captains who stumbled upon Pitcairn in the early nineteenth century gained no information on the sailor's fate, such that rumors of his survival and possible return to England continued to circulate as late as the 1820s, when Byron was composing the poem. One would think that the possibility of the continuing survival of the best known of the *Bounty* mutineers would have been appealing to Byron and the liberal agenda with which the poem and magazine are involved, yet Byron notably departs from this possibility. Dramatically asserting the poem's break with the actual history upon which the *Island* is based, Byron portrays Christian's death, and in so doing rejects the utopian opportunities likely expected of the *Liberal* and promised by the rumors of Christian's continued survival.

This egregious moment of fictionalization occurs in canto 4, after the battle between the navy and the mutineers, when the sailor, surrounded by soldiers and depleted of ammunition, first loads his rifle with a button in a final attempt at battle, and then jumps off a precipice to his death, in Manfred-like fulfillment of his earlier vow that "to be, / In life or death, the fearless and the free" (3.163–64). With his silent pacing, monadic isolation (unlike Torquil, Christian is not shown with a mate), and suicidal leap off a precipice, Christian is the most Byronic of the three male characters in the *Island.* That Byron kills him off, and in so doing departs from the careful attention to detail and historical accuracy that he characterizes in other portions of the poem, is intriguing. In its deliberate, self-conscious acceptance of impending death, the episode seems to allegorize the *Liberal*'s failure, and it also prefigures Byron's subsequent relegation of the poem to the vicissitudes of popular taste.

Another way to think about the episode, however, is simply as a decisive switch from history to fiction, and hence as a dramatization of Byron's changing notions of the agency of literary representation, and particularly the power of poem and magazine to combat contemporary imperial culture. As Bernard Beatty noted in an early analysis of the role of fiction in Byron's utopianism, the *Island* "tells us that we cannot return to Paradise in historical fact because attempting to do so renews our exclusion from it."[53] In other words, the only way to return to Tahiti—the real version of Paradise for the *Bounty* sailors—was to imagine it, because by the end of the eighteenth century, it was only in fantasy that it still existed. Such intentional turning away from historical fact as occurs in the poem recalls the "uncritical absorption in Romanticism's own self-representations" observed by Jerome McGann and is embodied in the various heroes whom the poem presents.[54] As Byron kills off Christian, and the poem suspends the known history of the *Bounty* to launch instead the new, purely imaginary story of survival that begins with Torquil's escape, the *Island* initiates a return to paradise that would otherwise be impossible. Indeed, this very possibility seems to depend upon Christian's death, as Christian himself seems to acknowledge to Torquil: "I must fall; but have you strength to fly? / 'Twould be some comfort still, could you survive" (3.158–59).

For Timothy Fulford, this turn by the *Island* away from history partakes in a retort to Byron's longtime poetic scapegoat, Southey, particularly the unabashedly jingoistic depiction of the South Seas that Southey had presented in his *Vision of Judgment*.[55] While this explanation certainly provides an important context to the contemporary South Sea representations to which Byron's poem adds, the poem is most important for the way in which the *Island* uses Christian's death to assert a shift away from history and into pure fiction, from literary identification with the revolutionary cause of the *Liberal* and the *Bounty* mutineers, and toward the different, subdued, quiet, and quiescent retreat of anonymity and exile. Such a shift by Byron toward a more removed, less active opposition to contemporary imperial power may differ dramatically from the actively anti-imperial contest in which poem and periodical were both originally conceived, but his intentions are still far less resigned than Mary Shelley's characterization of poem and magazine would have it. Rather than writing "tamely," as Shelley suggests, and ultimately abandoning literature for active political involvement, Byron in the *Island* reimagines literature as a last preserve from the material realities of everyday life. Such a characterization of poetry as a sanctuary from the ravages of contemporary culture is, of course, profoundly Romantic, but in Byron's case this belief by the time of the *Island* is further reinforced by the immense disappointments of his periodical venture. In the aftermath of the disillusionments causing his late declamation of a "lack of periodical talent," Byron saw the limits of even the most ambitious of periodicals. His insight is based on his recognition of the limitations of literature to impact the material world, and instead causes the poet to embrace a new version of poetry as an ideal preserve from everyday life.

Crucial to this idea of literary remove is the generic transition embodied in the replacement of the Byronic Christian with the almost saccharine Torquil, but it gains full realization in canto 4 when Neuha and Torquil escape the pursuing navy by diving deep underwater to hide in an island cave. Historical precedents for this plot device are numerous. A similar description of a cave occurs in Mariner's Tongan memoir, the most historically proximate source for Byron, and the episode also recalls older stories of New World encounter, such as the story of Inkle and Yarico, the native woman and European explorer who meet in a cave in a popular Renaissance-era travelers' tale, and even of Dido and Aeneas, who make love in a cave, and of whose story Inkle and Yarico's is likely a more recent adaptation. Yet, as Peter Hulme has pointed out, although these traditions may have some basis in fact, the persistence of certain elements of these stories throughout so many other subsequent travelers' tales shows how "during the colonial period large parts of the non-European world were *produced* for Europe through a discourse" of fictionalized, often romantic stories.[56] Although the *Island*'s episode is likely based upon any of the various historical anecdotes and fables of New World encounter that incorporate a cave, the emphasis in Byron's poem is on fiction, fantasy, and separation from history. The island outpost to which Torquil and Neuha escape is unnamed and uncharted when first introduced in the poem, and thus escapes the burdens of historical fact to which Byron had to answer in his depiction of Toobonai. (Indeed, precisely because it is fictional, it enjoys the obscurity that Tahiti, Toobonai, and even Pitcairn already lost.) More important, as the second island of the poem, and a hidden cave within an unknown and uncharted island, the island cave is a bower within a bower, and an extreme version of the romantic idyll that the *Bounty* mutineers had sought to find in Tahiti.

In a historically sensitive reading concerned only to locate the factual precedents for the plot and details of the *Island,* one might note that of all the geographic spaces described within the poem, the island cave comes closest to depicting the sanctuary that Christian and his comrades had found at Pitcairn and hence, in a sense, prophetically depicts an actuality that few Europeans yet knew. But rather than invite such a reading, the poem instead seems to emphasize a mythic significance to the island cave, one that returns to colonial allegory and conflates the spatial location with the body of the native female. Neuha's physique is frequently given an environmental cast. Early in the poem, we are told that this "infant of an infant world" is "like Night . . . / Or [a] cavern" (2.127, 129–30), and that this "daughter of the Southern Seas, / [was] Herself a billow in her energies" (2.141–12). The topographically objectifying rhetoric of these lines is a trope of orientalist writing, one that often occurs in the Oriental Tales. In the *Island,* however, these passages include an epic simile that graphically prefigures the means by which Neuha saves Torquil from the marauding navy. Just as she leads him to the underwater entrance to the hidden cave, Neuha's body is described as "Like coral reddening through the darken'd wave, / Which draws the diver to the crimson cave" (2.139–40). The image these lines provide is dramatically sexual, but as with the earlier inversion of colonial romance implied by Byron's emphasis on an active Neuha and an effeminate Torquil, both the prophetic depiction of the poem's climax and the episode itself are important for how they upend the usual conventions of colonial romance. Specifically, the passages use sex not as an act of conquest but as procreation. Inside the cave Neuha tends to her wounded lover by holding him to her breast, a pietà whose maternal dimensions are reinforced by the language of "nursling" (4.113) and "boy" (4.388) by which Torquil is described in the scenes inside the cave. Torquil is changing from lover to infant, and the entry into the vaginal cave is refigured from escape to insemination. The implication of such a passage is clear: the hidden cave so reminiscent of Neuha's body is a native womb, and Torquil's time within that cave a gestational duration that results in his racial reinvention. When the pair reemerge from the cave after the departure of the naval party, it is not a sole white survivor who comes out. Instead, Torquil returns as a native son and "son restored" (4.408). He may be the last survivor of the *Bounty* sailors who mutinied to remain in Tahiti, and the only white man left on Toobonai, but as far as Byron and the Toobonai islanders are concerned, Torquil's survival is dependent upon the wholesale erasure of his former racial identity.

A little more than a decade earlier, Mitford's South Sea poem, *Christina,* concluded with the mixed-race daughter of Fletcher Christian wedding a British sailor and returning with him to England. Based upon reports of the 1808 American "discovery" of Pitcairn, Mitford's poem responds to the settlement's miscegenation by imagining the effects of a dose of fresh white blood, and secures this symbolic repatriation by returning the couple to the north. Byron's poem, by contrast, ignores this more recent *Bounty* history, and in revisiting the earlier moment of the *Pandora* invasion, it embraces miscegenation as a means of erasing the outcome of that attack. Rather than rehabilitating the *Bounty* legacy with fresh infusions of northern culture, Byron asserts the end of the *Bounty*'s British identity and portrays the reinvention of its survivors as native Polynesians. This allegory of racial rebirth encapsulates the revolutionary utopianism with which the *Island* was conceived and which it still strived to achieve, despite its separation from the *Liberal*. By portraying Torquil's survival and implicit future in Toobonai, Byron does not imply the dominance of white culture and eventual dilution of native blood that might be expected in a similar scenario by Kipling, Haggard, or Stevenson; nor does the poem invite parallels to the actual history of John Adams, the patriarch who ruled Pitcairn as the last surviving *Bounty* sailor by the time of the nineteenth-century discovery of the island, and whose rigidly pious dominion over the mixed-race descendents of himself and the other sailors was the object of much colonial pride later in the century. Rather, in its explicitly sexual depiction of the inseminating and gestational process by which Torquil is reborn as a native son through his time inside "Neuha's cave" (4.414), the *Island* enacts a more thorough and complete defection from his British homeland than had ever been imagined when the *Bounty* sailors mutinied to become "men without country."

Byron's poem achieves this revolutionary vision of total and complete nonparticipation in the imperial processes then remaking the world, including the once unspoiled South Seas, by using fiction—and, more generally, the purely ideal nature of literary representation—to imagine a space where some version of the South Seas can still remain free from imperial transformation. The implicit significance of Neuha's cave, and Byron's Toobonai in general, is that the societies harbored in those locations are the peaceful, Pacific opposite of England, that martial and imperial isle so anxious to include those locations within its ever-expanding archipelago of power. Within the *Bounty* history, such a subversive image of British culture and identity has a historical precedent in "Belle Isle," the private island in the middle of Lake Windermere owned by distant relatives of the Christian family, and where, according to the popular rumors about the sailor's return to England, Fletcher was thought to have hidden himself. But in a more literary analogue, Byron's romantic idealization of the South Sea islands also has a variant in *Don Juan,* whose English cantos famously satirize British hypocrisy and social affectation, and which destroy one island so that Byron can idealize the other. (Indeed, in his broad diction and burlesque appearance, Ben Bunting seems to have been transported to the *Island* from the more prominent poem.)

The difference, of course, between *Don Juan* and the *Island* is the satiric and sentimental ethos that the two poems respectively inhabit. In the latter, smaller poem, Byron abandons the satiric assault attempted in *Don Juan* and instead aims for a more modest goal: the mere preservation of a space outside of contemporary history altogether. The poem *The Island* thus is not just *about* an island, but is also itself an island, in the sense that it is a text isolated from any larger literary mass. Removed from the *Liberal,* the *Island* became a self-contained, independent artifact, and a textual embodiment of the hidden cave at the center of the poem itself—a sanctuary hidden and unharmed by the depredations of contemporary society. In the artifactual conceits by which Keats, Lamb, and Hogg develop their exotic motifs, it is telling that Byron likens his work to an organic and topographical monument. Another pleasure-dome, but one not associated with empire and not even man-made, the island cave maintains late Romantic tendencies for literary materialism while using that convention to assert Byron's revisionary perspective.

Such an insight explains how the poem's separation from the magazine that could have enhanced its content instead could fulfill the poem's promise. The *Island*'s last-minute separation from the *Liberal* thus is not a sudden failure of faith, but rather a new strategy of imperial resistance equally as ardent as Byron had once envisioned by promising the poem for the periodical, but radically different in its perception of the ability of periodicals to effectively combat contemporary imperial power. The failure of the *Liberal* at the hands of both imperial bureaucrats and the "empire of sentiment" caused Byron to see the limitations of periodicals and the kind of textual campaign that distinct form of publication represented. Consequently, the *Island* itself presents a purely ideal and imaginary version of the South Seas, where the dream of the *Bounty* sailors still survives in the body of one man, and he and the other Toobonai Islanders still live in the one, literary *Island* that remains permanently protected from the devastation of imperial intrusion.

Indeed, if Byron's *Island* was the philosophical antithesis of the real island for which it was destined, the poem also survived as a last gasp of the revolutionary political idealism with which the *Liberal* had been conceived, and with which the periodical was in dire need of assistance. The hysterical response to the first news of the *Liberal*'s foundation had spawned a number of counterreactions, some of which picked up on the geopolitical conceits of the magazine. In London late in 1822, shortly after the first number of the *Liberal,* there appeared a printed but likely never published pamphlet entitled the *Illiberal: Verse and Prose from the North.* As might be guessed from its title, the pamphlet is a parody of the circumstances behind the production of the *Liberal,* and it includes a facetious dramatic dialogue—recalling the "Noctes" both in its fictional representation of literary personalities and in the conservative cast by which those characters are portrayed—in which Byron repents his works upon confrontation with Shelley's ghost.[57] A more interesting instance occurred with the *London Liberal; An Antidote to "Verse and Prose from the South,"* which appeared in January 1823, at exactly the same time as the *Liberal*'s second number. As in the *Illiberal,* the *London Liberal* co-opted the blend of territorial and political attributes by which the *Liberal* was defined, and it went one further in clearly identifying itself with the metropolitan center that the original *Liberal* had meant invade. An "antidote" to the liberal idealism by which Byron and his peers were thought to be infecting British shores, the *London Liberal* was explicit about its self-appointed importance. As if anticipating the censorship and political monitoring that the original *Liberal* suffered in regards to its correspondence and foreign distribution, the *London Liberal* promised to "keep a sharp look out a-head for the *Corsair* of Pisa, the most formidable, perhaps, of those rovers that infest the literary ocean."[58]

Amid this highly keyed, tense literary-political environment, the *Island*'s status as a text independent of the *Liberal* but deeply sympathetic with its ideals only becomes more meaningful and poignant. With its idyllic portrait of the remote South Seas, the poem reclaimed the revolutionary and utopian symbolism with which geography originally was invested in the *Liberal,* but which those satiric attacks spawned by the magazine's first issue had lately distorted. Moreover, because the poem survived the periodical and ultimately achieved a much vaster dissemination than had ever been possible for the *Liberal,* the *Island* negated whatever reactionary organization might have been incited by the works created to contest the *Liberal*'s founding. An antidote to an "Antidote," and a work that successfully infiltrated British and Continental reading markets when governments had actively suppressed transmission of the *Liberal* and its related correspondence, the *Island* realizes what the *Liberal* could not achieve. Its importance gives new weight to both works, and reiterates the significance of Byron's periodical collaboration.

Despite his proclaimed lack of talent for "the kinds of composition which is most acceptable to periodical readers," Byron exerts tremendous importance as the final case study of this book. In his unique independence of the periodical format, Byron stands at the era's most intriguing intersection between empire and periodicals, and presents the era's single most aggressive engagement of imperial motifs within the form. This is true even as his collaboration progressed, such that of all five case studies examined here, Byron also is the author whose collaboration with periodicals concludes most defiantly removed from that format. This arc in Byron's periodical engagement reflects his deep understanding, by the time of the *Island,* of the limits of periodicals—a position that also parallels his status as the era's most sophisticated critic of imperialism. It also provides, because of his acknowledged mastery of literary exoticism, Romanticism's strongest and most intriguing application of orientalism for imperial critique. His case is not entirely unique and exceptional. In both his opposition to imperialism and his eventual dismay over periodicals, Byron recalls some aspects of Hogg. Their parallels are charted in their mutual turn to pastoral, and in Byron's helplessness in the face of his previous literary achievements, these parallels even present an intriguing instance when the era's single most prominent literary celebrity has no more autonomy than a minor and marginalized author.[59] It is for these reasons that the era's "grand Napoleon of the realms of rhyme" remains one of the most compelling cases of late Romantic involvement with the post-Napoleonic periodicals.

No poem is an island, entire of itself. To further adapt Donne, every work intended for a periodical was once part of that culture, and hence a constitutive part of the vibrant literary landscape in which that work was composed and shaped. Byron's *Island* may seem a first glace a trivial poem, perhaps reminiscent of Lamb's essays in the precious sentimentality with which it is infused. But as can be seen in the poem's origins in the *Liberal* and that journal's radical identification with territorial space, it is a profound instance of the geographical exoticism common in late Romantic writing developed amid the periodicals. Whether inside the *Liberal* as originally intended or appearing, as it ultimately did, as a self-contained work, the poem demonstrates the paradoxical role of space in periodicals and exemplifies the extraordinary role of periodicals in late Romantic writing.

Conclusion

Space, Time, and the Periodical Collaborator

In *Romantic Genius and the Literary Magazine,* David Higgins argues that the solitary genius so sacred to Romantic ideals is a socially constructed phenomenon that owes as much to the extrinsic affirmations of the periodical press as it does to the intrinsic abilities of an individual author. According to Higgins, "Whether or not there is such a thing as 'genius' is perhaps less important than the fact [that] most people involved in the cultural field have believed . . . in its existence and value."[1] For Higgins, early-nineteenth-century periodicals are one of the most obvious and vital forms of that "cultural field," in which contemporary readers could find examples of such literary genius as well as follow an ongoing critical discourse on the characteristics and standards of what constituted that gift. Higgins goes on to show how the periodicals had further reason to stake a position in this discussion, as it provided a strategy of product differentiation within the fierce periodical marketplace.[2] This latter point looks back to Klancher in its account of the role of periodicals in forming and shaping British reading audiences, and in its synthesis of print capitalism with the traditionally transcendent concerns of Romanticism, Higgins's study provides a valuable precedent to my own. Like Higgins, I claim that magazines were an integral force in late Romantic writing, and I contest the received tradition that holds that the collective, corporate, and commercial format of publication is opposed to the promotion of the individual author who is so central to traditional Romantic notions of solitary genius. Unlike Higgins, however, I argue that this revisionary understanding of the role of periodicals in late Romantic writing also necessitates a major reconceptualization of the form's defining attribute. That is, in a massive revision of long-standing accounts of the chief attributes of periodicals and their place in Romantic and nineteenth-century literature, this book presents space as one of the form's defining attributes, and an element instrumental to authorial self-definition within that form.

This conceptual importance of space in periodicals has long gone unnoticed, no doubt because of ample evidence for the opposite aspect of time. Explicitly identified with time in their very name, periodicals were the object of Romantic distaste due to their serial and rapidly obsolescent nature—elements that must seem far closer to the "idle buzz of fashion" than to "the highest authority—that of time," to cite the comparison Hazlitt uses in one typically Romantic veneration of posterity.[3] James Mill was even more explicit in his criticism of the form. In his essay entitled "Periodical Literature" for the first number of the *Westminster Review,* Mill rued that "every motive . . . which prompts to the production of anything periodical, prompts to the study of immediate effect, of unpostponed popularity, of the applause of the moment."[4] Coming from an author whose early career largely took place amid the periodicals, Mill is acutely aware of the form's vulnerability to passing taste. His concerns are echoed by Thomas Macaulay, another Victorian sage whose career first began with contributions to the post-Napoleonic periodicals, and who harbored reservations about republishing his magazine essays. Periodical works, Macaulay acknowledged, "are not expected to be highly finished," and they have a natural life of "only six weeks." To republish his journalistic work, the author noted with chagrin, would be to "challenge[ ] comparison with the most symmetrical and polished of human compositions," and hence would do little to advance his reputation.[5]

Such prejudice among contemporary authors against the rapidly produced and easily disposable nature of periodical writing was widespread and reminds us of how closely the periodicals are identified with time. Indeed, it is worth noting that periodicals are so inextricably associated with time that the form is often considered, in a kind of reciprocal metonymy, an emblem of time itself. Long before Michael Woolf observed that the periodical constituted the "basic unit" of nineteenth-century history and culture, Thomas Carlyle and John Scott both cited periodicals as publications uniquely evocative of their historical moment.[6] In two separate contributions that are both entitled "Signs of the Times," the authors equate periodical publication with contemporary cultural developments in a way that prefigures the "empire of signs" explored in this book. For John Scott, then editor of the popular new *London Magazine,* signs of the times are the "local and temporary circumstances" that characterize modern life.[7] Scott proposes the topic for a series of essays that he hoped would become a mainstay of the magazine and would thereby illustrate the *London's* cultural modernity. Carlyle was even more specific on the importance of periodicals in modern life. Thus, in his (better-known) essay "Signs of the Times," which appeared later in the same decade in the *Edinburgh Review,* Carlyle notes that "every little sect among us . . . must have its Periodical, its monthly or quarterly Magazine."[8] In this astute, somewhat regretful observation on the pervasive growth of periodicals throughout contemporary culture, Carlyle reaffirms time as the defining attribute of the periodical format.

Yet if time is widely regarded as the defining attribute of periodicals, its corollary of space remains a prominent element of the periodical form, and one that suggests the different and unexpected opportunities available to authors who capitalized upon this alternate aspect of the format. The periodical essayist, Leigh Hunt once claimed in an issue of the *Examiner,* is a "writer who claims a peculiar intimacy with the public," and the periodical essay is a place where readers and authors can "reconnoitre each other with true English civility."[9] In this celebratory account of the cultural environs provided by the periodical form, Hunt invokes the familiar adage of periodicals as a republic of letters, but he also adapts the commonplace to suggest that the format provides a direct connection between author and reader. Such a comment, with its surprising assumption that periodicals can provide an intimacy that overcomes the actual increase in distance between authors and readers that occurred in this era of proliferating publication and mass distribution, represents a notable exception to the conventional notion of periodicals as an obstacle to Romantic ambition. In a distinctly nineteenth-century take on the eighteenth-century concept of periodicals as a literary analogue to civil society, Hunt exalts the milieu provided in magazine essays and other periodical publications, and he reiterates space as a factor of as much importance as the periodicals' more conventionally recognized attribute of time.

The five case studies of periodical collaborations by individual Romantic authors provided in this book have been an effort to demonstrate this strategic investment in space, and hence to illustrate, along with

Higgins, the crucial role of periodicals in the promotion of Romantic genius. In their mutual identification with a specific global location currently infused with topical significance, Keats, Lamb, Hogg, Landon, and Byron all demonstrate the importance of geography in contemporary periodical culture and stridently assert the power of the periodicals they hope to harness through their rhetorical identification of that process with imperialism, the era's most overt instance of spatial authority, and a compellingly topical paradigm of collective human power. Empire may be their overt theme, but in their disparate allusions to Greece, China, Egypt, Italy, and the South Seas, these authors reiterate the more general importance of space in the periodical press.

Such advantages to individual authors through these topographical motifs were also implicit in the general conceits of the form. If space is a crucial component of the periodical format, a fact that post-Napoleonic versions of the form often emphasized through metaphors comparing the form to a storehouse or site of artifacts and collections worthy of exhibition, late Romantic authors further capitalized upon that condition through the imperial and geographical motifs that pervade so many of their periodical-developed works. (One reason why Keats, Lamb, and Hogg are so exemplary in their periodical collaboration is that the exotic artifacts emblematizing their literary works build upon these geographical motifs both by borrowing the mystique of a specific territorial space and by emphasizing their place within the museological space of exhibition provided by the periodical form.) Indeed, even in derogatory descriptions of periodical collaboration, such as Keats's proud refusal to ever "mortgage [his] Brain to Blackwood," the temporal metaphor of financial accountability ("mortgage") is soon eclipsed by the spatial advantages of institutional sponsorship and exhibition that affiliation with a periodical magazine promises. In the perfect illustration of the synergy between periodical and individual author that occurred in his poems for the *Annals of the Fine Arts*—a synergy in which "essay or poem is to magazine as figure is to ground in the plastic arts"—Keats exemplifies the transcendent benefits of periodicals' thematization of space.[10]

Similar synergies of space and time are apparent in other periodical collaborations. In the archetypal collaboration of Lamb, for example, the temporal infinitude promised by a periodical's serial production is equated with the similarly relentless production of industrial manufacture and imperial export. Although time would seem to be the dominant aspect of such seriality, it is converted, in Lamb's thematic emphasis upon commodity culture and the British opening of China, into a territorial attribute—as the mounting inventories of china teacups infiltrate British borders at consumer behest—or into the space of the periodical essay itself, which for many *London* readers was the best part of the magazine, and the literary analogue of the *"'mighty heart'"* at the center of this "great Empire," as the magazine aimed to portray London.[11] Indeed, as Lamb lovingly dramatizes the images on the teacup in his essay's depiction of Elia's and Bridget's teatime conversation, his essay epitomizes Hunt's notion of the periodical essay as a place where readers "reconnoitre each other with true English civility."

Similarly, Byron, although exceptional in almost every other regard, exemplifies periodical collaboration in his prioritization of space over time. The prominent role of geography in both the *Liberal* and the *Island* clearly illustrates this criterion. Both works make their identification with the South a constitutive feature of their contents and political sympathies, encapsulating a literary and public celebrity long identified with global travel since *Childe Harold,* and which culminated in the poet's exile from England during which both publications were composed. This distinctive conflation of geography and textuality within the periodical texts only grew more important when Byron severed poem from periodical, and thereby left the idyllic space portrayed within the significantly named poem, *The Island,* to survive independently. As the poem literally became the distinct and isolated entity for which it is named, *The Island* epitomizes the importance of space in realizing periodical objectives of surviving through time.

Temporal qualities are less obvious in the other case studies, but this fact only reinforces the importance of space within periodicals. For Hogg, consistent with his oppositional position on periodicals, his "anti-Blackwoodian" novel ends in pastoral, thereby asserting his post-"Noctes" disillusionment with Edinburgh as well as recapitulating in literary genre the retreat from metropolitan culture that he undertook after his break with the magazine. Hogg depicts the prominent role of space in periodical power through the novel's allegorical mapping of the capital and various other Scottish locations, and he formally realizes the importance of space in periodical identity when his abandonment of magazines is commemorated with a new metropolitan affiliation with a London publisher. And in the most unusual use of space in the post-

Napoleonic periodicals, Landon reduces Italy's imperial topography to a mere prototype for the giftbooks' second-order style, and thereby evacuates space of its territorial or topographic qualities even as she reinforces its role within periodicals as a mode of authorial exhibition. This exceptional periodical collaboration—and least explicit connection of empire and periodicals—is, paradoxically, the most explicit demonstration of space within periodicals, as its figure for authorial self-exhibition that Landon exhibits throughout giftbooks graphically illustrates the spatial qualities inherent in the periodical form.

Indeed, time, in the sense of contemporary history, may have provided the vehicle for these authors' imperial rhetoric, but it also dictated when those conceits became unsustainable. Lamb's whimsically comic depiction of Chinese consumption in the "Dissertation upon Roast Pig" might not have been as funny a decade or two later, when Britain was embroiled in the Opium Wars. Champollion's premature death in 1832 may have been yet another instance of Romantic genius tragically cut short, but it also ensured the cessation of Hogg's literary allusions to Egypt. In calling attention to the differences between these works and the contemporary history to which they allude, I am less interested in testing their accuracy than in recognizing how that history forecast parallel developments in the literary works that history was summoned to represent. As military and government authority consolidated and intensified with each subsequent year, the empire that late Romantics once used to figure their periodical collaboration also began to predict its imminent failure. This is especially apparent in the South Sea history so crucial to Byron. In 1831, toward the end of the period examined in this book, the Pitcairn Islanders were forcibly returned to Tahiti by the British. The act, typically imperial in its indifference to cultural relativism and individual subjectivity, arguably was also prophetic of the subsequent century and a half of critical indifference to Byron's poem on the same topic, and which developed in part because of the poem's separation from the periodical in which that poem had been conceived.

Why then did Romantic and nineteenth-century authors turn to periodicals, and what did they find in the form that proved useful for their distinctly inward and personal concerns? In the case of one author closely preceding the figures in this study, the late-eighteenth-century poet William Cowper found newspapers to be inspirational texts in which information from various locations around the globe could be processed and considered in the retreat of Cowper's country drawing-room, and further contemplated and re-created in the space of Cowper's own reflective mind.[12] In this example, periodicals are the germ of Romantic introspection and subjectivity, or what Benedict Anderson, building upon Hegel, has memorably called the "lair of the skull."[13] In periodicals such as newspapers and magazines, the physical space of their pages may report on happenings in a vast array of places across the world, but they also function, in a fundamentally Romantic device, to stimulate the imagination or interior space of one's own mind. Like the travel narratives in *Purchas his Pilgrim* that sparked Coleridge's creation of "Kubla Khan," and as Lamb further realized in his reifying treatment of "Old China" in the *London Magazine,* it is the geographic space encompassed in periodicals that proved instrumental for late Romantic writers in the form.

Space, therefore, has always been important to the periodical form. It was so in early concepts of periodicals as a "republic of letters," and it only intensified in early-nineteenth-century approaches to periodicals as an "empire of signs," a phrase that emphasizes the correlation between literary-industrial acceleration and the general economic expansion of the era. The latter term, originally proposed by Klancher, and realized in the elaborate imperial motifs apparent in so many post-Napoleonic collaborations with periodicals, is particularly valuable because of its emphasis upon the highly commodified conditions of periodical publication and dissemination that the "literary republic" concept never adequately acknowledged. The many different forms of space within a periodical—which include the physical space of a periodical's pages, the geographical spaces referenced in their contents, the symbolic space of exhibition that the periodical aegis provides, and the social and cultural space conquered through dissemination of that mass-produced publication—make space the underlying objective and prevailing power activated by periodical collaboration. Far more so than time, then, it is space that ought to be celebrated as the latent quality of the format that provided such force and energy to the individual ambitions of Romantic authors.

This insight into the importance of space in post-Napoleonic periodicals also raises two more general points about the relationship of space to contemporary literature. First, the synthesis of material and ideal evident in these works reconceives long-standing notions about the politics and consequences of literary orientalism. Discourse and rhetoric may be intangible, but as Edward Said so masterfully demonstrated, the injuries of orientalism ultimately are always material. Yet in contrast to the literary exoticism that reflects contemporary empire in standard accounts of orientalism and imperialism, the kind of space invoked by most late Romantic contributors to the post-Napoleonic periodicals is often an anti-imperial emblem, either in the explicit sense of Byron's liberal activism or in the more general, professional sense of Hogg's and Landon's use of imperial rhetoric to convey the constraints and compromises of periodical collaboration. Thus, late Romantic allusions to empire and geography in the post-Napoleonic periodicals constitute a remarkable exception to much of the literature of the nineteenth century, the very era that Said indicts for its unreflective production of orientalist perceptions and imperial culture.[14] Although this study of empire within late Romantic periodical culture might initially appear to support materialist accounts of the role of periodicals in promulgating imperial and national culture, in fact this book reveals a different perspective. In a return to the profoundly idealistic concerns of high Romanticism, this study shows late Romantic writing in the post-Napoleonic periodicals to provide a last opportunity for an enthusiastic, uncomplicated use of imperial and oriental rhetoric. Indeed, it suggests that despite their overt uses of literary orientalism, many of these periodical contributors were astute critics of empire itself. Precisely because of their familiarity with the consequences and compromises of corporate collaboration, late Romantic contributors to the periodicals often were sophisticated opponents of empire, who employ orientalist language in ways that assail the capitalist processes and conditions that enable the politico-economic institution with which literary orientalism is traditionally associated.

In the second connection of space and literature in late Romantic writing among the post-Napoleonic periodicals, early-nineteenth-century British periodicals exhibit the same conceptual emphasis upon contemporary geopolitics and its role in shaping literary autonomy as do the authors, publishers, and culture makers of today. To put it another way, the political distribution of power that Pascale Casanova sees determining modern literary reception was as true two centuries ago as it is now, as individual periodical series distinguished themselves through strategic identification with specific global regions, and individual authors within those organs used those territorial motifs as metaphors by which to stake their claims to status within the British national metropole. Such gestures are most obvious in the case of geographically peripheral magazines, such as *Blackwood's* and the *Liberal,* whose respective identifications with the "South" or classical Greece and Egypt deliberately present them as cultural alternatives to London, but their insights are also true in the many allusions to imperialism deployed by individual periodical contributors. Like the "international literary sphere" that Casanova identifies within the world republic of letters, these early-nineteenth-century British authors invoke a global variety of geographical motifs as a means of rhetorically inflating their own published contribution. The value of their works, beyond the obvious relevance to Romantic and nineteenth-century literature, is that they invite a substantially different understanding of the uses of imperial history in literary history and criticism. Rather than merely exploring periodical contents for ethical commentary, this approach explores the psychic space of literary prestige as it was emblematized by empire. It synthesizes the traditionally ideal entities of literature with the fundamentally material concerns of empire, and tracks how individual works seek prestige within that space through self-conscious identification with contemporary world places.

"We will divide the world between us, like the Triumvirate," wrote Leigh Hunt to the Shelleys in 1821, in giddy anticipation of their plans for the *Liberal.*[15] In both his confidence and his rhetoric Hunt typifies the parallels between imperial and periodical production that prevailed in the post-Waterloo years, when the rapid expansion of the periodical press offered opportunities for self-promotion tantamount to empire itself. Although this book has focused on periodicals in particular, such rhetoric was so appealing that it pervaded the contemporary publishing industry at large. Many of the behaviors that we see in post-Napoleonic periodicals were apparent throughout the contemporary book trade, which mimicked the content and conventions of the industry's most profitable format. *The Private Memoirs and Confessions of a Justified Sinner* is a perfect example of this tendency, as the novel employs the miscellaneous style and Napoleonic motifs that Hogg fancied in his earlier periodical collaboration. In further illustration of this phenomenon, I would like to conclude with an instance of imperial rhetoric that does not pertain to individual contributions to periodicals, but instead demonstrates the pervasive importance of empire as a paradigm for conceptualizing power within the early-nineteenth-century British publishing industry at large.

The Edinburgh publishing magnate Archibald Constable often referred to himself and his competitors in nicknames derived from the imperial powers then conquering the globe. The firm of John Murray he called the "Emperor of the West," in cheeky salute to that firm's dominance in England, while his own local competitor, John Ballantyne, Constable dubbed the "Dey of All-jeers," in punning reference to that Edinburgh printer's jocular nature. Another London press, Longman and Co., Constable named "the Divan," after the royal assemblies in the Levant and other oriental regions, and for himself Constable used a variety of monikers, alternately going by the "Czar of Muscovy," to keep within the oriental theme, or affecting a classical tone by answering to "Hannibal," after the indomitable Carthaginian general and foe of Rome. Most topically, Constable liked to call himself the "Napoleon of Books," in a sobriquet that, like Byron's famous self-description as the "grand Napoleon of the realms of rhyme," crowned himself in a rhetorical self-investiture reminiscent of that for which his namesake was known.[16]

Possible sources for Constable's oriental rubrics are several. His sobriquets play upon the same metaphor of the "empire of the mind" then popular among contemporary periodicals, such as *Blackwood's,* that Klancher notes in his discussion of the early-nineteenth-century "empire of signs."[17] We also saw a contemporary analogy in the oriental rubrics for Edinburgh literati that Hogg employs in the Chaldee Manuscript. More graphically, Constable's description of himself and his fellow publishers divvying up the virtual territory of British reading audiences recalls Gillray's famous cartoon of Napoleon and Wellington carving up the globe. As such, the rubrics present Constable and his competitors as the literary equivalent of those powerful generals and conquerors.[18] But amid the extensive and varied imperial motifs throughout late Romantic collaborations with periodicals, Constable's oriental rubrics make most sense as a similar conceit, merely expanded in scope. (Constable was, after all, the publisher of the *Edinburgh Review,* the transformative periodical whose founding at the start of the century inaugurated the cultural omnipotence of periodicals for the next fifty years.) Like the periodical collaborations examined in this book, Constable's description of publishers as oriental empires is based upon comparisons of their mutual attributes of massification and rationalization. The only difference from periodicals in the case of Constable and his fellow publishers is that the motif is expanded from a periodical trend to a characteristic true of the whole of contemporary publishing.

Tellingly, this latter comparison of empire to contemporary British publishing reveals a crucial aspect of the imperial metaphor that was only implicit in periodical uses of that rhetoric. Constable's oriental rubrics play upon the metaphor "publishing empire" and assert the British publishing industry as a cultural and economic force comparable to empire itself. A colloquial term commonly used to signify the scope and power of media production, the phrase "publishing empire" plays upon the mutual objective of territorial conquest that print capitalism shares with empire.[19] It reprises the spatial emphasis that pervades late Romantic writing in the post-Napoleonic periodicals, and like that rhetorical trend, it references the print explosion after 1815 that made literary production such a compelling synecdoche for contemporary cultural and economic expansion. Like all of the geographical and exotic motifs in the various case studies explored in this book, the phrase uses this topical analogy to assert a transformative power for literary culture directly comparable to empire itself.

This, then, reveals the multiple advantages in the imperial and geographic rhetoric invoked by collaborators with the post-Napoleonic periodicals. By deploying topical geographies that implicitly likened periodical collaboration to imperial enterprise, late Romantic collaborators with the post-Napoleonic periodicals aimed to array themselves in the pomp and circumstance of empire itself. Like Constable and other contemporary publishers, these periodical contributors recognized that the extensive output of the post-Napoleonic print industry exercised a powerful effect on contemporary culture, complete with internal competition and audience diversification such that the literary production constituted a virtual world or simulacrum of territorial difference at large. Hence, their geographic and imperial motifs throughout their periodical and periodical-developed writing are, as in Constable's rubrics, an early and overdetermined instance of the colloquialism "publishing empire." For the late Romantic collaborators with the post-Napoleonic periodicals, this more specific venue might more accurately be rephrased as "periodical empire," in reference to their specific affiliation with the era's prevailing literary format and the genre arguably most directly analogous to imperial enterprise.

In summary, the echoes of imperial motifs in late Romantic collaborations with periodicals that Constable displays in his characterization of the British book trade reiterate the ubiquity of space as a conceptualizing mode throughout contemporary literary culture. That late Romantic, early-nineteenth-century periodicals were particularly visible sites of this overall literary trend only reaffirms their importance in the literary culture of the time, and shows the prescience of the periodical format in foreshadowing trends within literary culture at large, throughout that time and today. Both cases show space as a key element in individual self-promotion (even Constable's rubrics for publishers emphasize the person rather than the house, and therefore use empire as a figure for inflating the importance of the printer). In the periodical empire that developed in post-Napoleonic Britain, the entity that benefited most was the individual author, the very person usually thought to be lost in the corporate and collective nature of the periodical format, but whose upward mobility through affiliation with that format actually legitimated the era's pervasive imperial metaphor.

Notes

Introduction

1. Altick, *English Common Reader,* 329–30. For more recent studies of the impact of periodicals in the Romantic era, see Higgins, *Romantic Genius,* and Wheatley, Introduction.

2. John Keats to Charles Wentworth Dilke, September 22, 1819 (*Letters,* 2: 178–79).

3. Bayley, *Imperial Meridian,* 250. For studies of more explicit moments of territorial coverage in contemporary periodicals, see Demata, "Prejudiced Knowledge," and Webb, "Great Theatre."

4. *Examiner,* January 11, 1818, 24; Shelley, "Ozymandias," lines 2, 1 (*Shelley's Poetry and Prose,* 103).

5. "North America—President's Message," "The latest advices of the state of affairs in New Guyana," "Distressed Seamen, and Distress of the Poor in General" (*Examiner,* January 11, 1818, 19–22; 23; 17–18).

6. Anderson, *Imagined Communities,* 33.

7. Volney, *Ruins,* 13. This volume is a facsimile of an 1890 edition that reprints the English translation supervised by Volney and that was originally published in Paris in 1802.

8. The suspicions and distaste harbored by the high Romantics is well known. See, for example, Latané, "Birth of the Author"; Manning, "Wordsworth in the *Keepsake*"; Newlyn, *Reading, Writing, and Romanticism.*

9. Klancher, *English Reading Audiences,* 81.

10. Ibid., 56.

11. Habermas, *Structural Transformation.*

12. Klancher, *English Reading Audiences,* 51.

13. Ibid., 51, 7, 67, 20.

14. Ibid., 58, 66, 72.

15. Ibid., 72.

16. Ibid., 66.

17. See Colla, *Conflicted Antiquities;* Gidal, *Poetic Exhibitions;* Jenkins, *Archeologists and Aesthetes.*

18. Jasanoff, *Edge of Empire.*

19. See, for example, Clifford, *Predicament of Culture;* Coombes, *Reinventing Africa;* Mitchell, *Colonising Egypt.*

20. Pascoe, *Hummingbird Cabinet,* 5.

21. Graham, *English Literary Periodicals.* See also Fader, *Periodical Context;* Fader and Bornstein, *British Periodicals.*

22. For a brief but illuminating glimpse into some of the titles of periodicals in the eighteenth and early nineteenth centuries, see appendix 8 of St. Clair, *Reading Nation,* 572–77. For a more comprehensive survey of the various periodicals within each era, see Sullivan, *British Literary Magazines,* vols. 1–2.

23. Fraser, Green, and Johnston, *Gender and the Victorian Periodical,* 83.

24. Jasanoff, *Edge of Empire,* 6.

25. "Characteristics of the Present State," 1. See also Marchand, *Athenaeum.*

26. "Characteristics of the Present State," 2.

27. Klancher, *English Reading Audiences,* 102.

28. Haydon, *Autobiography,* 1: 235.

29. *Annals of the Fine Arts* 3, no. 8 (1818): 171–72: Keats, "On Seeing the Elgin Marbles," lines 1, 9, 12 (*Poems,* 93); "To Haydon with a Sonnet Written on Seeing the Elgin Marbles," lines 1–2 (*Poems,* 94).

30. On the case to repatriate the Elgin Marbles, see Hitchens, *Imperial Spoils,* and Tournikiotis, *Parthenon and Its Impact.*

31. Keats, "On Seeing the Elgin Marbles," line 5.

32. Keats, "On First Looking into Chapman's Homer," lines 11, 14 (*Poems,* 64); Pratt, *Imperial Eyes.*

33. See Heringman, "Stones So Wondrous Cheap"; Larrabee, *English Bards and Grecian Marbles;* Scott, "Beautiful Ruins."

34. Hemingway, "Academic Theory" and *Landscape Imagery.*

35. See "Arrival of a colossal Head, said to be of Memnon," *Annals of the Fine Arts* 3, no. 10 (1818): 494–98; and "Colossal Head said to be of Memnon," 3, no. 2 (January 1819): 589–92.

36. See, for example, Fraser, Green, and Johnston, *Gender and the Victorian Periodical,* 16; Higgins, *Romantic Genius,* 7; Wheatley, Introduction, 7.

37. Parker, *Literary Magazines,* 1.

38. "Notices of Works in Hand," *Annals of the Fine Arts* (March 1817): 159–71.

39. See the sonnets "Upon the Sight of a Beautiful Picture" and "To B. R. Haydon, Esq.," which appeared in *Annals of the Fine Arts* (January 1818): 561.

40. Franta, "Keats and the Review Aesthetic."

41. Keats, "On a Grecian Urn," *Annals of the Fine Arts* 4, no. 15 (January 1820): 638–39. The poems on Greek artifacts were not Keats's only contributions to the *Annals.* "Ode to a Nightingale" appeared a few issues earlier (4, no. 13 [1819]: 354–56).

42. Keats, "Ode on Indolence," lines 5–7 (*Poems,* 375).

43. "Every reader of the Ode notices the emphasis that Keats throws on the silence of the Urn, with the words 'quietness', 'silence', 'unheard melodies', 'soft pipes', 'ditties of no tone', 'silent', and 'silent form'" (Jack, *Keats and the Mirror of Art*, 214).

44. Fraser, Green, and Johnston, *Gender and the Victorian Periodical;* Gilmartin, *Print Politics;* Haywood, *Revolution in Popular Literature.*

45. It might also, if looking toward the end of the century, examine the imperial fiction first published in magazines by authors such as Conrad and Hugh Clifford: see, for example, Dryden, "At the Court of *Blackwood's.*"

46. See, for example, Barrell, *Infection of Thomas De Quincey;* Russett, *De Quincey's Romanticism;* Rzepka, *Sacramental Commodities.*

47. Said, *Orientalism*, 73, 22.

48. For recent efforts to repatriate cultural patrimony, see Appiah, "Whose Culture Is It?"

49. Cannadine, *Ornamentalism*, 172.

50. Ibid., 10.

51. Majeed, *Ungoverned Imaginings.*

52. Leask, *British Romantic Writers;* Makdisi, *Romantic Imperialism.*

53. Cronin, *Romantic Victorians;* Nemoianu, *Taming of Romanticism.* See also Tucker, "House Arrest."

54. For an excellent review of the transformative shift to visuality in the late Romantic period, see Wood, *Shock of the Real.*

55. Habermas makes frequent use of the phrase. See also Klancher, "Discriminations,"; Warner, *Letters of the Republic.*

56. Casanova, *World Republic.*

57. Ibid., 81, 320.

58. Bourdieu, *Field of Cultural Production* and *Rules of Art.*

59. Casanova, *World Republic*, 354.

One. China for Sale

1. See, for example, Monsman, *Confessions of a Prosaic Dreamer.* For studies emphasizing Lamb's authorship as a product of literary collaboration, see Aaron, *Double Singleness*, and Hickey, "Double Bonds."

2. Lamb's blank verse tragedy, *John Woodvil*, was never performed, and although published in 1802, was damned by critics included in the *Edinburgh Review.* His short comedy *Mr. H——* failed miserably at its single performance in 1806. His poetry, included in a two-volume collected works in 1818, gained mixed reviews, and because critical response to volumes was warmer for its prose works, the 1818 volumes marked a definitive transition from Lamb's early efforts at poetry and toward prose.

3. Hazlitt, *Spirit of the Age*, 348.

4. Sullivan, *British Literary Magazines*, 2: 288.

5. "Prospectus," 57.

6. Bauer, *London Magazine.*

7. Qtd. in Shattock, *Politics and Reviewers,* 16.

8. Bauer, *London Magazine,* 70.

9. Schoenfield, "Voices Together," 261, 265.

10. See, for example, Kevin Gilmartin, who effectively demonstrates the "inconsistency in radical discourse"; or David Higgins and Robert Morrison, who separately show how the high Tory *Blackwood's* became a surprising defender of the radical Shelley; or Nanora Sweet, who reads the dialectical clash of Tory, Whig, and Radical discourses in the *New Monthly* (Gilmartin, *Print Politics,* 59; Higgins, *Romantic Genius,* 19–23; Morrison, "William Blackwood," 38; Sweet, "*New Monthly Magazine*").

11. "The Old Benchers at the Inner Temple," *London Magazine,* September 1821; *Works,* 82–91. Rather than citing the commonly used Lucas edition, textual quotations used in this chapter are drawn from the versions first published in the *London,* both because many essays were rewritten for the collation in the volumes *Elia* and *Last Essays of Elia* and to emphasize their contemporary appearance in periodicals. Subsequent quotations are cited parenthetically in the text.

12. De Quincey's collaboration with the *London* is discussed in Morrison, "Opium-Eaters."

13. Lamb, "Recollections of the South Sea House," 142; *Works,* 1–7, as "The South-Sea House."

14. Lamb, "Oxford in the Vacation"; *Works,* 7–12.

15. Charles Lamb to William Ayrton, April 18, 1817 (*Letters,* 3: 242).

16. Lamb, "Old China"; *Works,* 247–52.

17. Sekora, *Luxury.*

18. On the eighteenth-century transformation of consumer culture, see Brewer and Porter, *Consumption;* Weatherill, *Consumer Behaviour.*

19. Campell, *Romantic Ethic.*

20. Plumb, "Royal Porcelain Craze."

21. For the scapegoating of female consumers during chinamania, see Kowaleski-Wallace, *Consuming Subjects,* 57–69.

22. See the play *The Coffee-House Politician,* first performed in 1730 as *Rape upon Rape* (Fielding, *Complete Works,* 9: 96).

23. See *Tatler* 23 (May 31–June 2, 1709); *Spectator* 247 (December 13, 1711); 252 (December 19, 1711); 299 (February 12, 1719); 326 (March 14, 1712). For a general review of periodicals in the eighteenth-century culture of consumption, see Raven, "Defending Conduct and Property."

24. Pater, "The Character of the Humourist: Charles Lamb," in *Fortnightly Review,* September 1, 1878, 466–74, rpt. in *Nineteenth-Century Literature Criticism,* 10: 397.

25. Haven, "Romantic Art," 142.

26. Marx, *Capital,* 1: 163.

27. Charles Lamb to Thomas Manning, May 10, 1806 (*Letters of Charles and Mary Anne Lamb,* 2: 226).

28. Marx, *Capital,* 1: 163.

29. De Quincey, "Confessions," 3: 442–43; Pope, "Rape of the Lock," lines 105–17.

30. Lamb, "Mrs. Battle's Opinions" and "Dissertation upon Roast Pig"; *Works,* 32–37, 120–26.

31. "The salient features of the traditional English 'Willow pattern' design are building in the centre or the to the right of centre, a prominent Willow tree and two or three figures crossing a bridge to the left, away from the building, two doves being normally placed in the sky above the fleeing lovers" (Godden, *Caughley and Worcester Porcelains,* 15). See also Carswell, *Blue and White;* Moore, *Old China Book.*

32. Lovejoy, "Chinese Origin of Romanticism." See also Honour, *Vision of Cathay;* Impey, *Chinoiserie;* Porter, "Peculiar but Uninteresting Nation"; Spence, *Chan's Great Continent.*

33. Coleridge, "Kubla Khan, or A Vision in a Dream."

34. In 1818, for example, upon the publication of his *Works,* the *British Critic* described Lamb's poetry as "awkward and unsuccesful imitations" of Wordsworth." Similarly, in 1823, when the essays were collected into a volume, the *Monthly Review* noted that in the past Lamb's writing was often confused with that of Charles Lloyd, who bore the same initials (Reiman, *Romantics Reviewed,* A.1: 161; A.2: 773).

35. See, for example, Aaron, *Double Singleness.*

36. McFarland, *Romantic Cruxes.*

37. Lamb, "Witches, and Other Night-Fears"; *Works,* 65–70.

38. See, for example, Charles Lamb to Robert Lloyd, February 7, 1801 (*Letters of Charles and Mary Anne Lamb,* 1: 270–71).

39. Lamb, "Recollections of Christ's Hospital"; *Works,* 12–22, as "Christ's Hospital Five and Thirty Years Ago." For a different reading of the Christ's Hospital essay, but which still emphasizes that Lamb's essays "need to be read in their original periodical form," see Treadwell, "Impersonation and Autobiography."

40. Lamb, "Blakesmoor in H——shire"; *Works,* 153–57.

41. Porcelain's dynamic history—from costly item of fashion to everyday houseware to prized object of connoisseurship—is detailed in Joanna Baillie's fascinating poem "Lines to a Teapot." In prescient description of what the anthropologist Igor Kopytoff would later call the "cultural biography" of an object, Baillie's poem depicts the trajectory of a porcelain teapot from Chinese artisan, British importer, wealthy buyer, poor home, and ultimately back to genteel collectors.

42. Lowes, *Road to Xanadu;* Shaffer, *"Kubla Khan";* Hayter, *Opium;* Milligan, *Pleasures and Pains;* Richardson, *British Romanticism;* Schneider, *Coleridge, Opium, and Kubla Khan.*

43. Beetham, "Towards a Theory of the Periodical," 29.

44. Abrams, "Structure and Style," 202.

45. Bauer, *London Magazine,* 68.

46. See, for example, Charles Lamb to Bernard Barton and Lucy Barton, December 1, 1824 (*Letters,* 2: 446–48).

47. For accounts of the opening of China initiated by Raffles, see Bayley, *Imperial Meridian*, 64–67, 98–99. See also Greenberg, *British Trade.*

48. "Cho-fang" is another Elian pun. The term is likely a transliteration of *chī fàn,* which means "to eat" in Chinese.

49. Hulme, *Colonial Encounters.*

50. Howard, *Chinese Armorial Porcelain,* 108–13.

51. "Pottery and Porcelain," 33.

52. Liu, "Robinson Crusoe's Earthenware Pot." Lamb's co-optation of Chinese superiority at porcelain firing also anticipates a similar revision in British narratives about glass production. See Armstrong, *Victorian Glassworlds.*

53. Robinson, "Ode on a 'New Etrurian' Urn" and "Question of the Imprint of Wedgwood."

54. Wynter, *Introduction to European Porcelain,* 191.

55. Gigante, "Lamb's Low-Urban Taste."

Two. Deciphering *The Private Memoirs*

1. See, for example, Bloedé, "Hogg's *Private Memoirs*"; Gifford, *James Hogg,* 142–43; Miller, *Doubles,* 1–20, 16–17.

2. "New Publications, with Critical Remarks: 'The Private Memoirs and Confessions of a Justified Sinner,'" in *New Monthly Magazine* 11 (November 1, 1824): 506, rpt. in *Nineteenth-Century Literature Criticism,* 4: 278. Redekop, "Beyond Closure."

3. See, for example, Kiely, *Romantic Novel in England,* 208–32.

4. [Hogg], *Private Memoirs,* 169. All subsequent page citations are noted in the text.

5. "On the Cockney School of Poetry," 40, 39.

6. Wheatley, "Blackwood's Attacks" and "Paranoid Politics."

7. Duncan, "Edinburgh."

8. For an excellent discussion of this contradiction in *Blackwood's,* see Dart, "Romantic Cockneyism."

9. [Hogg], "Verses."

10. [Hogg], "Translation from an Ancient Chaldee Manuscript." Subsequent quotations are cited within the text and, in keeping with the biblical format, are noted by chapter and verse.

11. James Hogg to William Blackwood, September 25, 1817 (*Collected Letters,* 1: 303).

12. On the cultural authority accorded English in Enlightenment Scotland, see Crawford, *Devolving English Literature;* Crawford, *Scottish Invention of English Literature;* Sorensen, *Grammar of Empire.*

13. James Hogg to William Blackwood, September 25, 1817 (*Collected Letters,* 1: 303).

14. De Sacy is occasionally corrupted as "De Lacy" in pirated American versions of the *Noctes Ambrosianae.*

15. On Sylvestre de Sacy, see Said, *Orientalism.*

16. James Hogg to William Blackwood, September 25, 1817 (*Collected Letters,* 1: 303).

17. Leask, *British Romantic Writers,* 8.

18. Budge, *Rosetta Stone;* Parkinson, *Cracking Codes.*

19. Southey, *Letters from England,* 449.

20. Altick, "William Bullock"; Carrott, *Egyptian Revival;* Curl, *Egyptian Revival;* Porterfield, *Allure of Egypt;* Saglia, "Consuming Egypt."

21. Hughes, "James Hogg."

22. Matthews, "Egyptians in Scotland."

23. Parsons, "Parodic Background"; Pittock, *Invention of Scotland,* 37.

24. Grant, "Sphinx in the North."

25. On the auld alliance, see Macdougall, *Antidote to the English;* Bonner, "Scotland's 'Auld Alliance.'"

26. Pittock, *Celtic Identity* and *Poetry and Jacobite Politics.*

27. Editorship of *Blackwood's* was often more fluid. For a convincing argument that the publisher William Blackwood continued to be as involved in editing as Wilson, see Parker, *Literary Magazines,* 199n12, and Morrison, "William Blackwood."

28. James Hogg to William Blackwood, October 19, 1817 (*Collected Letters,* 1: 304–5).

29. Walter Scott to William Blackwood, November 1817 (*Letters,* 5: 6).

30. [Napier], *Hypocrisy Unveiled,* 5–6.

31. Bauer, *London Magazine.*

32. See 2.1: "Now, behold, as soon as they were gone, he sat down in his inner chamber, which looketh towards the street of Oman, and the road of Gabriel, as thou goest up into the land of Ambrose." These claims of origin may or may not have been true. In her history of the press, Margaret Oliphant notes that the sodden carousing in Edinburgh was a fiction invented in the relative calm of suburban Chiefswood (*Annals of a Publishing House,* 1: 261).

33. See, in addition to Murphy and Schoenfeld, Russett, "Gothic Violence."

34. Murphy, *Poetry as an Occupation,* 120.

35. Smith, *Scottish Literature,* 1972.

36. Daiches, *Paradox of Scottish Culture,* 22.

37. Watson, *Revolution,* 173.

38. Trumpener, *Bardic Nationalism.*

39. Strout, "Hogg's 'Chaldee Manuscript.'"

40. On Constable's oriental nicknames, see Mackenzie, *Noctes Ambrosianae,* 1: xix–xx, n. 4.

41. Similarly, in the "Memoir" prefixed to his later *Altrive Tales,* Hogg describes the Chaldee Manuscript as having been "interlarded" "with a good deal of devilry" (Hogg, *Altrive Tales,* 1832, cited in Strout, "Hogg's 'Chaldee Manuscript,'" 706).

42. Although Bainbridge does not dwell on the Rosetta Stone in particular, the rich history of Romantic identification with Napoleon is recounted in Bainbridge, *Napoleon and English Romanticism.*

43. Mason, "Three Burials."

44. The four court scenes in the novel are (1) George's trial for assaulting Wringhim at Arthur's Seat (34–36); (2) Drummond's trial (in absentia) for George's murder (38–39); (3) the arraignment and subsequent trial of Bell Calvert for theft (45–63); and (4) the trial for Blanchard's murderer, in which an innocent man is convicted (98).

45. Wortham, *Genesis of British Egyptology,* 69–83. Such commitment to hieroglyphs as a secret code may be another reason for the popularity of Egyptian motifs among Scottish Freemasonry, and it may also account for certain details within *The Private Memoirs.* One surname adopted by Wringhim in the course of his flight from Gil-martin is "Cowan," presumably a corruption of his given name, "Colwan," but also a derogatory term used to identify those not initiated into Freemasonry (146). Although it is understandably difficult to ascertain whether Hogg was a Mason, such clues provide further precedents for his Egyptian motifs, and certainly reiterate the use of Scottish nationalist sentiment to portray his exclusion from the Edinburgh elite.

46. Said, *Orientalism,* 80–88.

47. Simpson, *Romanticism, Nationalism.*

48. Colla, *Conflicted Antiquities;* Redekop, "Beyond Closure," 161.

49. To demonstrate the discursive shift that occurs within a single individual, here is the dialogue, annotated according to the punctuation and speech tags given in the text:

> (1) "Where will the ravens find a prey the night?"
> (2) "On the lean crazy souls o' Auchtermuchty," quo the thither.
> (1) "I fear they will be o'er weel wrappit up in the warm flannens o' to mak a meal o'," quo the first. "Whaten vile sounds are these that I hear coming bumming up the hill?"
> (2) "O these are the hymns and praises o' the auld wives and creeshy louns o' Auchtermuchty, wha are gaun crooning their way to heaven; an' gin it warna for the shame o' being beat, we might let our great enemy tak them. For sic a prize as he will hae! Heaven, forsooth! What shall we think o' heaven, if it is to be filled wi' vermin like thae, amang whom there is mair poverty and pollution, than I can name."
> (1) "No matter for that," said the first, "we cannot have our power set at defiance; though we should put them in the thief's hole, we must catch them, and catch them with their own bait too. Come all to church to-morrow, and I'll let you hear how I'll gull the saints of Auchtermuchty. In the mean time, there is a feast on the Sidlaw hills tonight, below the hill of Macbeth,—Mount, Diabolus, and fly." (137)

The dialogue is seeded with quotations and puns: the first corbie puns on how he'll "gull" some victims, and the whole conversation concludes with a command—

"Mount, Diabolus, and fly"—familiar to readers from Scott's poem *The Lay of the Last Minstrel* (in the *Lay,* it is spoken by a knight to his mount, possibly suggesting Hogg's burlesque of Scott in his reduction of chivalric romance to an absurd scene between two birds).

50. Duncan, *Scott's Shadow;* Fielding, *Writing and Orality.*

51. Campbell, "Hogg and the Bible," 23.

52. [Hogg], "Scots Mummy."

53. North debuted in *Blackwood's* in the series "Christopher in the Tent," which appeared in August and September 1819, and which included many other characters that would soon appear in the "Noctes Ambrosianae."

54. Thus, when recounting the conversation between himself and North, the Shepherd speaks and even thinks in dialect: "'Gude sauf us, Christy's mair nor half seas ower!' thinks I; 'but I maunna pretend no to understand him. . . . Ay, ye're no far wrang, man,' I says." But as the letter proceeds from their conversation to the Scots Mummy tale, Hogg's voice notably shifts to standard English: "But at length [I heard] a subject that hit my fancy to a hair; and the moment that I first heard the relation, I said to myself, 'This is the very thing for old Christy.'"

55. Russett, *Fictions and Fakes;* Stewart, *Crimes of Writing.*

56. Murphy, "Impersonation and Authorship." See also Mackenzie, "History of Blackwood's," xi.

57. Schoenfield, "Butchering James Hogg."

58. Garside, "Hogg and the Blackwoodian Novel," 13.

59. Byron to John Murray, September 23, 1822 (*Letters,* 10: 40).

60. James Hogg to William Blackwood, October 19, 1817 (*Collected Letters,* 1: 305).

61. Parker, *Literary Magazines,* 15.

62. Altick, *Presence of the Present.* See also Mayo, *English Novel in the Magazines.*

63. Price, *Anthology and the Rise of the Novel.*

64. Beetham, "Towards a Theory of the Periodical," 27.

65. Klancher, *English Reading Audiences,* 51.

Three. "But Another Name for Her Who Wrote"

1. [Thackeray], "Word on the Annuals."

2. An exception is noted by Fernandez, "Graven Images." However, the poem that Fernandez discusses is only a single poem in Landon's vast corpus.

3. In addition to Leighton and Stephenson, below, see also Mellor, *Romanticism and Gender,* 110–24; Armstrong, *Victorian Poetry;* Francis, "Letitia Landon"; Linkin, "Romantic Aesthetics." For Landon's objectification specifically in the periodical press, see Sanders, "Meteor Wreaths."

4. [Bulwer-Lytton], "Romance and Reality," 546.

5. Altick, *English Common Reader,* 362–63; Graham, *English Literary Periodicals,* 368–69. See also Terence Hoagwood and Kathryn Ledbetter, who view the annuals

as a "distinctly different genre" that "deserve[s] to be studied as a unique publishing phenomenon" (*"Colour'd Shadows"*, 77). On the annuals' adverse effect on poetry production and sales, see also Erickson, *Economy of Literary Form*, 29–33.

6. Beetham, "Towards a Theory of the Periodical," 23. Joanne Shattock makes a similar point about bound reprints of reviews asserting their "non-ephemerality" (*Politics and Reviewers*, 109).

7. Linley, "Centre That Would Not Hold."

8. "The basic unit for the study of Victorian cultural history is the individual issue of a Victorian periodical" (Woolf, "Charting the Golden Stream," 27).

9. Eliot, *Middlemarch*, 237.

10. Ibid., 235.

11. Tucker, "House Arrest," 526.

12. Pascoe, *Romantic Theatricality*, 229–43.

13. Prins, *Victorian Sappho*, 191–209.

14. Cronin, *Romantic Victorians*, 95; Leighton, *Victorian Women Poets*, 61.

15. Although McGann is speaking specifically of Landon's poems for the *Literary Gazette*, he sees those contributions as having "forecast the coming of the gift books and annuals" (*Poetics of Sensibility*, 146, 144).

16. "Corinne at the Cape of Misena," *Amulet*, 1832. Textual quotations are from the reprint in Landon, *Selected Writings*, 142–46, lines 1–3. Hereafter cited in text by line number.

17. Letitia Landon to Charles Heath, May 19, no year. Original at Huntington Library, in Daniel Maclise, *A Gallery of Illustrious Literary Characters* (London: Chatto and Windus, 1873).

18. [Hunt], "Pocket-Books and Keepsakes," 14.

19. Rappoport, "Buyer Beware," 454, 467.

20. Craciun, *Fatal Women*, 198.

21. Hofkosh, *Sexual Politics*, chap. 4; Lawford, "Bijoux beyond Possession"; Taylor, "Barrett Browning's Subversion."

22. Klancher, *English Reading Audiences*, 9.

23. Rappoport, "Buyer Beware," 461.

24. Stephenson, *Letitia Landon*, 72.

25. As further illustration of the reductively visual manner in which Staël relies upon the Roman setting to portray Corinne's fame, note the rigidly taxonomic arrangement by which the crowning ceremony at the Capitol is described. Inside the Capitol, Corinne and the senator who is to crown her are "in the center of the hall . . . surrounded by his brothers in office; on one side, all the cardinals and most distinguished ladies of Rome; on the other, the members of the Academy; while the opposite extremity was filled by some portion of the multitude who had followed Corinne [through the streets to the ceremony]. The chair destined for her was placed a step lower than that of the senator." In the rigid visual arrangement of the participants described in this scene, Staël demarcates a spatial hierarchy that suggests the Capitol's function as a physical stage, where Roman architecture is the background for cultural and historical greatness (*Corinne*, 21).

26. Braudy, *Frenzy of Renown,* 55–189.

27. See Davidoff and Hall, *Family Fortunes,* 160–61.

28. Moers, *Literary Women,* 181.

29. Landon to S. C. Hall, 1837 (*Letters,* 167).

30. "L." [Landon], "Rome."

31. Landon, *Improvisatrice,* lines 1–3. Hereafter cited in text by line number.

32. "Advertisement," ibid.

33. Riess, "Laetitia Landon," 817.

34. For example, Leighton, *Victorian Women Poets,* 59; Miller, *Margaret Fuller,* xxi.

35. Buzard, *Beaten Track;* O'Connor, *Romance of Italy.* See also Brand, *Italy and the English Romantics.*

36. Simone Balayé, *Les Carnets de Voyage de Mme. De Staël,* 1616, cited in Vallois, "Voice as Fossil," 51.

37. For example, Moskal, "Lady Morgan's Travel Books."

38. See, for example, Hemans's "The Indian Woman's Song," from *Records of Women,* or Wordsworth's "The Complaint of a Forsaken Indian Woman," from *Lyrical Ballads,* a poem about a Native American "Indian" but also a typically nineteenth-century consideration of the fate of widows in exotic cultures.

39. Mackenzie, *Noctes Ambrosianae,* 1: 466 (no. 16, August 1824).

40. See, for example, Emma Francis, who claims that the Improvisatrice is "one of Landon's most intense preoccupations" with the "space created by the dialogue between visual and written texts" ("Letitia Landon," 108).

41. "Review of the Improvisatrice," 157.

42. The title and translation credits to this edition of Staël's *Corinne* further illustrate Landon's identification with Corinne. The volume's title page includes the byline "Translated by Isabel Hill, with Metrical Versions of the Odes by L. E. Landon," and two of the four translated odes include annotations that remind the reader of Landon's involvement. Such repeated allusion to Landon makes her contribution a point of attraction in the edition—after all, in 1833 such contributions from the "English Corinne" would have distinguished the volume from the many other editions of the novel available at that time. Indeed, in the odes that repeat Landon's translation credit, those credits assert her involvement at the cost of the narrative fiction. The "Chant of Corinne at the Capitol" has a footnote that reminds readers that the passage was "Translated by Miss L. E. Landon" (25), and hence contradicts the novel's claim that the text is Corinne's own improvisation. "Corinne's Chant in the Vicinity of Naples" goes even further and includes the "L.E.L." initials at the end of the ode, and thereby suggests that Landon is the author of that text (223). By thus disrupting the fiction of Corinne's improvisation, these credits to Landon all but displace Staël as the authorial referent of the novel.

43. Montwieler, "Laughing at Love."

44. [Johnstone], "Books of the Season," 678.

45. Said, *Culture and Imperialism,* 97.

46. [Thackeray], "Word on the Annuals," 762.

47. Landon, "Macao," rpt. in Leader and Haywood, *Romantic Period Writings,* 208–9.

48. Landon, "The Chinese Pagoda," rpt. in Leader and Haywood, *Romantic Period Writings,* 210–11.

49. Stephenson, *Letitia Landon,* 143.

50. Jump, "False Prudery," 12.

51. Letitia Landon to Anna Thomson, Summer 1831 (*Letters,* 66).

52. Letitia Landon to Anna Maria Hall, August 1833 (*Letters,* 91).

53. [Thackeray], "Word on the Annuals," 763.

54. Lootens, "Receiving the Legend."

55. Ibid., 245.

56. [Thackeray], "Word on the Annuals," 763.

Four. Only "a Little Above the Usual Run of Periodical Poesy"

1. Byron, *Childe Harold's Pilgrimage: A Romaunt,* 3 (in *Complete Poetical Works,* vol. 2), quoting from Fougeret de Monbron, *Le Cosmopolite,* 1753.

2. For example, neither Jerome McGann nor Jerome Christensen discuss the *Liberal* at any significant length in their seminal studies of Byron; Fred Rosen completely overlooks the magazine in his discussion of Byron's politics, despite Rosen's specific focus on the poet's place in the history of British liberalism; and even Herman Ward's 1973 study devoted to Byron's relationship with magazines focuses on his relationship with reviews but barely considers the *Liberal.* See Christensen, *Lord Byron's Strength;* McGann, *Fiery Dust;* Rosen, *Bentham, Byron, and Greece;* Ward, *Byron and the Magazines.* Similarly, if Byron criticism considers the *Island* at all, the poem is "a rattling good yarn," a "mixed bag," or "a flawed poem of great interest." See Fleck, "Romance in Byron's *The Island,*" 165; McGann, *Fiery Dust,* 193; Woodring, *Politics in English Romantic Poetry,* 222.

3. Byron to Leigh Hunt, July 25, 1823 (*Letters,* 10: 90).

4. Byron, *Don Juan,* 11.55.8 (in *Complete Poetical Works,* vol. 5).

5. Byron to John Hunt, March 17, 1823 (*Letters,* 10: 123).

6. Byron, *English Bards,* line 60 (in *Complete Poetical Works,* 1: 227–64).

7. Byron to John Cam Hobhouse, July 2, 1811; Byron to Thomas Moore, December 25, 1820 (*Letters and Journals,* 2: 55–56; 7: 254).

8. Graham, *English Literary Periodicals,* 286.

9. The *OED* provides only one instance (from an 1820 article in the *Edinburgh Review*) of the word that antedates the periodical the *Liberal.* For further etymology, and one that includes the magazine among other political terminology of the eighteenth and nineteenth centuries, see Williams, *Keywords,* 179–81.

10. [Hunt], "Preface," vii. Interestingly, the contemporary *New Monthly Magazine* claimed a similar conflation of literature and politics. See Sweet, "*New Monthly Magazine.*"

11. *Windsor Eton Express and General Advertiser,* January 12, 1822, 3, qtd. in Bebbington, "Most Remarkable Man."

12. William Wordsworth to Walter Savage Landor, April 20, 1822 (Wordsworth, *Letters,* 4: 124); "Memoirs of the Living Poets," col. 826.

13. *Blackwood's,* March 1822, qtd. in Marshall, *Byron, Shelley, Hunt.*

14. Review of the *Liberal, New European Magazine,* October 1822, 354–63, in Reiman, *Romantics Reviewed,* B, 5: 1845. "Letter from London," *Blackwood's,* vol. 11 (1822): 237, cited in Hogg, "Contemporary Reception." Similarly, the *London Literary Gazette* referred to the magazine as "the grand Pisan Conspiracy."

15. [Hunt], "Preface," vii.

16. Ibid.

17. Franklin, "Cosmopolitanism and Catholic Culture." Franklin also notes the symbolic significance of Byron's translation of Pulci in the *Liberal*'s fourth and final issue. See also Saglia, "Mediterranean Unrest."

18. Marshall, *Byron, Shelley, Hunt,* 89.

19. Higgins, *Romantic Genius,* 123. Higgins specifically discusses Hazlitt's famous essay "My First Acquaintance with Poets," which appeared in the *Liberal*'s third issue, but his claim might be true of the magazine as whole.

20. Mazzeo, "Mixture of All the Styles."

21. For Gilmartin, the *Liberal* was "an impressive if finally imperfect effort to join the popular radical hostility of the 1810s . . . to an emerging, proto-Arnoldian sense of liberalism" (*Print Politics,* 211).

22. For an interesting comparative case of literary and political "triangulation," see the discussion of British interest in South America in the *New Monthly Magazine* by Sweet, "Hitherto Closed."

23. Marshall, *Byron, Shelley, Hunt,* 133–34.

24. "Review.—the Liberal," col. 1142.

25. The objections to Byron's association with Hunt were class-based, and they extended to Hazlitt. See Wu, "Talking Pimples."

26. Marshall, *Byron, Shelley, Hunt,* 25.

27. Ibid., 71.

28. Lamb, *Preserving the Self;* Rennie, *Far-Fetched Facts;* Smith, *European Vision.* For a postcolonial revision of European historiography of the South Seas, see Obeyesekere, *Apotheosis of Captain Cook.*

29. Calder, "The Island."

30. Dening, *Mr. Bligh's Bad Language,* 113.

31. Fulford, Lee, and Kitson, "Banks, Bligh, and the Breadfruit," "Sir Joseph Banks."

32. Dening, *Mr. Bligh's Bad Language,* 24.

33. For the *Bounty* history, see, in addition to the sources previously mentioned, Caroline Alexander, *Bounty.*

34. Southey, "A Vision of Judgment," 10: 236.

35. Byron, *The Island* (in *Complete Poetical Works,* 7: 26–74). Subsequent refer-

ences are cited in text by canto and line number. Burke, *Reflections,* 232. The parallels between Bligh and Antoinette are often uncanny. When his men rejected the pumpkin that Bligh served instead of bread, the captain indifferently responded that "they would eat grass."

36. On the "paradox" that breadfruit, "the very symbol of free and unencumbered life," supported slavery, see Dening, *Mr. Bligh's Bad Language,* 13.

37. Studies of this convention are legion. See Ashcroft, Griffiths, and Tiffin, *Empire Writes Back;* Lewis, *Gendering Orientalism;* McClintock, *Imperial Leather;* Young, *Colonial Desire.*

38. See, for example, Addison, "Elysian and Effeminate"; Addison, "Gender and Race"; Franklin, *Byron's Heroines,* 89–98.

39. Byron to Count Alfred d'Orsay, April 22, 1823 (*Letters,* 10: 156).

40. See Christensen, *Lord Byron's Strength;* McGann, *Don Juan in Context.*

41. Review of *The Island, New European Magazine* 3 (July 1823): 47–51 (quote on 51), rpt. in Reiman, *Romantics Reviewed,* B, 5: 1870; Coleridge, *Works of Lord Byron,* 5: 615n1.

42. Hazlitt, *Spirit of the Age,* 104.

43. Leigh Hunt to Elizabeth Kent, April 7, 1823, cited in Marshall, *Byron, Shelley, Hunt,* 178n40.

44. Byron to Douglas Kinnaird, March 8, 1823 (*Letters,* 10: 117).

45. Schmidt, "Bligh, Christian, Murray, and Napoleon," *Byron Journal.* See also Dening, *Mr. Bligh's Bad Language,* 302.

46. Byron, *English Bards,* 228 (Preface).

47. Byron to John Cam Hobhouse, July 6 1821 (*Letters,* 8: 148).

48. Mary Shelley to John Murray, June 10, 1832 (*Letters,* 2: 163–64).

49. Byron, *Island,* 144n1.

50. See, for example, Fleck, "Romance in Byron's *The Island.*"

51. James Hogg to William Blackwood, October 19, 1817 (*Collected Letters,* 1: 305).

52. Byron's depiction of Torquil may have been influenced by George Stewart and Peter Haywood, the two well-born midshipmen aboard the *Bounty.* Both young men adapted easily to life on Tubuai, as the *Pandora* sailors later recalled the wails of Stewart's native wife, who attempted to follow the departing vessel in her canoe. Byron would have been familiar with their history, as Heywood's family conducted a successful and carefully orchestrated campaign to pardon the young sailor from the likely death sentence for mutiny. However, as indicated by Torquil's name, Byron's emphasis in the character is on the fictional and intertextual rather than the historical representation of Bligh and Christian.

53. Beatty, "Fiction's Limit and Eden's Door," 24.

54. McGann, *Romantic Ideology,* 1.

55. Fulford, "Poetic Hells and Pacific Edens."

56. Hulme, *Colonial Encounters,* 2; emphasis in the original.

57. Marshall, *Byron, Shelley, Hunt,* 120–21, 217–27.

58. Ibid., 121–26; see also 228–37.
59. Kahn, "Pastoral Byron."

Conclusion

1. Higgins, *Romantic Genius,* 9.
2. Ibid., 4.
3. Hazlitt, "On the Living Poets," 220, 222. See also Bennett, *Romantic Poets.*
4. [Mill], "Periodical Literature," 207.
5. Thomas Macaulay to Macvey Napier, June 24, 1842 (*Letters,* 4: 40).
6. Woolf, "Charting the Golden Stream," 27.
7. [J. Scott], "Signs of the Times," 154.
8. [Carlyle], "Signs of the Times," *Edinburgh Review* 49 (1829). Quotations are from Carlyle, *Works of Thomas Carlyle,* 27: 61.
9. [Hunt], "On Periodical Essays," *Examiner,* January 10, 1808, rpt. in *Hunt's Literary Criticism,* 77, 79.
10. Parker, *Literary Magazines,* 1.
11. "Prospectus," 57.
12. Goodman, "Loophole in the Retreat." See also Ellison, "News, Blues, and Cowper's Busy World."
13. Anderson, *Imagined Communities,* 35.
14. Said, *Culture and Imperialism.*
15. Leigh Hunt to Percy and Mary Shelley, September 21, 1821 (*Correspondence,* 1: 172).
16. Mackenzie, *Noctes Ambrosianae,* 1: xix–xx, n. 4.
17. Klancher, *English Reading Audiences,* 58.
18. James Gillray, "The Plumb-Pudding in Danger," 1805. In the picture, Napoleon is shown slicing off a hefty portion of Europe, in graphic depiction of his territorial seizures, while Pitt has fork and knife stuck deep into the Atlantic Ocean, in vivid demonstration of British naval supremacy.
19. Appropriately, in exemplification of the various meanings of "imperialism," the *American Heritage Dictionary,* 4th ed., gives "publishing empire" as one example of this usage.

Bibliography

Aaron, Jane. *A Double Singleness: Gender and the Writings of Charles and Mary Lamb.* Oxford: Clarendon Press, 1991.

Abrams, M. H. "Structure and Style in the Greater Romantic Lyric." In *Romanticism and Consciousness: Essays in Criticism,* edited by Harold Bloom, 201–29. New York: W. W. Norton, 1970.

Addison, Catherine. "'Elysian and Effeminate': Byron's *The Island* as a Revisionary Text." *SEL* 35 (1995): 687–706.

———. "Gender and Race in Byron's *The Island* and Mitford's *Christina." Antipodes* 18, no. 1 (2004): 72–76.

Alexander, Caroline. *The Bounty: The True Story of the Mutiny on the Bounty.* New York: Penguin, 2003.

Altick, Richard D. *The English Common Reader: A Social History of the Mass Reading Public, 1800–1900.* Chicago: University of Chicago Press, 1957.

———. *The Presence of the Present: Topics of the Day in the Victorian Novel.* Columbus: Ohio State University Press, 1991.

———. "William Bullock and the Egyptian Hall." In *The Shows of London,* 235–52. Cambridge, MA: Harvard University Press, 1978.

Anderson, Benedict. *Imagined Communities: Reflections on the Origin and Spread of Nationalism.* Revised ed. 1991. Reprint, London: Verso, 1996.

Appiah, Kwame Anthony. "Whose Culture Is It?" *New York Review of Books* 53, no. 2 (2006): 38–41.

Armstrong, Isobel. *Victorian Glassworlds: Glass Culture and the Imagination, 1830–1880.* Oxford: Oxford University Press, 2008.

———. *Victorian Poetry: Poetry, Poetics and Politics.* London: Routledge, 1993.

Ashcroft, Bill, Gareth Griffiths, and Helen Tiffin. *The Empire Writes Back: Theory and Practice in Post-Colonial Literatures.* 2nd ed. New York: Routledge, 2002.

Baillie, Joanna. "Lines to a Teapot." In *The Dramatic and Poetical Works of Joanna Baillie,* 799–801. London: Longman, Brown, Green, and Longman's, 1851.

Bainbridge, Simon. *Napoleon and English Romanticism.* Cambridge: Cambridge University Press, 1995.

Barrell, John. *The Infection of Thomas De Quincey: A Psychopathology of Imperialism.* New Haven, CT: Yale University Press, 1991.

Bauer, Josephine. *The London Magazine, 1820–29.* Copenhagen: Rosenkilde and Bagger, 1953.

Bayley, C. A. *Imperial Meridian: The British Empire and the World, 1780–1830.* London: Longman, 1989.

Beatty, Bernard. "Fiction's Limit and Eden's Door." In *Byron and the Limits of Fiction,* edited by Bernard Beatty and Vincent Newey, 1–38. Totowa, NJ: Barnes & Noble Books, 1988.

Bebbington, W. G. "The Most Remarkable Man of His Age: Byron in *the Windsor and Eton Express and General Advertiser.*" *Keats-Shelley Memorial Bulletin* 7 (1956): 27–31.

Beetham, Margaret. "Towards a Theory of the Periodical as a Publishing Genre." In *Investigating Victorian Journalism,* edited by Laurel Brake, Aled Jones, and Lionel Madden, 19–32. New York: St. Martin's Press, 1990.

Bennett, Andrew. *Romantic Poets and the Culture of Posterity.* Cambridge: Cambridge University Press, 1999.

Bloedé, Barbara. "James Hogg's *Private Memoirs and Confessions of a Justified Sinner:* The Genesis of the Double." *Etudes Anglaises* 16 (1973): 174–86.

Bonner, Elizabeth. "Scotland's 'Auld Alliance' with France, 1295–1560." *History* 84, no. 273 (1999): 5–30.

Bourdieu, Pierre. *The Field of Cultural Production: Essays on Art and Literature.* Translated by Randal Johnson. New York: Columbia University Press, 1993.

———. *The Rules of Art: Genesis and Structure of the Literary Field.* Translated by Susan Emanuel. Stanford, CA: Stanford University Press, 1996.

Brand, C. P. *Italy and the English Romantics: The Italianate Fashion in the Early Nineteenth-Century England.* Cambridge: Cambridge University Press, 1957.

Braudy, Leo. *The Frenzy of Renown: Fame and Its History.* Oxford: Oxford University Press, 1986.

Brewer, John, and Roy Porter, eds. *Consumption and the World of Goods.* London: Routledge, 1993.

Budge, E. A. Wallis. *The Rosetta Stone.* New York: Dover Publications, 1989.

[Bulwer-Lytton, Edward]. "Romance and Reality." *New Monthly Magazine* 32, no. 132 (December 1831): 545–51.

Burke, Edmund. *Reflections on the Revolution in France, 1790.* Edited by J. C. D. Clark. Palo Alto, CA: Stanford University Press, 2001.

Buzard, James. *The Beaten Track: European Tourism, Literature, and the Ways to Culture, 1800–1918.* Oxford: Oxford University Press, 1993.

Byron, George Gordon, Lord. *Byron's Letters and Journals.* Edited by Leslie A. Marchand. 10 vols. Cambridge, MA: Harvard University Press, 1973–1980.

———. *The Complete Poetical Works.* Edited by Jerome McGann. 7 vols. Oxford: Clarendon Press, 1980–93.

Calder, Angus. "'The Island': Scotland, Greece and Romantic Savagery." In *Byron and Scotland: Radical or Dandy?* edited by Angus Calder, 132–50. Totowa, NJ: Barnes and Noble Books, 1989.

Campell, Colin. *The Romantic Ethic and the Spirit of Modern Consumerism.* Oxford: B. Blackwell, 1987.

Campbell, Ian. "James Hogg and the Bible." *Scottish Literary Journal* 10, no. 1 (1983): 14–29.

Cannadine, David. *Ornamentalism: How the British Saw Their Empire.* Oxford: Oxford University Press, 2001.

[Carlyle, Thomas]. "Signs of the Times." In *The Works of Thomas Carlyle,* 56–82. New York: Charles Scribner's Sons, 1899.

Carrott, Richard G. *The Egyptian Revival: Its Sources, Monuments, and Meaning, 1801–1858.* Berkeley: University of California Press, 1978.

Carswell, John, ed. *Blue and White: Chinese Porcelain and Its Impact on the Western World.* Chicago: University of Chicago Press, 1985.

Casanova, Pascale. *The World Republic of Letters.* Translated by M. B. DeBevoise. Cambridge, MA: Harvard University Press, 2004.

"Characteristics of the Present State of English Literature." *Athenaeum,* January 2, 1828, 1–2.

Christensen, Jerome. *Lord Byron's Strength: Romantic Writing and Commercial Society.* Baltimore, MD: Johns Hopkins University Press, 1993.

Clifford, James. *The Predicament of Culture: Twentieth-Century Ethnography, Literature, and Art.* Cambridge, MA: Harvard University Press, 1988.

Coleridge, Ernest Hartley, ed. *The Works of Lord Byron.* 13 vols. 1902. Reprint, London: John Murray, 1924.

Coleridge, Samuel Taylor. "Kubla Khan: or, A Vision in a Dream." In *Poetical Works,* edited by J. C. C. Mays, 509–14. Princeton, NJ: Princeton University Press, 2001.

Colla, Elliott. *Conflicted Antiquities: Egyptology, Egyptomania, Egyptian Modernity.* Durham, NC: Duke University Press, 2007.

Coombes, Annie E. *Reinventing Africa: Museums, Material Culture, and Popular Imagination in Late Victorian and Edwardian England.* New Haven, CT: Yale University Press, 1994.

Craciun, Adriana. *Fatal Women of Romanticism.* Cambridge: Cambridge University Press, 2003.

Crawford, Robert. *Devolving English Literature.* New York: Oxford University Press, 1992.

———, ed. *The Scottish Invention of English Literature.* Cambridge: Cambridge University Press, 1998.

Cronin, Richard. *Romantic Victorians: English Literature, 1824–1840.* New York: Palgrave, 2002.

Curl, James Stevens. *The Egyptian Revival.* New York: Routledge, 2005.

Daiches, David. *The Paradox of Scottish Culture: The Eighteenth-Century Experience.* London: Oxford University Press, 1964.

Dart, Gregory. "Romantic Cockneyism: Hazlitt and the Periodical Press." *Romanticism* 6, no. 2 (2000): 143–62.

Davidoff, Leonore, and Catherine Hall. *Family Fortunes: Men and Women of the English Middle Class, 1780–1850.* Chicago: University of Chicago Press, 1987.

Demata, Massimiliano. "Prejudiced Knowledge: Travel Literature in the *Edinburgh Review.*" In *British Romanticism and the Edinburgh Review,* edited by Massimiliano Demata and Duncan Wu, 82–101. New York: Palgrave, 2002.

Dening, Greg. *Mr. Bligh's Bad Language: Passion, Power and Theatre on the Bounty.* Cambridge: Cambridge University Press, 1992.

De Quincey, Thomas. "Confessions of an English Opium-Eater." In *Collected Writings of Thomas De Quincey,* edited by David Masson, 209–449. Edinburgh: Adam and Charles Black, 1890.

Dryden, Linda. "At the Court of *Blackwood's:* In the Kampong of Hugh Clifford." In *Print Culture and the Blackwood Tradition, 1805–1930,* edited by David Finkelstein, 215–35. Toronto: University of Toronto Press, 2006.

Duncan, Ian. "Edinburgh, Capital of the Nineteenth Century." In *Romantic Metropolis: the Urban Scene of British Culture, 1780–1840,* edited by James Chandler and Kevin Gilmartin, 45–64. Cambridge: Cambridge University Press, 2005.

———. *Scott's Shadow: The Novel in Romantic Edinburgh.* Princeton, NJ: Princeton University Press, 2007.

Eliot, George. *Middlemarch.* Edited by Gregory Maertz. Peterborough, Ontario: Broadview, 2004.

Ellison, Julie. "News, Blues, and Cowper's Busy World." *Modern Language Quarterly* 62, no. 3 (2001): 219–37.

Erickson, Lee. *The Economy of Literary Form: English Literature and the Industrialization of Publishing, 1800–1850.* Baltimore, MD: Johns Hopkins University Press, 1996.

Fader, Daniel. *The Periodical Context of English Literature, 1709–1907.* Ann Arbor, MI: University Microfilms, 1971.

Fader, Daniel, and George Bornstein. *British Periodicals of the 18th and 19th Centuries.* Ann Arbor, MI: University Microfilms, 1972.

Fernandez, Jean. "Graven Images: The Woman Writer, the Indian Poetess, and Imperial Aesthetics in L.E.L.'s 'Hindoo Temples and Palaces at Madura.'" *Victorian Poetry* 43, no. 1 (2005): 35–52.

Fielding, Henry. *The Complete Works of Henry Fielding.* Edited by William Ernest Henley. 16 vols. London: William Heinemann, 1903.

Fielding, Penny. *Writing and Orality: Nationality, Culture, and Nineteenth-Century Scottish Fiction.* Oxford: Oxford University Press, 1996.

Fleck, P. D. "Romance in Byron's *The Island.*" In *Byron: A Symposium,* edited by J. D. Jump, 163–83. New York: Barnes and Noble Books, 1975.

Francis, Emma. "Letitia Landon: Public Fantasy and the Private Sphere." *Essays and Studies* (1998): 93–115.

Franklin, Caroline. *Byron's Heroines.* Oxford: Clarendon Press, 1992.

———. "Cosmopolitanism and Catholic Culture: Byron, Italian Poetry, and *The*

Liberal." In *British Romanticism and Italian Literature: Translating, Reviewing, Rewriting,* edited by Laura Bandiera, 255–68. Amsterdam: Rodopi, 2005.

Franta, Andrew. "Keats and the Review Aesthetic." *Studies in Romanticism* 38 (1999): 343–64.

Fraser, Hilary, Stephanie Green, and Judith Johnston. *Gender and the Victorian Periodical.* Cambridge: Cambridge University Press, 2003.

Fulford, Tim, Debbie Lee, and Peter J. Kitson. "Banks, Bligh, and the Breadfruit: Slave Plantations, Tropical Islands and the Rhetoric of Romanticism." In *Literature, Science and Exploration in the Romantic Era,* 108–26. Cambridge: Cambridge University Press, 2004.

———. "Sir Joseph Banks and His Networks." In *Literature, Science and Exploration in the Romantic Era,* 33–45. Cambridge: Cambridge University Press, 2004.

Fulford, Timothy. "Poetic Hells and Pacific Edens." *Romanticism on the Net,* no. 32–33 (2003–4).

Garside, Peter. "Hogg and the Blackwoodian Novel." *Studies in Hogg and his World* 15 (2004): 5–20.

Gidal, Eric. *Poetic Exhibitions: Romantic Aesthetics and the Pleasures of the British Museum.* Lewisburg, PA: Bucknell University Press, 2001.

Gifford, Douglas. *James Hogg.* Edinburgh: Ramsay Head Press, 1976.

Gigante, Denise. "Lamb's Low-Urban Taste." In *Taste: A Literary History,* 89–116. New Haven, CT: Yale University Press, 2005.

Gilmartin, Kevin. *Print Politics: The Press and Radical Opposition in Early Nineteenth-Century England.* Cambridge: Cambridge University Press, 1996.

Godden, Geoffrey A. *Caughley and Worcester Porcelains, 1775–1800.* New York: Frederick A. Praeger, 1969.

Goodman, Kevis. "The Loophole in the Retreat: The Culture of News and the Early Life of Romantic Self-Consciousness." *South Atlantic Quarterly* 102, no. 1 (2003): 25–52.

Graham, Walter. *English Literary Periodicals.* New York: Thomas Nelson and Sons, 1930.

Grant, Eric. "The Sphinx in the North: Egyptian Influences on Landscape, Architecture and Interior Design in Eighteenth- and Nineteenth-Century Scotland." In *The Iconography of Landscape: Essays on the Symbolic Representation, Design, and Use of Past Environments,* edited by Denis Cosgrove and Stephen Daniels, 236–53. Cambridge: Cambridge University Press, 1988.

Greenberg, Michael. *British Trade and the Opening of China, 1800–1842.* Cambridge: Cambridge University Press, 1951.

Habermas, Jürgen. *The Structural Transformation of the Public Sphere: An Inquiry into a Category of Bourgeois Society.* Translated by Thomas Burger with the assistance of Frederick Lawrence. 8th ed. Cambridge: MIT Press, 1996.

Haven, Richard. "The Romantic Art of Charles Lamb." *ELH* 30, no. 2 (1963): 137–46.

Haydon, Benjamin Robert. *The Autobiography and Memoirs of Benjamin Robert Haydon.* Edited by Tom Taylor. New edition. 2 vols. New York: Harcourt, Brace, 1926.

Haywood, Ian. *The Revolution in Popular Literature: Print, Politics, and the People, 1790–1860.* Cambridge: Cambridge University Press, 2004.

Hayter, Alethea. *Opium and the Romantic Imagination.* London: Faber, 1968.

Hazlitt, William. "On the Living Poets." In *Lectures on the English Poets,* 220–56. London: Oxford University Press, 1924.

———. *The Spirit of the Age.* New York: Derby and Jackson, 1859.

Hemingway, Andrew. "Academic Theory versus Association Aesthetics: The Ideological Forms of a Conflict of Interests in the Early Nineteenth Century." *Ideas and Production,* no. 5 (1988): 18–42.

———. *Landscape Imagery and Urban Culture in Early Nineteenth-Century Britain.* Cambridge: Cambridge University Press, 1992.

Heringman, Noah. "'Stones So Wondrous Cheap.'" *Studies in Romanticism* 37, no. 1 (1998): 43–63.

Hickey, Alison. "Double Bonds: Charles Lamb's Romantic Collaborations." *English Literary History* 63 (1996): 735–71.

Higgins, David. *Romantic Genius and the Literary Magazine: Biography, Celebrity, Politics.* Routledge, 2005.

Hitchens, Christopher. *Imperial Spoils: The Curious Case of the Elgin Marbles.* New York: Hill and Wang, 1988.

Hoagwood, Terence Allan, and Kathryn Ledbetter. *"Colour'd Shadows": Contexts in Publishing, Printing, and Reading Nineteenth-Century British Women Writers.* New York: Palgrave, 2005.

Hofkosh, Sonia. *Sexual Politics and the Romantic Author.* Cambridge: Cambridge University Press, 1998.

Hogg, James. *The Collected Letters of James Hogg.* Edited by Gillian Hughes. 3 vols. Edinburgh: Edinburgh University Press, 2004.

[Hogg, James]. *The Private Memoirs and Confessions of a Justified Sinner.* Edited by P. D. Garside. Edinburgh: Edinburgh University Press, 2002.

———. "A Scots Mummy." *Blackwood's Magazine,* August 1823, 188–90.

———. "Translation from an Ancient Chaldee Manuscript." *Blackwood's Magazine,* October 1817, 89–96.

———. "Verses. Recited by the Author, in a Party of His Countrymen, on the Day That the News Arrived of Our Final Victory over the French." *Edinburgh Monthly Magazine,* April 1817, 72.

Hogg, James. "Contemporary Reception of 'The Liberal.'" *Byron Journal* 7 (1979): 61–75.

Honour, Hugh. *The Vision of Cathay.* New York: Icon Editions, 1961.

Hood, Thomas. "A Sentimental Journey, from Islington to Waterloo Bridge." *London Magazine,* March 1821, 508–15.

Howard, David Sanctuary. *Chinese Armorial Porcelain.* London: Faber, 1974.

Hughes, Gillian. "James Hogg, and Edinburgh's Triumph over Napoleon." *Scottish Studies Review* 4, no. 1 (2003): 98–111.

Hulme, Peter. *Colonial Encounters: Europe and the Native Caribbean, 1492–1797.* New York: Routledge, 1986.

Hunt, Leigh. *The Correspondence of Leigh Hunt. Edited by His Eldest Son.* 2 vols. London: Smith, Elder and Co., 1862.

[Hunt, Leigh]. "On Periodical Essays." In *Leigh Hunt's Literary Criticism,* edited by Lawrence Huston Houtchens and Carolyn Washburn Houtchens, 77–79. New York: Columbia University Press, 1956.

———. "Pocket-Books and Keepsakes." In *Keepsake,* 1–18. London: Thomas Davidson, 1828.

———. "Preface." *Liberal,* October 1822, v–xii.

Impey, Oliver. *Chinoiserie: The Impact of Oriental Styles on Western Art and Decoration.* London: Oxford University Press, 1977.

Jack, Ian. *Keats and the Mirror of Art.* Oxford: Clarendon Press, 1967.

Jasanoff, Maya. *Edge of Empire: Lives, Culture, and Conquest in the East, 1750–1850.* New York: Knopf, 2005.

Jenkins, Ian. *Archeologists and Aesthetes in the Sculpture Galleries of the British Museum, 1800–1939.* London: British Museum Press, 1992.

[Johnstone, Christian Isobel]. "The Books of the Season." *Tait's Edinburgh Magazine* 4, no. 47–48 (November–December 1837): 678–88; 792–97.

Jump, Harriet Devine. "'The False Prudery of Public Taste': Scandalous Women and the Annuals, 1820–1850." In *Feminist Readings of Victorian Popular Texts: Divergent Femininities,* edited by Emma Liggins and Daniel Duffy, 1–17. Aldershot: Ashgate, 2001.

Kahn, Arthur D. "The Pastoral Byron: Arcadia in *The Island.*" *Arcadia* 8 (1973): 274–83.

Keats, John. *The Letters of John Keats, 1814–1821.* Edited by Edward Hyder Rollins. 2 vols. Cambridge, MA: Harvard University Press, 1958.

———. *The Poems of John Keats.* Edited by Jack Stillinger. Cambridge, MA: Harvard University Press, 1978.

Kiely, Robert. *The Romantic Novel in England.* Cambridge: Harvard University Press, 1972.

Klancher, Jon. "Discriminations, or Romantic Cosmopolitans in London." In *Romantic Metropolis: The Urban Scene of British Culture, 1780–1840,* edited by James Chandler and Kevin Gilmartin, 65–82. Cambridge: Cambridge University Press, 2005.

———. *The Making of English Reading Audiences, 1790–1832.* Madison: University of Wisconsin Press, 1987.

Kopytoff, Igor. "The Cultural Biography of Things: Commoditization as Process." In *The Social Life of Things,* edited by Arjun Appadurai, 64–91. Cambridge: Cambridge University Press, 1986.

Kowaleski-Wallace, Elizabeth. *Consuming Subjects: Women, Shopping, and Business in the Eighteenth Century.* New York: Columbia University Press, 1997.

Lamb, Charles. "Blakesmoor in H——shire." *London Magazine,* September 1824, 225–28.

———. "A Dissertation upon Roast Pig." *London Magazine,* September 1822, 245–48.

———. *The Letters of Charles Lamb, to Which Are Added Those of His Sister Mary Lamb.* Edited by E. V. Lucas. 3 vols. New Haven, CT: Yale University Press, 1935.

———. *The Letters of Charles and Mary Anne Lamb.* Edited by Edwin W. Marrs Jr. 3 vols. Ithaca, NY: Cornell University Press, 1975–78.

———. "Mrs. Battle's Opinions on Whist." *London Magazine,* February 1821, 161–65.

———. "Old China." *London Magazine,* March 1823, 269–72.

———. "Oxford in the Vacation." *London Magazine,* October 1820, 365–69.

———. "Recollections of Christ's Hospital." *London Magazine,* November 1820, 139.

———. "Recollections of the South Sea House." *London Magazine,* August 1820, 142–46.

———. "Witches, and Other Night-Fears." *London Magazine,* October 1821, 384–87.

———. *The Works of Charles and Mary Lamb.* Edited by E. V. Lucas. 5 vols. London: Methuen, 1903; New York: AMS Press, 1968.

Lamb, Jonathan. *Preserving the Self in the South Seas, 1680–1840.* Chicago: University of Chicago Press, 2001.

Landon, Letitia. "The Chinese Pagoda." In Zachary Leader and Ian Haywood, eds., *Romantic Period Writings, 1798–1832: An Anthology,* 210–11. London: Routledge, 1998

———. *The Improvisatrice.* New York: Woodstock Books, 1996.

———. *Letitia Elizabeth Landon: Selected Writings.* Edited by Jerome McGann and Daniel Riess. Peterborough, Ontario: Broadview, 1997.

———. *Letters by Letitia Elizabeth Landon.* Edited by F. J. Sypher. Ann Arbor, MI: Scholars' Facsimiles and Reprints, 2001.

———. "Macao." In Zachary Leader and Ian Haywood, eds., *Romantic Period Writings, 1798–1832: An Anthology,* 208–9. London: Routledge, 1998.

———. "Rome." *Literary Gazette,* March 11, 1818, 173.

Larrabee, Stephen A. *English Bards and Grecian Marbles; the Relationship between Sculpture and Poetry, Especially in the Romantic Period.* Port Washington, NY: Kennikat Press, 1964.

Latané, David E. "The Birth of the Author in the Victorian Archive." *Victorian Periodicals Review* 22 (1989): 109–17.

Lawford, Cynthia. "Bijoux beyond Possession: The Prima Donnas of L.E.L.'s Album Poems." In *Women's Poetry, Late Romantic to Late Victorian: Gender and Genre, 1830–1900,* edited by Isobel Armstrong and Virginia Blain, 102–14. New York: St. Martin's Press, 1999.

Leask, Nigel. *British Romantic Writers and the East: Anxieties of Empire.* Cambridge: Cambridge University Press, 1992.

Leighton, Angela. *Victorian Women Poets: Writing against the Heart.* Charlottesville: University Press of Virginia, 1992.

Lewis, Reina. *Gendering Orientalism: Race, Femininity and Representation.* London: Routledge, 1996.

Linkin, Harriet K. "Romantic Aesthetics in Mary Tighe and Letitia Landon: How Women Poets Recuperate the Gaze." *European Romantic Review* 7, no. 2 (1997): 159–88.

Linley, Margaret. "A Centre That Would Not Hold: Annuals and Cultural Democracy." In *Nineteenth-Century Media and the Construction of Identities,* edited by Laurel Brake, Bill Bell, and David Finkelstein, 54–74. Hampshire: Palgrave, 2000.

Liu, Lydia H. "Robinson Crusoe's Earthenware Pot: Science, Aesthetics, and the Metaphysics of True Porcelain." In *Romantic Science: The Literary Forms of Natural History,* edited by Noah Heringman, 139–71. Albany: SUNY Press, 2003.

Lootens, Tricia. "Receiving the Legend, Rethinking the Writer: Letitia Landon and the Poetess Tradition." In *Romanticism and Women Poets: Opening the Doors of Reception,* edited by Harriet Kramer Linkin and Stephen C. Behrendt, 242–59. Lexington: University Press of Kentucky, 1999.

Lovejoy, Arthur O. "The Chinese Origin of Romanticism." In *Essays in the History of Ideas,* 99–135. New York: Capricorn Books, 1960.

Lowes, John Livingston. *The Road to Xanadu; a Study in the Ways of the Imagination.* Revised ed. Boston: Houghton Mifflin, 1964.

Macaulay, Thomas. *The Letters of Thomas Babington Macaulay.* Edited by Thomas Pinney. 6 vols. London: Cambridge University Press, 1974–81.

Macdougall, Norman. *An Antidote to the English: The Auld Alliance, 1295–1560.* East Linton, Scotland: Tuckwell Press, 2001.

Mackenzie, R. Shelton. "History of Blackwood's Magazine." In *Noctes Ambrosianae,* edited by R. Shelton Mackenzie, 1: v–xxviii. New York: Redfield, 1854.

———, ed. *Noctes Ambrosianae.* 5 vols. New York: Redfield, 1854.

MacKenzie, John M. *Orientalism: History, Theory and the Arts,* 1995.

Majeed, Javed. *Ungoverned Imaginings: James Mill's "The History of British India and Orientalism."* Oxford: Clarendon Press, 1992.

Makdisi, Saree. *Romantic Imperialism: Universal Empire and the Culture of Modernity.* Cambridge: Cambridge University Press, 1998.

Manning, Peter J. "Wordsworth in the *Keepsake,* 1829." In *Literature in the Marketplace: Nineteenth-Century British Publishing and Reading Practices,* edited by John O. Jordan and Robert L. Patten, 44–73. Cambridge: Cambridge University Press, 1995.

Marchand, Leslie A. *The Athenaeum; a Mirror of Victorian Culture.* New York: Octagon Books, 1971.

Marshall, William H. *Byron, Shelley, Hunt and the Liberal.* Philadelphia: University of Pennsylvania Press, 1960.

Marx, Karl. *Capital.* Translated by Ben Fowkes. Vol. 1. New York: Vintage, 1977.

Mason, Michael York. "The Three Burials in Hogg's *Justified Sinner." Studies in Scottish Literature* 13 (1978): 15–23.

Matthews, William. "The Egyptians in Scotland: The Political History of a Myth." *Viator* 1 (1970): 289–306.

Mayo, Robert D. *The English Novel in the Magazines, 1740–1815.* Evanston, IL: Northwestern University Press, 1962.

Mazzeo, Tilar J. "'A Mixture of All the Styles': Colonialism, Nationalism, and Plagiarism in Shelley's Indian Circle." *European Romantic Review* 8, no. 2 (1997): 155–68.

McClintock, Anne. *Imperial Leather: Race, Gender, and Sexuality in the Colonial Conquest.* New York: Routledge, 1995.

McFarland, Thomas. *Romantic Cruxes: The English Essayists and the Spirit of the Age.* Oxford: Clarendon Press, 1987.

McGann, Jerome. *Don Juan in Context.* Chicago: University of Chicago Press, 1976.

———. *Fiery Dust: Byron's Poetic Development.* Chicago: University of Chicago Press, 1968.

———. *The Poetics of Sensibility: A Revolution in Literary Style.* Oxford: Clarendon Press, 1996.

———. *The Romantic Ideology: A Critical Investigation.* Chicago: University of Chicago Press, 1983.

Mellor, Anne K. *Romanticism and Gender.* New York: Routledge, 1993.

"Memoirs of the Living Poets of Great Britain (Byron)." *Imperial Magazine* 4, no. 44 (September 1822): cols. 816–26.

[Mill, James]. "Periodical Literature: Edinburgh Review." *Westminster Review* 1 (January 1824): 206–68.

Miller, Karl. *Doubles: Studies in Literary History.* Oxford: Oxford University Press, 1985.

Miller, Perry, ed. *Margaret Fuller, American Romantic: A Selection from Her Writings and Correspondence.* 1963. Reprint, Ithaca, NY: Cornell University Press, 1970.

Milligan, Barry. *Pleasures and Pains: Opium and the Orient in Nineteenth-Century British Culture.* Charlottesville: University Press of Virginia, 1995.

Mitchell, Timothy. *Colonising Egypt.* Cambridge: Cambridge University Press, 1988.

Moers, Ellen. *Literary Women.* New York: Doubleday, 1976.

Monsman, Gerald. *Confessions of a Prosaic Dreamer: Charles Lamb's Autobiography.* Durham, NC: Duke University Press, 1984.

Montwieler, Katherine. "Laughing at Love: L.E.L. and the Embellishment of Eros." *Romanticism on the Net,* nos. 29–30 (2003).

Moore, N. Hudson. *The Old China Book, Including Staffordshire, Wedgwood, Lustre, and Other English Pottery and Porcelain.* New York: Tudor Publishing, 1944.

Morrison, Robert. "Opium-Eaters and Magazine Wars: De Quincey and Coleridge in 1821." *Victorian Periodicals Review* 30 (Spring 1997): 27–40.

———. "William Blackwood and the Dynamics of Success." In *Print Culture and the Blackwood Tradition, 1805–1930,* edited by David Finkelstein, 21–48. Toronto: University of Toronto Press, 2006.

Moskal, Jeanne. "Lady Morgan's Travel Books." In *Romantic Women Writers: Voices and Countervoices,* edited by Paula R. Feldman and Theresa M. Kelley, 171–93. Hanover, NH: University Press of New England, 1995.

Murphy, Peter T. "Impersonation and Authorship in Romantic Britain." *ELH* 59 (1992): 625–49.

———. *Poetry as an Occupation and an Art in Britain, 1760–1830.* Cambridge: Cambridge University Press, 1993.

[Napier, Macvey]. *Hypocrisy Unveiled, and Calumny Detected: In a Review of Blackwood's Magazine.* Edinburgh: Pillans, 1818.

Nemoianu, Virgil. *The Taming of Romanticism: European Literature and the Age of Biedermeier.* Cambridge, MA: Harvard University Press, 1984.

Newlyn, Lucy. *Reading, Writing, and Romanticism: The Anxiety of Reception.* Oxford: Oxford University Press, 2000.

Nineteenth-Century Literature Criticism. Detroit: Gale Research Company, 1981–.

Obeyesekere, Gananath. *The Apotheosis of Captain Cook: European Mythmaking in the Pacific.* Princeton, NJ: Princeton University Press, 1992.

O'Connor, Maura. *The Romance of Italy and the English Political Imagination.* New York: St. Martin's Press, 1998.

Oliphant, Mrs. (Margaret). *Annals of a Publishing House: William Blackwood and His Sons, Their Magazine and Friends.* 2nd ed. 3 vols. New York: AMS Press, 1974.

"On the Cockney School of Poetry." *Blackwood's Magazine,* October 1817, 38–41.

Parker, Mark. *Literary Magazines and British Romanticism.* Cambridge: Cambridge University Press, 2000.

Parkinson, Richard. *Cracking Codes: The Rosetta Stone and Decipherment.* London: British Museum Press, 1999.

Parsons, Coleman O. "The Parodic Background of 'The Chaldee Manuscript.'" *Studies in Scottish Literature* 24 (1989): 221–25.

Pascoe, Judith. *The Hummingbird Cabinet: A Rare and Curious History of Romantic Collectors.* Ithaca, NY: Cornell University Press, 2006.

———. *Romantic Theatricality: Gender, Poetry, and Spectatorship.* Ithaca, NY: Cornell University Press, 1997.

Pittock, Murray G. H. *Celtic Identity and the British Image.* Manchester: Manchester University Press, 1999.

———. *The Invention of Scotland: The Stuart Myth and the Scottish Identity, 1638 to the Present.* London: Routledge, 1991.

———. *Poetry and Jacobite Politics in Eighteenth-Century Britain and Ireland.* Cambridge: Cambridge University Press, 1994.

Plumb, J. H. "The Royal Porcelain Craze." In *In the Light of History,* 57–69. Boston: Houghton Mifflin, 1973.

Pope, Alexander. "The Rape of the Lock." In *The Poems of Alexander Pope,* vol. 2: *The Rape of the Lock and Other Poems,* edited by Geoffrey Tillotson, 125–212. London: Routledge, 1993.

Porter, David. "A Peculiar but Uninteresting Nation: China and the Discourse of Commerce in Eighteenth-Century England." *Eighteenth-Century Studies* 33, no. 2 (1999–2000): 181–99.

Porterfield, Todd. *The Allure of Egypt: Art in the Service of French Imperialism, 1798–1836.* Princeton, NJ: Princeton University Press, 1998.

"Pottery and Porcelain." *Household Words,* October 4, 1851, 32–37.

Pratt, Mary Louise. *Imperial Eyes: Travel Writing and Transculturation.* New York: Routledge, 1992.

Price, Leah. *The Anthology and the Rise of the Novel: From Richardson to George Eliot.* Cambridge: Cambridge University Press, 2000.

Prins, Yopie. *Victorian Sappho.* Princeton, NJ: Princeton University Press, 1999.

"Prospectus." *London Magazine,* 1820, iv–viii.

Rappoport, Jill. "Buyer Beware: The Gift Poetics of Letitia Elizabeth Landon." *Nineteenth-Century Literature* 58, no. 4 (2004): 441–73.

Raven, James. "Defending Conduct and Property: The London Press and the Luxury Debate." In *Early Modern Conceptions of Property,* edited by John Brewer and Susan Staves, 301–22. London: Routledge, 1995.

Redekop, Magdalene. "Beyond Closure: Buried Alive with Hogg's *Justified Sinner.*" *ELH* 52 (1985): 159–84.

Reiman, Donald H., ed. *The Romantics Reviewed: Contemporary Reviews of British Romantic Writers.* 9 vols. New York: Garland, 1972.

Rennie, Neil. *Far-Fetched Facts: The Literature of Travel and the Idea of the South Seas.* Oxford: Oxford, 1995.

"Review of the Improvisatrice." *European Magazine,* August 1824, 156–60.

"Review.—the Liberal." *Imperial Magazine* 4 (December 1822): cols. 1139–42.

Richardson, Alan. *British Romanticism and the Science of the Mind.* Cambridge: Cambridge University Press, 2001.

Riess, Daniel. "Laetitia Landon and the Dawn of English Post-Romanticism." *SEL* 36, no. 4 (1996): 807–27.

Robinson, Dwight E. "Ode on a 'New Etrurian' Urn: A Reflection of Wedgwood Ware in the Poetic Imagery of John Keats." *Keats-Shelley Journal* 12 (1963): 11–35.

———. "A Question of the Imprint of Wedgwood in the Larger Poems of Keats." *Keats-Shelley Journal* 16 (1967): 23–28.

Rosen, Fred. *Bentham, Byron, and Greece: Constitutionalism, Nationalism, and Early Liberal Political Thought.* Oxford: Clarendon Press, 1992.

Russett, Margaret. *De Quincey's Romanticism: Canonical Minority and the Forms of Transmission.* Cambridge: Cambridge University Press, 1997.

———. *Fictions and Fakes: Forging Romantic Authenticity, 1760–1845.* Cambridge: Cambridge University Press, 2006.

———. "The Gothic Violence of the Letter: Naming the Scotch Novelist." In *Fictions and Fakes: Forging Romantic Authenticity, 1760–1845,* 155–91. Cambridge: Cambridge University Press, 2006.

Rzepka, Charles J. *Sacramental Commodities: Gift, Text, and the Sublime in De Quincey.* Amherst: University of Massachusetts Press, 1995.

Saglia, Diego. "Consuming Egypt: Appropriation and the Cultural Modalities of Romantic Taste." *Nineteenth-Century Contexts* 24, no. 3 (2002): 317–32.

———. "Mediterranean Unrest: 1820s Verse Tragedies and Revolutions in the South." *Romanticism* 11, no. 1 (2005): 99–113.

Said, Edward. *Culture and Imperialism.* New York: Knopf, 1994.

———. *Orientalism.* New York: Knopf, 1994.

Sanders, Valerie. "'Meteor Wreaths': Harriet Martineau, 'L.E.L.', and Fraser's Magazine." *Critical Survey* 13, no. 2 (2001): 42–61.

Schmidt, Arnold A. "Bligh, Christian, Murray, and Napoleon: Byronic Mutiny from London to the South Seas." *Byron Journal* 32, no. 1 (2004): 21–30.

Schneider, Elisabeth. *Coleridge, Opium, and Kubla Khan.* New York: Octagon Books, 1966.

Schoenfield, Mark L. "Butchering James Hogg: Romantic Identity in the Magazine Market." In *At the Limits of Romanticism: Essays in Cultural, Feminist, and Materialist Criticism,* edited by Mary A. Favret and Nicola J. Watson, 207–24. Bloomington: Indiana University Press, 1994.

———. "Voices Together: Lamb, Hazlitt, and the *London.*" *Studies in Romanticism* 29 (1990): 257–72.

Scott, Grant F. "Beautiful Ruins: The Elgin Marbles Sonnet in Its Historical and Generic Contexts." In *The Sculpted Word: Keats, Ekphrasis, and the Visual Arts,* 45–67. Hanover, NH: University Press of New England, 1994.

[Scott, John]. "The Signs of the Times." *London Magazine,* February 1821, 153–61.

Scott, Walter. *The Letters of Sir Walter Scott.* Edited by H. J. C. Grierson. 12 vols. London: Constable, 1933.

Sekora, John. *Luxury: The Concept in Western Thought, Eden to Smollett.* Baltimore, MD: Johns Hopkins University Press, 1977.

Shaffer, E. S. *"Kubla Khan" and the Fall of Jerusalem: The Mythological School in Biblical Criticism and Secular Literature, 1770–1880.* Cambridge: Cambridge University Press, 1975.

Shattock, Joanne. *Politics and Reviewers: The Edinburgh and the Quarterly in the Early Victorian Age.* New York: Leicester University Press, 1989.

Shelley, Mary. *The Letters of Mary Wollestonecraft Shelley.* Edited by Betty T. Bennett. 3 vols. Baltimore, MD: Johns Hopkins University Press, 1980–88.

Shelley, Percy Bysshe. *Shelley's Poetry and Prose.* Edited by Donald H. Reiman and Sharon B. Powers. New York: Norton, 1977.

Simpson, David. *Romanticism, Nationalism, and the Revolt against Theory.* Chicago: University of Chicago Press, 1993.

Smith, Bernard. *European Vision and the South Pacific.* 2nd ed. New Haven, CT: Yale University Press, 1985.

Smith, G. Gregory. *Scottish Literature: Character and Influence.* London: Macmillan and Co., 1972.

Sorensen, Janet. *The Grammar of Empire in Eighteenth-Century British Writing.* Cambridge: Cambridge University Press, 2000.

Southey, Robert. *Letters from England.* Edited by and with an introduction by Jack Simmons. London: Cresset Press, 1951.

———. "A Vision of Judgement." In *The Poetical Works of Robert Southey, Collected by Himself,* 189–256. London: Longman, Brown, Green, and Longmans, 1842.

Spence, Jonathan D. *The Chan's Great Continent: China in Western Minds.* New York: Norton, 1998.

Staël, Madame de. *Corinne; or, Italy.* Translated by Isabel Hill with Metrical Versions of the Odes by L. E. Landon. New York: A. L. Burt, n.d.

St. Clair, William. *The Reading Nation in the Romantic Period.* Cambridge: Cambridge University Press, 2004.

Stewart, Susan. *Crimes of Writing: Problems in the Containment of Representation.* New York: Oxford University Press, 1991.

Stephenson, Glennis. *Letitia Landon: The Woman Behind L.E.L.* Manchester: Manchester University Press, 1995.

Strout, Alan Lang. "James Hogg's 'Chaldee Manuscript.'" *PMLA* 65, no. 5 (1950): 695–718.

Sullivan, Alvin, ed. *British Literary Magazines.* 4 vols. Vol. 2: *The Romantic Age, 1789–1836.* Westport, CT: Greenwood Press, 1983.

Sweet, Nanora. "'Hitherto Closed to British Enterprise': Trading and Writing the Hispanic World circa 1815." *European Romantic Review* 8, no. 2 (1997): 139–47.

———. "The *New Monthly Magazine* and the Liberalism of the 1820s." In *Romantic Periodicals and Print Culture,* edited by Kim Wheatley, 147–62. London: Frank Cass, 2003.

Taylor, Beverly. "Elizabeth Barrett Browning's Subversion of the Giftbook Model." *Studies in Browning and His Circle* 20 (1993): 62–69.

[Thackeray, William Makepeace]. "A Word on the Annuals." *Fraser's Magazine* 16 (1837): 757–63.

Tournikiotis, Panayotis, ed. *The Parthenon and Its Impact in Modern Times.* Athens: Melissa Publishing House, G. Rayas and Co., 1994.

Tucker, Herbert F. "House Arrest: The Domestication of English Poetry in the 1820s." *New Literary History* 25 (1994): 521–48.

Treadwell, James. "Impersonation and Autobiography in Lamb's Christ's Hospital Essays." *Studies in Romanticism* 37 (Winter 1998): 499–521.

Trumpener, Katie. *Bardic Nationalism: The Romantic Novel and the British Empire.* Princeton, NJ: Princeton University Press, 1997.

Vallois, Marie-Claire. "Voice as Fossil. Madame De Staël's *Corinne or Italy:* An Archaeology of Feminine Discourse." *Tulsa Studies in Women's Literature* 6, no. 1 (1987): 47–60.

Volney, C. F. *The Ruins, or, Meditation on the Revolutions of Empires: And the Law of Nature.* Baltimore, MD: Black Classic Press, 1991.

Ward, Herman M. *Byron and the Magazines, 1806–1824.* Salzburg: Institut für English Sprache und Literatur, 1973.

Warner, Michael. *The Letters of the Republic: Publication and the Public Sphere in Eighteenth-Century America.* Cambridge: Harvard University Press, 1990.

Watson, Nicola J. *Revolution and the Form of the British Novel, 1790–1825.* Oxford: Clarendon Press, 1994.

Weatherill, Lorna. *Consumer Behaviour and Material Culture in Britain, 1660–1760.* New York: Routledge, 1988.

Webb, Timothy. "A 'Great Theatre of Outrage and Disorder': Figuring Ireland in the *Edinburgh Review,* 1802–29." In *British Romanticism and the Edinburgh Review,* edited by Massimiliano Demata and Duncan Wu, 58–81. New York: Palgrave, 2002.

Wheatley, Kim. "The Blackwood's Attacks on Leigh Hunt." *Nineteenth-Century Literature* 47, no. 1 (1992): 1–31.

———. Introduction to *Romantic Periodicals and Print Culture,* edited by Kim Wheatley, 1–18. London: Frank Cass, 2003.

———. "Paranoid Politics: The *Quarterly* and *Edinburgh* Reviews." *Prose Studies* 15, no. 3 (1992): 319–43.

Williams, Raymond. *Keywords: A Vocabulary of Culture and Society.* Revised ed. New York: Oxford University Press, 1985.

Wood, Gillen D'Arcy. *The Shock of the Real: Romanticism and Visual Culture, 1760–1860.* New York: Palgrave, 2001.

Woodring, Carl. *Politics in English Romantic Poetry.* Cambridge, MA: Harvard University Press, 1970.

Woolf, Michael. "Charting the Golden Stream." *Victorian Periodicals Newsletter,* no. 13 (1971): 23–38.

Wordsworth, William. *The Letters of William and Dorothy Wordsworth.* Edited by Ernest de Selincourt and arranged, revised, and edited by Alan G. Hill. 2nd ed. 7 vols. Vol. 4. Oxford: Clarendon Press, 1978.

———. *The Prelude.* Edited by Ernest de Selincourt. Oxford: Clarendon, 1959.

Wortham, John David. *The Genesis of British Egyptology, 1549–1906.* Norman: University of Oklahoma Press, 1971.

Wu, Duncan. "Talking Pimples: Hazlitt and Byron in Love." *Romanticism* 10, no. 2 (2004): 158–72.

Wynter, Harriet. *An Introduction to European Porcelain.* London: Arlington Books, 1971.

Young, Robert J. C. *Colonial Desire: Hybridity in Theory, Culture and Race.* London: Routledge, 1995.

Index